# The Shaping of
# Environmentalism
# in America

# The Shaping of Environmentalism in America

Victor B. Scheffer

UNIVERSITY OF WASHINGTON PRESS

*Seattle and London*

Library of Congress Cataloging-in-Publication Data

Scheffer, Victor B.
    The Shaping of environmentalism in America/Victor B. Scheffer.
    p.  cm.
    Includes bibliographical references and index.
    ISBN 0–295–97060–X (alk. paper)
    1. Environmental policy—United States—History.  2. Environmental protection—United States—History.  3. Human ecology—United States—History.  I. Title.
HC110.E5S39  1991
363.7'07'0973—dc20                         90-40577
                                                    CIP

*I think that some of the people who warn us about environmental crisis have got their perspectives wrong. Indeed, I think they are wrong to call it a crisis at all. A crisis is a situation that will pass; it can be resolved by temporary hardship, temporary adjustment, technological and political expedients. What we are experiencing is not a crisis: it is a climacteric. For the rest of man's history on earth, so far as one can foretell, he will have to live with problems of population, of resources, of pollution.*[1]

Eric Ashby (1978)

# Contents

# *Preface*

I write of a social revolution. I write especially for readers who suppose that environmentalism is a word deeply rooted in the American vernacular. It is not. It was seldom used before the appearance of Rachel Carson's *Silent Spring:* the 1962 book that challenged the chemical poisoners and what they were doing to the beauty and the life-support bases of our nation. A profound revolution followed. I don't mean that Miss Carson's book was responsible, only that it was one of the first shots fired.

I offer an informal view of thought and action attending the environmental movement in the United States, especially during its formative years, 1960 to 1980, when its direction and leadership were clearly established. *Environmentalism* as a movement—and a budding social science, a field of political management, a philosophy, and a religion—was firmly in place. However, the movement met with notable setbacks during the Reagan regime, 1981 to 1989, and I conclude the narrative with an epilogue wherein environmental events during that regime are highlighted.

New information pertinent to the movement will continue to be uncovered. Thus, not until 1984—forty years after the event—did we learn that babies born in the Love Canal district, when active dumping of chemical wastes was taking place, were abnormally small. It took two generations to understand the hazard posed by airborne asbestos fibers; in 1985, the Manville Corporation was faced with $29 billion in claims stemming from asbestos-related diseases incurred in earlier years. World industrialists released millions of tons of seemingly inert chlorofluorocarbons (aerosols and the like) into the atmosphere before they agreed in 1985 that these were destroying stratospheric ozone and thereby admitting dangerous radiations from the sun. Many generations will pass before we grasp the enormity of chemical pollution of America's aquifers and estuaries. And the full effects of nuclear testing in the 1950s upon genetic lines can only be known by persons living far beyond our time.

The term "environmental" first entered Bell Telephone's Yellow Pages in 1963, while "environment" as a special section first entered the *Britannica Book of the Year* in 1972.[2] But the central idea of environmentalism—respect for nature—had been evolving in American thought for well over a century. Witness Cooper's *The Pioneers* and *The Prairie*, Thoreau's *Walden*, and Marsh's *Man and Nature*.[3]

If you are looking for other source materials on the early environmental movement you will find them listed in two excellent Smithsonian bibliographies, *A Search for Environmental Ethics: An Initial Bibliography* (1980) and *The Natural Environment: An Annotated Bibliography on Attitudes and Values* (1984).[4] These describe 1,303 books and articles published from 1945 to 1983. While they emphasize ethics, rather than environmental biology and engineering, they usefully cover the environmental age. You will find contemporary sources in periodicals listed in library catalogs under the heading "environment," such as *Environment, Environment Abstracts, Environmental Ethics, Environmental Forum, The Environmental Index, Environmental Law, Environmental Periodicals Bibliography, The Environmental Professional, Environmental Review*, and *Journal of Environmental Education*. See also the annual reports of the President's Council on Environmental Quality.

•   •   •

I thank Michael J. Bean, editor (1983) of the *Yale Law Journal*, for help with environmental law, and James L. Olsen, Jr., for help in locating publications in the National Academy of Sciences files. I thank the librarians, invariably kind, who helped me at the University of Washington and other Puget Sound libraries. It is a measure of the broad sweep of the environmental movement that its literature must be searched for under architecture, business administration, engineering, geography, health sciences, law, the natural sciences, philosophy, political science, religion, and sociology. Even poetry. And I thank the millions of people largely unknown to me who are acting from conscience to work for a cleaner, safer, and more beautiful world. They perceive that mankind must quit trying to conquer natural ecosystems and, rather, treat them with respect; must live more soberly among them than in the past. Some are dreamers and others crusaders; most are simply the more thoughtful and considerate members of your community and mine. Their collective effort is shaping environmentalism.

# Awareness of Planet Earth

# 1

# *The Roots of Environmentalism*

Environmentalism has roots in conservation: the preservation and careful use of natural resources. However, in the years after World War II, we Americans learned that trusting in conservation alone would not enable us to survive indefinitely in surroundings which daily were growing more dangerous, ugly, and impoverished. We learned that conservation as a policy is not wrong, only incomplete. We took a broader look around us and found a new guide in ecology: the study of the relationships between living organisms and their surroundings. Thus, environmentalism is rooted in both conservation and ecology.

"Conservation" had been coined during the administration of Theodore Roosevelt (1901–09) by a forester, Gifford Pinchot. During the first half of the twentieth century, when the great federal agencies for managing public parks, forests, soils, water, and wildlife were taking shape, Americans increasingly saw outdoor men in uniform: park rangers, foresters, reclamation engineers, and game wardens. Enlightened citizens designed less wasteful ways of using natural resources. And the public conscience was stirring; the old belief that property rights are absolute was giving way to the belief that some things belong to all. Yet, while the conservation textbooks of the day dealt at length with the wise use of resources, they rarely touched on famine, the burgeoning of human populations, urban blight, the pollution of air and water, the hazard of anthropogenic chemicals, and the disappearance of old wilderness. They dealt piecemeal with human surroundings. They focused on the *what* and *how* of managing natural resources but seldom on the *why?*

According to historian Samuel P. Hays, the so-called Progressive Conservation Movement (1890–1920) was not a grassroots movement but a scientific one. It "neither arose from a broad popular outcry, nor centered its fire primarily upon the private corporation. . . . Conservation leaders sprang from such fields as hydrology, forestry, agrostology [grass botany], geology, and anthropology. Vigorously active in professional circles in the national capital, these leaders brought the ideals and practices of their crafts into federal resource policy."[1]

"Ecology" had been coined even earlier. Ernst Haeckel, biologist and philosopher, introduced it in his book, *General Morphology of Organisms* (1866). Its use gradually spread through botany, zoology, entomology, oceanography, limnology, and other life sciences. Charles Elton, one of the founders of scientific ecology, defined it broadly as "a knowledge of natural history."[2] He explained that ecologists have always been among us, from primitive ages when men and women first began to put two and two together to interpret their surroundings. Thus environmentalism, rooted in ecology, is a return to first principles.

Writer John Steinbeck and ecologist Ed Ricketts sailed leisurely to the Gulf of California in the spring of 1940 to study marine life. There they found organic domains wholly new to the man of letters, if not to the ecologist. While Ricketts explained various animal adaptations for survival, Steinbeck listened and marveled. Later, in *Sea of Cortez*, he penned a poetic definition of ecology. "Our fingers turned over the stones and we saw life that was like our life. . . . The tide pool stretches both ways, digs back to electrons and leaps space into the universe and fights out of the moment into non-conceptual time. Then ecology has a synonym which is ALL."[3]

In the 1960s, ecology became a household word. It was introduced by career biologists who, having identified abuses of the environment, cried alarm at what they saw. It was sold to the public by those in particular who foresaw the social destiny of their science. They warned that man cannot forever disobey the ancient organic laws that govern all others of the multimillion living species. By 1964, explained ecologist Eugene Odum, ecology was beginning to achieve "a maturity, a cohesiveness, and an importance in human affairs that is new."[4] Botanist Pierre Dansereau urged, "Let us therefore consider the emergence of ecology as a great intellectual adventure, to be compared with the development of organic evolution and of nuclear physics. [It has] served as a training ground for the release of a newfound science to society as a whole."[5]

The most influential among the career ecologists were those who insisted that respect for the biosphere, like respect for justice, must continuously have a place in law and government. They insisted that people are *entitled* to clean and beautiful surroundings. They insisted that protection of the environment is nonnegotiable. And they were articulate; they deliberated how best they might carry the special, arcane, or technical concepts of ecology into the mainstream of American thought. They were fired by missionary zeal to explain new ecological values which were in fact as old as life itself. They called upon citizens at large to question the wisdom of governments and business corporations which had long controlled the use of America's natural resources. Marston Bates was one such ecologist. In his classic, *The Forest and the Sea* (1960), he concluded that "man's destiny is tied to nature's destiny and the arrogance of the engineering mind does not change this. Man may be a very peculiar animal, but he is still a part of the system of nature."[6] He later added: "Ecology may well be the most important of the sciences from the viewpoint of long-term human survival, but it is among those least understood by the general public."[7]

The contributions of an earlier and more specialized sort of ecology to a later and more popular one are illustrated by the history of The Nature Conservancy, an "organization committed to the preservation of natural diversity by protecting lands and the life they harbor." It started in 1917 as a committee, within the young Ecological Society of America, to preserve endangered wildlands. Practicing ecologists had seen in dismay the rolling grasslands of the Central States succumb, one by one, to the plow, to overgrazing, and to suburban and industrial sprawl. Only fragments of the native pastures upon which the shaggy bison had grazed could be found in fenced pioneer cemeteries, in military reservations, and on railroad embankments. In 1931, the Ecological Society established a second committee—on the study of plant and animal communities—and in 1946 the members of the two committees joined as an independent group of twelve members for which they coined the name, The Nature Conservancy (TNC). Rachel Carson watched the growth of TNC and, before her death in 1964, provided generously for it in her will. Without a paid staff until 1967, TNC received in that year a powerful boost from the Ford Foundation and, by 1970, was managing a revolving fund of $4.5 million.[8] It grew influential because it understood that, in capitalistic America, title to land carries great potential for social change. To date, TNC has saved over 3 million acres of land.

Although professionals introduced the word ecology to the people, it was the people who demanded the impressive political improvements that were to characterize the environmental age. It was the daily commuters who drove with smarting eyes through city smog . . . the mothers who learned that DDT was present in their breasts and that arsenic from smelter smoke was accumulating in the bodies of their children . . . the poultrymen who wondered why eggshells broke more easily than they used to . . . the fishermen who saw trout streams, once pure, now running brown . . . the farmers who wondered where all the bluebirds had gone, and why the water level in the wells had dropped and why the water tasted queer . . . and those of us who learned that the whale hunters, having reduced two species of whales to commercial extinction, had turned to killing others at the rate of more than 60,000 a year. It was the families who looked in vain for open beaches where they could dig clams and build sand castles. They were disappointed because, of the 21,000 miles of seashore along the contiguous United States, only 7 percent were now open to public recreation. The environmental revolution was triggered by outrage tinged with regret.

One historian of the revolution has written that "the turning point, when people had had enough, came in 1969, a year that included the Santa Barbara oil spill, the seizure of eleven tons of coho salmon in Wisconsin and Minnesota because of excessive DDT concentrations, application for permission to build a trans-Alaska pipeline, and the burning of the Cuyahoga River in Cleveland."[9] In July of that year, radio and TV stations in California announced: "The children of Los Angeles are not allowed to run, skip, or jump inside or outside on smog alert days by order of the Los Angeles Board of Education and the County Medical Association."[10]

Contributing to public outrage was increasing awareness of outdoor surroundings, thanks to television and the automobile. Under-Secretary of the Interior John C. Whitaker put it this way: "As Americans traveled in their automobiles, which had doubled in number from 1950 to 1970, they saw garish road signs, fields of junked automobiles, choked and dying streams, overgrazed and eroded hills and valleys, and roadsides lined with endless miles of beer cans, pop bottles, and the tinfoil from candy wrappers and cigarette packages. They could no longer move a few hundred miles West; the frontiers were gone."[11]

• • •

Who were the first marchers in the environmental movement? They came from everywhere: zoologists, poets, engineers, mystics, public-health nurses, "flower children," economists, bureaucrats, farmers, homemakers, demographers, professors, and students. Especially students. Like a patriotic surge, the movement swept across boundaries of age, sex, intellect, and social class. The young were the shock troops. It has always been the young who can af-

ford the luxury of ideals and can easily fall in love with the image
of what *Homo sapiens* might be. It is they who can believe in many
possible worlds. They had lost confidence in the wisdom of their
elders. They asked one another, "What the hell is going on?" And
their political influence was growing, for they were more numerous in the population and better educated than their parents. They
were the war boom babies. Their population increased 50 percent
between 1960 and 1970 (from 16.5 million to 24.7 million).[12] Moreover, in 1960 only 13 percent of persons in ages twenty to twenty-
four were in college; in 1970, 23 percent.[13] Thus, the distance between the young activists and their parents was an educational, as
well as a generational, gap. The 26th Amendment, ratified in 1971,
lowered the voting age from twenty-one to eighteen years, thereby
creating 11 million new voters, all young.

Robert Cahn, Pulitzer Prize journalist, tells a delightful story about
the power of environmentally turned-on children.[14] When a New
York corporation proposed to build a nuclear plant on the shore of
Lake Cayuga, it steamrolled the opposition. Then the opposition
reacted; it drafted a careful statement of environmental impacts,
including radioactive and thermal pollution of the lake. It mailed
the statement, not to the corporation's board of directors, but to
their children who were away at college. An accompanying letter
stated (in so many words): "When you come home for Christmas,
ask your father to reconsider building the plant." The scheme
worked. Three of the fathers subsequently met with the full board
and recommended that the project be canceled, and so it was.

The role of older Americans in the environmental movement was
slightly different. They had watched their surroundings worsen and
had been forced to accept a declining standard of living. Many
longed, naively, for a return to the pastoral America that Norman
Rockwell used to paint for the covers of the *Saturday Evening Post.*
Ecology, the miracle science, now promised to bring back the landscapes they remembered. I don't mean that the role of older Americans was any less important than that of younger ones—only less
intense. Sociologist Joseph Harry makes the telling point that the
big-name environmental organizations in 1974 were substantially
the same as those preexisting in 1950.[15] In other words, the bridge
between the earlier conservationists and the later environmentalists was continuous.

•   •   •

If religion can be defined simply as a binding philosophy, the
start of environmentalism was a religious reformation; an epi-

phany; an awakening to desecrated surroundings. It stimulated the writing of countless folk songs and at least one ecology hymnal wherein new words were set to old songs. Thus—to the tune of "Battle Hymn of the Republic"—

> Mine eyes have seen the fury of the spoiling of the earth;
> Seen the promise of a future that was dead before its birth;
> Where the heraldings of plenty were the harbingers of dearth,
> As we go marching on. . . .[16]

The religious undertone had begun faintly to sound long before the environmental age. John Muir, contemplating the Sierra Nevada, wrote in 1901: "Benevolent, solemn, fateful, pervaded with divine light, every landscape glows like a countenance hallowed in eternal repose; and every one of its living creatures, clad in flesh and leaves, and every crystal of its rocks, whether on the surface shining in the sun or buried miles deep in what we call darkness, is throbbing and pulsing with the heartbeats of God."[17] And in 1923, botanist Liberty Hyde Bailey campaigned for a visionary Society of the Holy Earth whose "principle of union will be the love of the Earth, treasured in the hearts of men and women." Although he was not destined to found that society, he lived a rich life by its principles, dying at age ninety-six revered by his students and respected by scientists throughout the world.[18]

In our own time, René Dubos, biologist and Pulitzer Prize winner, could speak easily of a theology of the earth and could urge us to use the earth reverently.[19] Gordon Harrison, of the Ford Foundation, could write that "Nature seen from the vantage point of the civilized life has for many people an esthetic appeal at least equivalent in spiritual values to great art, and the vision of the wild as God's handiwork is quite sufficient motivation for many who wish to preserve it against the desecration of highways, power lines or subdivisions."[20] Historian Lynn White concluded a 1967 essay with these oft-repeated words: "Both our present science and our present technology are so tinctured with orthodox Christian arrogance toward nature that no solution for our ecologic crisis can be expected from them alone. Since the roots of our trouble are so largely religious, the remedy must also be essentially religious, whether we call it that or not."[21] (One reason the seed of environmentalism found fertile ground on college campuses may have been that it offered a religion to young persons who, through a liberal education, were moving beyond dependence upon gods. They were looking for guidance from natural, not supernatural, wisdom.)

As the environmentalists learned more about Planet Earth they chose it as an ikon. They chose well, for Earth is a word rich in meanings both concrete and abstract. The first *Whole Earth Catalog* was published in 1968; Friends of the Earth was founded in 1969; Earth Day—a high point in the environmental movement—was celebrated nationwide in 1970; Earth First!, a radical environmental group, was founded in 1971; and the book, *Only One Earth*, opened the great UN Conference on the Human Environment in 1972. By featuring the globe on which we walk, the environmentalists reminded us of its treasures and showed us where we were losing them.

Environmentalism is the resurgence of an old understanding: that the living world is a continuous and responsive, self-renewing and virtually closed system. As poet Robinson Jeffers put it:

> . . . Integrity is wholeness,
>   the greatest beauty is
> Organic wholeness, the wholeness of life and
>   things, the divine beauty of the universe.
>   Love that, not man
> Apart from that, or else you will share man's
>   pitiful confusions, or drown in despair when
>   his days darken.[22]

•　•　•

I don't wish to leave the impression that environmentalism swept across America without resistance. It was opposed by those who perceived it as a threat to the profit system or to the growth of technology in an engineered world, or simply as a new cause coming on stage in a drama already crowded with causes. The opponents viewed with skepticism the pure intent of environmentalism to be *a movement toward understanding humankind's natural bases of support while continuously applying what is learned toward perpetuating those bases.* The opponents seemed not to understand that environmentalism is a morality of life or death for the human race.

So, environmentalists were not always welcomed. They were perceived by some as simply a new and disruptive breed, or as another claimant group like homosexuals, old people, taxpayers, and the handicapped. In 1966, "environmental science" was blasted in a *Science* magazine editorial as "one of the newest fads in Washington—and elsewhere."[23] The writer feared that government was about to take responsibility for all of man's surroundings "in the heavens, beneath the sea, and upon and under the dry land." (Not a bad idea.) As recently as 1982, actor Robert Redford offered Washington State University and the University of Idaho $400,000 to open an Institute for Resource Management which would help graduates study earthkeeping. In the planning stage, the Institute drew fire from Idaho reactionaries who feared that "it could thrust Idaho into a role of environmental advocacy."[24]

Early opposition to environmentalism came from the business world: from manufacturers, corporate leaders, owners of extractive industries, land developers, and a few economists. By and large, these groups were against government interference with freedom to use one's "own" property. Witness Julian L. Simon, a specialist in mail-order marketing and a senior fellow at the Heritage Foundation. In the late seventies he began to lecture on his favorite themes: that the ultimate human resource is imagination; that energy, food, and materials are not finite in any meaningful way; and that using resources will not slow the future of economic progress. He argued that "the future is likely to be decreasingly perilous because our powers to manage our environment have been increasing throughout human history."[25]

Simon continued to press his claim that all's well and is getting better. In a co-authored book, *The Resourceful Earth,* he offered two statements which are patently untrue:[26]

1. "An increased rate of [species] extinction cannot be ruled out if tropical deforestation is severe, but no evidence about linkage has yet been demonstrated." (In fact, an estimated 40 to 50 percent of all living species depend absolutely upon tropical forests. Destroying their habitat *will* destroy species: the known and the never-to-be-known.)

2. "The [global] fish catch, after a pause, has resumed its long upward trend." (Doubtful. The fishing nations, by stepping up their effort, by reducing waste, by increasing the take of less desirable species, and by expanding aquaculture, managed to increase world production between 1971 and 1982 by about 2 percent a year. But the law of diminishing returns holds good. There is no possibility that the fish catch will follow a "long upward trend.")

E. F. Schumacher, British economist and renowned champion of the "small is beautiful" economy, concluded that successful businessmen are often astonishingly primitive. They fit into a "simplified version of the world and are satisfied with it. And when the real world occasionally makes its existence known and attempts to force upon their attention a different one of its facets, one not provided for in their philosophy, they tend to become quite helpless and confused. They feel exposed to incalculable dangers and 'unsound' forces and freely predict general disaster."[27]

Schumacher's conclusion might, I think, be extended. Corporations—by and large—have rarely been willing to pay the costs of maintaining a healthy and enduring environment. Although businessmen are ideologically opposed to reducing the principal fund, they seem willing, with scarcely a twinge of conscience, to reduce the principal represented by the earth itself. The tension between business interests and environmental interests which has characterized the environmental movement was inevitable. It resulted from a profound difference of opinion as to how humankind should use the biosphere.

Distrust of environmentalism appeared in a second group: the technology-dependent. These included "hard" scientists and engineers such as industrial chemists, oil geologists, physicists, and others working outside the life sciences. A common theme in their opposition was that, because our inventiveness has always enabled us to overcome nature, it always will. But, one wonders, did they really believe that newfound technologies would enable us to advance forever while ignoring or defying Barry Commoner's Four Laws of Ecology?

> Everything is connected to everything else.
> Everything must go somewhere.
> Nature knows best.
> There is no such thing as a free lunch.[28]

When the harmful health effects of industrial chemicals were first being publicized in the 1960s, hard scientists were among the leading disparagers of environmentalism. John Maddox, a theoretical physicist, accused Rachel Carson of playing a literary trick on her readers. "The most seriously misleading part of the narrative is the use of horror stories about the misuse of DDT to create an impression that there are no safe uses worth consideration." Miss Carson's sin was the use of "calculated overdramatization." Maddox explained the difference between his personal optimism and that of the environmentalists: the "prophets of doom." He concluded that, "in the metaphor of spaceship earth, mere housekeeping needs courage. The most serious worry about the doomsday syndrome is that it will undermine our spirit."[29]

Granted that gloomy environmentalists exist; they at least understand the importance of *carrying capacity* in land management.

11

Consider, if you will, this prediction offered by Maddox in 1972: "But famine is now an unreal scarecrow. There is a good chance that the problems of the 1970s and 1980s will not be famine and starvation but, ironically, the problems of how best to dispose of food surpluses in countries where famine has until recently been epidemic." And ". . . there is no reason to complain at the way in which dams such as the Aswan Dam are known to fill with silt and eventually become unproductive of electricity—this, after all, is what used to happen to beaver dams on a much smaller scale."[30]

J. Peter Vajk, space technology analyst, studied computer models developed for the Club of Rome's widely read *Limits to Growth* (1972). He found them too pessimistic; misleading because they failed to credit the full potential of future innovation and creativity. He argued that we Earthlings can find a positive future by departing the womb of earth for outer space. "With virtually unlimited solar energy available in space, we eventually could build countless new settlements [there], with the total land area ultimately available *many thousands of times* greater than the total surface area of the entire planet Earth." We could be space-mining the asteroids and visiting the planets in craft powered by mass drivers, ion engines, and solar sails. Meanwhile, those of us left behind could be drawing limitless energy beamed from solar-cell satellites traveling in geosynchronous orbit 36,000 miles above us.[31] Vajk's arguments—blending science and philosophy—for enlarging the human environment were ably reasoned, but they missed the point. Until we have learned to live with nature on the planet which gave us birth and have learned as social organisms to respect one another and coexist in peace, it is certain that we cannot trust ourselves to found civilizations among the stars. The heavenly body which first we must make livable is the one beneath our feet.

"Like all the healing arts," wrote humanist Theodore Roszak in 1972, "ecology is through and through judgemental in character. . . . [It] is the closest our science has come to an integrative wisdom. It, and not physics, deserves to become the *basic* science of the future."[32]

Opposition to environmentalism came also from religious bigots. It was perpetuated by the notion that anything not covered in the Bible must be either untrue or evil. In 1971 Richard Neuhaus, a Lutheran minister, bitterly attacked the environmentalists as nature worshippers. He lumped Thoreau, John Muir, Hitler, and the ancient Canaanites as typical of their idolatrous kind.[33] Other ministers, less outspoken but equally sincere, denounced the environmental movement as "an American heresy" and as "a sort of

*Technological Man*

13

mindless ecological imperative . . . ultimately reactionary and antihuman, as well as anti-Christian."[34]

Once, after writer Joseph Wood Krutch had spoken from a Tucson radio station, an irate woman phoned in to denounce him for blasphemy. "Only man, she said, was valuable in God's sight, whereas I [Krutch] had put myself on the devil's side when I had confessed that I should not like to see even such 'noxious' creatures as the tarantula and the scorpion totally exterminated." Krutch silenced her by pointing out that the God of the Bible had carefully provided, through the agency of Noah, for the preservation of *all* species.[35]

Yale professor Stephen Kellert studied the influence of a person's religious background on his or her concern for the ethical treatment of animals. He found a marked difference in attitude between persons who attended church at least once a week and those who rarely or never attended. Most church participants regarded animals from a "utilitarian" perspective; most nonparticipants from a "humanistic" one. Kellert sought to understand the difference. Perhaps, he concluded, it stemmed from "the notion of a single God endowed with human image and characteristics, and the related belief that only man possesses the capacities for reason and immortality." Moreover, because idolatry is an abomination in Judeo-Christian theology, "the fundamental communality of humans and animals was regarded with grave concern by many strong adherents of traditional religious thought." In contrast, nonchurchgoers more easily accepted animals into the spiritual collective which comprises all life.[36]

It would have been, I suppose, the disciples of the most narrowly doctrinaire religions who spoke most loudly against environmentalism. On the other hand, the moderate National Council of Churches adopted in 1979 a clear policy statement on "the ethic of ecological justice." It expanded the definition of *neighbor* "to encompass all humans in past, present and future generations, as well as the rest of creation." Energy use, said the Council, "must not exceed the limited natural resources available, or overtax the ability of the environment to absorb pollution." The Council came out strongly against nuclear power on the grounds that it is inherently dangerous and can lead to the proliferation of weapons. The Council's vote on this ecological White Paper was 120 for, 26 against, 1 abstention.[37]

Timothy O'Riordan, a British environmentalist of uncommon vision, concluded in 1976:

At its heart environmentalism preaches a philosophy of human conduct that many still find difficult to understand, and those who are aware seemingly find unattainable. As we face the final quarter of the 20th century with growing uncertainty and increasing fears about the permanence of our institutions and the threat of violence and strife, the search for the environmentalist perspective may well come to dominate our total consciousness.[38]

# 2

# *The Societal Background*

The sixties and early seventies were shocking times.[1] Future historians may find it hard to envision the anger released as elements in our society fought to win freedom of opportunity and constitutional rights for themselves and for others. They struggled to change outmoded attitudes and institutions. They set themselves against received authority. They demanded that scientists and technologists rise from their workbenches to accept social responsibility. The ferment of the times would later be called the liberation movements. The environmental movement, while peripheral to those others, attracted many of the same activists: the thoughtful kinds who in every generation have seen no distinction between injustice to men and injustice to the earth. What the environmentalists and the liberationists shared in common was a fierce devotion to moral principles. They campaigned for what they perceived to be good.

The liberation movements brought rapid improvements. Having sacrificed during World War II for the freedom of humans abroad, we Americans turned to liberating humans at home: blacks, Native Americans, Hispanic Americans, Asian Americans, women, gays and lesbians, the physically handicapped, and the old. These were groups who, for generations past, had endured civil and economic inequality. And our concern even spread to the animals with whom we share the earth. We asked, "Do they not deserve rights resembling ours?" Many of us worked for freedom-of-information laws that would oblige government to account for its actions. We pushed for truth in advertising, and made consumerism—the protection of the interests of consumers—a popular word.

And when, in 1968, we saw the first images of Earth entire we thought of our lonely position in the universe, of our duty to the only home we shall ever have, and of our desperate need to survive as civilized beings here. One of the most stirring passages in the literature of the age was penned by poet Archibald MacLeish as he contemplated photographs taken from out beyond the moon:

> To see the earth as we now see it, small and blue and beau-
> tiful in that eternal silence where it floats, is to see our-
> selves as riders on the earth together, brothers on that bright
> loveliness in the unending night—brothers who *see* now they
> are truly brothers.[2]

The anger expressed by the sixties generation, said MacLeish, "was
not a resentment of our human life but a resentment *on behalf* of
human life; not an indignation that we exist on the earth but that
we *permit* ourselves to exist in a selfishness and wretchedness and
squalor which we have the means to abolish."[3]

• • •

For some of us, the zanier aspects of the sixties and seventies
are sharpest in memory: The four young men from Liverpool who
incited in 1964 the disorder called Beatlemania. The flower children
of Haight-Ashbury and Woodstock. The magic day of the great
Human Be-In described as "ending with 100,000 stoned revolu-
tionaries watching a parachutist floating through the afternoon sky
like an Icarus studiously making a deal with gravity."[4] And everywhere the hippies, hitchhiking, sleeping in parks and on beaches,
and clustering for mutual comfort in the grubbier corners of our
cities. A columnist for the *San Francisco Chronicle* wrote that "if the
hippies have done nothing else—and if they do nothing else—they
have made the rest of us reexamine our lives, look again at what
we are doing and why we are doing it."[5]

One thermometer of the fever of the times was the increase in
little newspapers with such names as *Rising Up Angry, Straight Creek
Journal, Quicksilver Times, Xanadu, Off Our Backs, Kudzu,* and *Prairie
Fire.* A journalism professor estimated that by 1969, the numbers
of such papers had risen to 500, with 4.5 million readers.[6] The
offbeat *Whole Earth Catalogs* were published in California from 1968
to 1981 (and revived in 1986). Profusely illustrated, they told where
to obtain plans for adobe and solar houses. They told where to buy
goats, guitars, kerosene lamps, motorcycle tires, pots, prayer lan-
terns, puppets, recipes for hangover melancholia, contraceptives,
sleeping bags, and vitamins, as well as books on desert survival,
doctoring, and dowsing. As we now turn the pages of these mav-
erick catalogs, we can better understand the hippies. We can feel
the fresh winds that stirred them.

Some individuals in the counterculture obeyed a pastoral impulse; they returned to the land. They rejected artificial and complex styles of living in favor of ones more natural and simple. "The

back-to-the-landers," wrote Carol Polsgrove, editor of *Mother Jones* magazine, "remind us that we can live in a circumscribed place, with a few people we know well, with a minimum of getting and spending—and be happy. They remind us that there is more than one sort of human society."[7] In 1971, fifteen men and women established a commune on 670 acres of scenic woodland and grassland in the Coast Range of northern California. Barbara Dean, one of the founders, told how she and her companions—all novices to the open country—met the challenges of subsisting on the fruits of their own labors and (equally difficult) of living with one another. At last report, the commune was thriving, and Ms. Dean was living under an oak tree in a yurt covered with burlap bags stiffened with cement.[8]

Herbert Marcuse became one of the gurus of the environmental movement; Wendell Berry one of its poets laureate. Marcuse, a visionary teacher at the University of California, was called by the *New York Times* "the most important philosopher alive." He preached the erotic possibilities of human life and approved militant, but nonviolent, action by the young. The young understood perfectly when he said, "If someone has to study a textbook on sexual behavior in order to learn how to make love to his wife or girl, something is wrong with him."[9] (The American Legion demanded he be fired from his teaching post.) Marcuse astutely foresaw the implications of the student revolt for the environmental movement. The revolt, he insisted, would have to accomplish a radical transformation of the very institutions and enterprises which waste our resources and pollute the earth. Heady stuff for students.

Wendell Berry, farmer and teacher as well as poet, predicted in 1971 that the environmental movement would ultimately be seen as the logical culmination of the civil rights and peace movements.

> They have the same cause, and that is the mentality of greed and exploitation. The mentality that exploits and destroys the environment is the same that abuses racial and economic minorities, that imposes on young men the tyranny of the military draft, that makes war against peasants and women and children with the indifference of technology. The mentality that destroys a watershed and then panics at the threat of flood is the same mentality that gives institutionalized insult to black people and then panics at the prospect of race riots. It is the same mentality that can mount deliberate warfare against a civilian population and then express moral shock at the logical consequences of such warfare at My Lai. We would be fools to believe that we could

solve any one of these problems without solving the others.[10]

The explosive rise of environmentalism angered some of the activists who were already deeply involved with Vietnam, civil rights, and poverty. These maintained that, while Nixon was plotting to carry the war into Laos and the police were clubbing blacks in the street, Planet Earth should wait its turn for attention. Indeed, *Ramparts* magazine editorialized that any analogy between the upcoming Earth Day teach-ins of 1970 and the various ongoing Vietnam teach-ins was "obscene." *Ramparts* complained that, while the sponsors of the Vietnam teach-ins were working at great odds "against the lies and opposition of the government, university administrations and the media," the sponsors of Earth Day were being blessed by Senator Gaylord Nelson, Nixon's Department of Health, Education, and Welfare, and well-funded conservation foundations.[11]

In 1970, The *Christian Century* quoted Douglas Moore, of the Washington Black United Front, as having called Ralph Nader "the biggest damn racist in the United States . . . more responsible than any man for perverting the war on poverty to the war on pollution."[12] But there was not, in fact, contradiction between the antipoverty and the antipollution movements. Both were aspects of a common program of reconstruction. The leaders of the two groups were similar in wanting to break through barriers of indifference and outright hostility to effect changes in the human condition. They were similar in the dedication and courage they displayed. That is to say, the social and economic preconditions for both the environmental and the liberation movements were basically the same.

It is understandable that the environmental movement should have offered the Johnson and Nixon administrations a domestic program which would divert attention from Vietnam. Both presidents endorsed the movement. And it is understandable that a young man sentenced to possible death in Vietnam, or denied his civil rights, should fault his government for showing more interest in endangered wolves and pupfish than in guaranteeing simple justice. But hindsight enables us to see that the dual and separate movements toward environmental health and societal health proceeded concurrently. The underprivileged and dispossessed among us will always complain, I suppose, that undue attention is being given to environmental issues, while others—mostly the better-off—will counter that earthkeeping is a perennial and fundamental responsibility. Earthkeeping has never needed, nor will it need, justification.

**Vietnam and the Student Revolt.** Our undeclared war in southeastern Asia began as a confused dream and became a nightmare that lasted sixteen years, from 1959 to 1975 (counting between the dates when the first and last American soldiers were killed). It was our longest war. It worried four presidents—Kennedy, Johnson, Nixon, and Carter—took 58,132 American lives, cost $100 billion, and left some of us doubting that ever again could we believe our own government. In 1972, the *New Yorker* editorialized: "Is it necessary, this week, to add that Vietnam, where we have turned half a nation into a purgatory (one part prison and torture chamber, one part lunatic asylum, one part whorehouse, and the rest a graveyard), where we have made an assault of unprecedented magnitude on the land, and where, in the process, we have damaged our language with propaganda and undermined our own laws, is the place where we Americans are, hacking away most vigorously at our parent, the Earth?"[13]

During the height of the war, environmentalists were distressed to learn of a new weapon developed for use in Vietnam: a chemical defoliant (Agent Orange) dropped from aircraft to destroy enemy crops and ambush-concealing vegetation. It contained traces of dioxin, which can poison directly or can cause miscarriage and birth defects such as spina bifida. From 1961 to 1971, the Army dropped about *20 million gallons* of the agent on the green fields and forests of Vietnam.[14] In 1984, after prolonged litigation, seven American manufacturers of Agent Orange volunteered to compensate war veterans for delayed-effect injuries from contact with the agent. While admitting no liability, the companies agreed out of court to establish a fund of $180 million—which could accumulate to $250 million within six years—for treatment of cancer, liver and nerve damage, persistent skin rashes, emotional difficulties, and other injuries. About 15,000 veterans, comprising U.S., Australian, and New Zealand soldiers, were plaintiffs in that class-action suit.[15] The United States rarely allows its own military to sue in civil court for casualties of war. In early 1989, however, a federal judge ordered the government to reexamine Agent Orange injury claims put forth by more than thirty thousand veterans. The outcome of the case will have important legal implications.

Vietnam was the principal cause of the student revolt of the sixties. Antagonism to the war extended to military research on campus and to the granting of academic credit for R.O.T.C. training.

Credit, explained the students bitterly, for learning state-of-the-art ways to kill, maim, destroy, and deceive. Violence erupted in the mid-sixties at scores of American colleges and universities. Students occupied campus buildings, set fire to libraries, destroyed research files, hurled obscenities (and worse) at speakers, and fought with police. Although the violence touched no more than one in fifty institutions, some had prestigious names like Harvard, Dartmouth, Columbia, Stanford, and the University of California at Berkeley.

In 1969, John Seeley, dean of Santa Barbara's Center for the Study of Democratic Institutions, dissected the causes of the student revolt. Among them, he concluded, were "the drift of war toward biocide; the mindless spoliation of nature and probable poisoning of the environment; the total corruption of men's minds by mass propaganda in small matters and large; the progressive alienation, constriction, and truncation of the human being [and] the dominance of technological thoughtways in which means float free of, or determine, ends."[16]

Then, on a warm spring Monday on the campus of Kent State University, there occurred an act of violence that pierced the heart of the nation. On May 4, 1970, twenty-eight national guardsmen opened fire on a group of unarmed students protesting the invasion of Cambodia, killing four and wounding nine. The newsphoto of Mary Vecchio weeping over the body of a fallen student is one that Americans would not soon forget.[17]

The student revolt lasted roughly a decade, from 1964 to 1973, by which time the more important grievances had been dealt with. And the 26th Amendment, ratified in 1971, had enfranchised youth in ages eighteen to twenty years, thus quieting their objection, "If we're old enough to fight and die we're old enough to vote."

I return to Archibald MacLeish, who understood the students because he was wise and humane and was a student himself throughout life: "If a generation is bold enough to face up to the truth about its troubles—bold enough to accept the truth, grow angry, rage—it may arrive at a state of honest indignation, violent revulsion against a dirty past, which will renew the future and give its aspirations hope."[18]

**The Struggle for Black Civil Rights.** In 1954, I was eating breakfast in a Washington, D.C., restaurant near a table occupied by two Southerners. I could hear them discussing the headlines in the morning news. Said one slowly, "It was the only thing to do, but God what a pity!" He spoke of the Warren Court's decision, *Brown* *v. Board of Education of Topeka*, the bold statement that established a legal base from which black Americans could reach upward for equality of opportunity. The ensuing years were years of national testing for white, as well as black, Americans—years in which charity and hatred were redefined.

The awesome influence of television, then scarcely a decade old, was demonstrated during the civil rights movement. Sociologist Daniel Bell recalls that "the sight on national television of police dogs snarling at Martin Luther King in Birmingham, Alabama, could raise a national storm of protest and within a day or two 10,000 persons could fly to Alabama to join him in a march of protest."[19] In February 1960, blacks at a Greensboro, North Carolina, lunch counter refused to leave when they were denied service, and so triggered the first of many "sit-ins." By October of that year, lunch counters in more than a hundred Southern cities had been integrated. "Merchants, with almost visible relief, dropped the encrusted restrictions of two centuries."

Older Americans remember the rioting in Biloxi when blacks tried to bathe at "public" but segregated city beaches . . . when children were afraid to enter Southern schools without protection from federal marshals . . . when "freedom riders" were beaten unconscious for trying to drink from whites-only fountains at an Alabama bus depot . . . when James H. Meredith was denied admission to the University of Mississippi . . . when four black girls in white Sunday dresses were bombed to death in a church in Birmingham . . . when Martin Luther King was killed by a sniper . . . when twenty-six persons died in Newark riots and forty in Detroit . . . when the National Guard was called to quell fighting in Boston after the court had ordered black children bused to predominantly white schools. Older Americans remember.

The editors of *Life*, looking back at the sixties, agreed that the single event most representative of those turbulent years was the rioting in the Watts district of Los Angeles during August 1965. "It was Watts, sudden and violent, that finally ripped the fabric of lawful democratic society and set the tone of confrontation and open revolt so typical of our present time [1969]."[20]

But irreversible steps toward racial equality *were* gradually taken. Schools, universities, and public facilities *were* integrated. The Civil Rights Acts of 1960 and 1964, and the Voting Rights Act of 1965, promised a new day for blacks. The Fair Housing Act (1968) abolished discrimination in 80 percent of U.S. housing. The 24th Amendment abolished the poll tax, originally designed to disenfranchise the Southern poor (mostly blacks). Robert C. Weaver became in 1966 American's first black cabinet member; Thurgood Marshall in 1967 the first black on the Supreme Court. Whereas there had been two black congressmen in 1960, there were seventeen in 1980. *Brown v. Board of Education* had given blacks a powerful assist by offering them equal opportunity to learn; the important Civil Rights Act of 1964 offered them equal opportunity to live and work where they chose. It touched the lives of every American and cleared the way for thousands of middle-class blacks to obtain decent jobs and housing. "Equal opportunity acts" in 1974 spelled out the rights of all citizens to an education and to commercial credit. Affirmative action to erase inequalities in hiring soon became, under Lyndon Johnson, a national policy.

"The reawakening of moral zeal," concluded writer Charles Morris, "was the finest achievement of the civil rights movement. The stark courage of the SNCC [Student Nonviolent Coordinating Committee] kids, the mute force of a quarter million marchers, the cadenced rhythms of the black spirituals, the shining, transcendent glory of stoic resistance to hoses, clubs, and dogs, all stirred sensibilities dulled by the technocratic reductionist creed."[21]

**The Feminist Movement: Sisterhood.** When my father was a boy, the Supreme Court upheld a state law denying women the right to practice law, explaining that "the natural and proper timidity and delicacy which belongs to the female sex evidently unfits it for many of the occupations of civil life." As recently as 1961, the court permitted the exclusion of women from jury duty on grounds of sex, citing their role as "the center of home and family life" (a decision reversed in 1975). But, in the 1960s, women moved swiftly to recognize their own worth as human beings and to accept, equally with men, the full responsibilities of citizens. Women began to gain exceptional political power when they launched the "new feminist movement."

In 1975, the International Women's Year, sponsored by the United Nations, was celebrated with meetings in many parts of the world. The most notable was The Tribune, held in Mexico City and attended by more than five thousand. During 1975, wrote columnist Abigail McCarthy, "for the first time in the history of the world, women *representing their countries* met in international conferences in which they outnumbered men, and gave consideration to their own destinies."[22] And in 1977, a spectacular National Women's Conference, funded by the U.S. government, convened in Houston. More than 1,400 voting delegates discussed legalized abortion, lesbian rights, the Equal Rights Amendment (ERA), and other issues of interest to women. On one occasion, three hundred outraged "pro-life" and "pro-family" delegates quit the convention floor, singing "God Bless America" to prove that their kind of patriotism was purer than that of the delegates left behind.

During the sixties and seventies, feminists successfully lobbied for national legislation and administrative changes, some revolutionary. Who, for example, could have predicted that the federal government would legislate a girl's right, equal to a boy's, to participate in school athletics? In the summer before his death, President John F. Kennedy signed the Equal Pay Act of 1963, requiring equal pay for equal work regardless of sex. The Civil Rights Act of 1964 banned, among other practices, male/female help-wanted advertisements. Executive Order 11246 (1965) and its Amendment 11375 (1967) banned sex discrimination in colleges, in most federally assisted educational programs, in the federal government, and by federal contractors. In 1965, the Supreme Court struck down an ancient Connecticut law prohibiting birth-control devices, thus establishing a woman's broad "right to privacy." The Equal Employment Opportunity Act (1972) eased litigation in cases of employment discrimination, and the hotly argued ERA (1972) was sent to the states for approval. In 1973, the Supreme Court ruled that states may not prevent a woman from having an abortion during the first six months of pregnancy. That ruling, based on *Roe v. Wade* and *Doe v. Bolton*, fanned the flames of a controversy which may survive far beyond our time. (It was ably described in Barbara Milbauer's book, *The Law Giveth: Legal Aspects of the Abortion Controversy*.)[23]

Back to the ERA. It was only twenty-four words: "Equality of rights under the law shall not be denied or abridged by the United States or by any state on account of sex." Its opponents—including, oddly, many women—felt that it threatened the familiar, homey America where a woman knew her place and was content to stay there. After bitter controversy, time ran out in 1982 for the ERA. It had received only thirty-five of the necessary thirty-eight state ratifications. But it may yet become law, for a 1984 Louis Harris poll indicated that 63 percent of women and 58 percent of men favored it.[24]

The feminist movement remains healthy and lively, supported by an ideology, a literature, and political clout. Except for a dwindling number of male-dominated organizations, including private clubs, fundamentalist churches, hard-hat labor unions, and lawmaking cliques, women are increasingly held to be "as good as men." As newswoman Shana Alexander wrote in 1975, "No one in this country is a full citizen until he or she is accorded the same rights, privileges as every other citizen. Laws that treat men and women differently—whether the differences are discriminatory or 'protective'—raise basic questions about the status of women as full citizens."[25]

**The Demand for Accountability.** As environmentalism gained new followers, they demanded of government and of industry changes that would bring healthier surroundings, not only out-of-doors but in the home and workplace. They newly realized their status as consumers, and introduced the word "consumerism." They called for freedom of information in those areas vital to public health which had been hidden from them on the excuse of national security or trade secrecy. They demanded public participation in government decision making. They demanded openness in the affairs of the various Establishment bodies which their money supported and which, in turn, strongly influenced their daily lives. They demanded *accountability*.

I don't mean that their demands appeared *de novo* in the sixties. As early as 1936, the Consumers Union of the United States, a nonprofit membership group, had begun to test merchandise and to publicize its findings. It became widely known as a champion of truth in advertising and, by 1960, its monthly *Consumer Reports* had attained a circulation of 865,000.[26]

The founder of the consumer rights movement in America—and still its best-known activist—was Ralph Nader. "When Nader's book *Unsafe at Any Speed* first appeared in 1965," reported Mark Sullivan, "the author was so unknown that General Motors, whose Corvair automobile was the target of the attack, hired a special investigator to determine who he was and what he was really up to. He was found to be a modest young bachelor and recent graduate of Harvard Law School who appeared to be up to nothing more than being concerned over the safety, health, and rights of individual citizens living in a world dominated by business and government interests."[27] *Unsafe at Any Speed* provoked within the auto industry howls of rage like those which had been provoked within the chemical industry by the publication of *Silent Spring*. Nader urged the government to require safety standards on everything from brake performance to windshields. Within a year after the appearance of his book, Congress passed the National Traffic and Motor Vehicle Safety Act of 1966 which gave the federal government authority to establish and enforce automobile safety standards. Nader, by then established as Mr. Consumer, continued to write books and to lecture, using his royalties to finance research and lobbying. Lasting monuments to his zeal and industry are the Center for Science in the Public Interest and dozens of Public Interest Research Groups (PIRGs).

Interest in consumerism swelled concurrently with interest in environmentalism. Among the laws passed between 1966 and 1972 were the National Traffic and Motor Vehicle Safety Act of 1966, the Fair Packaging and Labeling Act (1966), the Wholesome Meat Act (1967), the Consumer Credit Protection ("Truth in Lending") Act (1968), the Wholesome Poultry Products Act (1968), the landmark Occupational Safety and Health Act of 1970 (OSHA), and the Consumer Product Safety Act (1972). A new federal bureau, the Consumer Protection and Environmental Health Service, was launched in 1971. Thanks to legislation, Americans were now able to buy safer autos and to be informed of the octane ratings of auto fuels. They learned which food additives were hazardous. They gained new protection from deceptive advertising. When, in 1972, the *Britannica Book of the Year* introduced a section on Consumer Affairs, it signaled the coming of age of a new power group within our society.

•   •   •

The landmark Freedom of Information Act was passed during the presidency of Lyndon B. Johnson. At its core were these words: "Except as otherwise required by statute, matters of official record shall be made available, in accordance with published rule, to persons properly and directly concerned, except information held confidential for good cause found." Those mainly responsible for drafting its terms were journalists engaged in a running battle with the Pentagon over restrictions placed on news from Vietnam, and with judges over restrictions on the publication of crime news considered prejudicial to fair trial. The 1966 act opened many government records to the public while withholding a few, such as military security papers and personnel and medical records, so it nicely balanced the citizen's right to know with his or her right to privacy. A person denied information could sue the reluctant agency in federal court.

Environmentalists saw at once that the act would be invaluable to them. It would, for example, give them access to the facts essential for winning court cases in which government agencies (such as the Army Corps of Engineers) were suspected of environmental malpractice. Moreover, the Freedom of Information Act and its later amendments guaranteed that "a person suffering legal wrong be-

*Ralph Nader*

cause of agency action . . . is entitled to judicial review thereof." When amendments to the Freedom of Information Act were passed by Congress in 1974, President Gerald Ford vetoed them on the grounds that they were "simply unrealistic." Congress overrode his veto. The 1976 Government in the Sunshine Act was the last in a series of accountability laws. It declared that the public "is entitled to the fullest practicable information regarding the decision-making processes of the Federal Government. It is the purpose of this Act to provide the public with such information while protecting the rights of individuals and the ability of the Government to carry out its responsibilities."

**The Liberation of Animals.** "Either love . . . is something which we share with animals or it is something which does not really exist in us," wrote Joseph Wood Krutch, drama critic and self-taught naturalist.[28] Because human life depends in one way or another upon nonhuman animals, should we not respect them? Should we not concede them rights, or preemptive claims to life, approaching those that we ourselves enjoy? Such questions have been voiced from the time when the Christian radical, Francis of Assisi, preached the equality of all living forms. Although he failed in his time, the world eventually heard his message. With the coming of environmentalism the message was accepted as scripture in the animal liberation, or animal rights, movement.

The movement shares with the Western "humane societies" concern for the welfare of animals, but is ideologically more deeply rooted, more complete. While its disciples try to spare animals pain and fear they ask, *Why* are we doing so? They value the animal more or less independently of its material contribution to mankind. The future of endangered species is a shared concern of activists in both the animal liberation and environmental camps. And logically so, for those who seek justice for the individual are likely to campaign as well for the preservation of the whole species of which the individual is a part.

The animal liberation movement is fairly new. The Society for Animal Protective Legislation was founded in 1955 by a steadfast humanitarian, Christine Stevens. The Society for Animal Rights was incorporated in 1959 and began in 1980 to publish the *Animal Rights Law Reporter*. A Universal Declaration of the Rights of Animals— issued in London in 1978 over the signatures of two million—affirmed that "all animals are born with an equal claim on life and the same rights to existence. . . . The rights of animals, like human beings, should enjoy the protection of the law."[29] The Society for the Study of Ethics and Animals and the Scientists Center for Animal Welfare were founded in 1979. Both the Animal Rights Network and the Attorneys for Animal Rights were also founded in 1979. By early 1983, nineteen American colleges would be offering courses on ethics and animals.[30]

One measure of the growth of the animal liberation movement was the increase of public interest from 1960 to 1980 in benign, or appreciative, uses of wildlife. The number of camera safaris rose meteorically.[31] State wildlife agencies began to develop "nongame wildlife" or "watchable wildlife" programs. (Nongame species include kingfishers, herons, eagles, owls, prairie dogs, chipmunks, wolves, flying squirrels, and other species not traditionally killed for sport or for the market.) By 1986, more than thirty states would be funding nongame programs through "checkoffs" on state income tax forms, for a total revenue of $9 million.

In the spring of 1972, law professor Christopher D. Stone published in the *Southern California Law Reporter* an article that posed a startling question: "Should Trees Have Standing? Toward Legal Rights for Natural Objects." Stone suggested that, because all things in nature (including animals) are vulnerable to damage by humans, perhaps they deserve to be regarded as "jural persons" having the right, equally with faceless corporations, to sue for justice. The proposition gave rise to furious discussion. Thirteen years later, Stone published a book-length revision: "a more expansive inquiry into the legal and moral status of what I call unconventional entities generally—not merely lakes and mountains, but robots and embryos, tribes and species, future generations and artifacts."[32]

In 1970, Richard D. Ryder, a clinical psychologist, coined a word which was to enter the Oxford English Dictionary: "speciesism."[33] It means bias toward the interests of one's own species and against members of other species, and is analogous with racism and sexism. Peter Singer, Australian philosopher, became one of the leaders of the animal liberation movement. He concluded in 1975 that

> the environmental movement . . . has led people to think about our relation with other animals in a way that seemed impossible only a decade ago. To date environmentalists have been more concerned with wildlife and endangered species than with animals in general, but it is not too big a jump from the thought that it is wrong to treat whales as giant vessels filled with oil and blubber to the thought that it is wrong to treat pigs as machines for converting grains to flesh.[34]

He contended that animals have rights which humans are morally obligated to respect. But, when we *must* treat one species at the expense of another, we should sacrifice the one having the lesser capacity to suffer. (Singer, by the way, is a vegetarian.) He wrote in 1973 that "if possessing greater intelligence does not entitle one human to exploit another, why should it entitle humans to exploit nonhumans?"[35]

I recall an experiment performed in the 1950s which could not be repeated openly in America today because it would call for the prolonged suffering of several hundred animals. It was carried out at Johns Hopkins University School of Medicine. A physiologist dropped rats, one by one, into swirling water-baths of various temperatures to learn how long each could swim before it drowned. He hoped to find a difference in endurance under stress between tame and wild rats. He found that "the average survival times were directly related to the temperature of the water."[36] One rat clung to life for eighty-one hours, or more than three days. Tame rats survived longer than wild ones, perhaps because they trusted people. Curiously, a few rats died when they first touched the water, or even while they were being held. From these observations the researcher gained insight into the sudden death, or voodoo, phenomenon: a way of dying in which the victim suddenly "gives up." Before each rat died, its pulse and breathing rate slowed and its temperature dropped, while its heart filled with blood. The researcher concluded that sudden death is apparently "a result of hopelessness; this seems to involve overactivity primarily of the parasympathetic system."

But was it necessary to cause intense suffering to confirm what had been known to nurses and doctors for centuries?

# AREAS OF ENVIRONMENTAL CONCERN

# 3

# Croplands, Rangelands, and Forests

In the 1960s we newly recognized certain areas of concern which were geographical: where America had been poisoned, or worn threadbare, or buried under wastes, or bereft of biodiversity, or exploited beyond carrying capacity. We recognized other areas which were conceptual: where ingrained attitudes toward our surroundings threatened to block remedial action. These various areas of concern can be arranged in about a dozen categories: croplands, rangelands, and forests; natural lands; the ocean; fresh water resources; air quality; mineral resources; energy resources; control of the atom; society's wastes and poisons; endangered species; and the human population. Their boundaries overlap. Wastes and poisons, for example, are a concern deserving singular attention yet one that impinges upon all the others. I offer in this chapter a brief description of each area of concern.

Farm experts began pointing in the 1960s to symptoms of cropland abuse which could no longer be ignored. These included soil loss through erosion, exhaustion of soil fertility, soil salination from irrigation water, pollution of soils by biocides, sedimentation of water-storage reservoirs, and falling water tables. Moreover, the growth of cropland area was barely keeping pace with the growth of the human population. At least one million acres were disappearing yearly under roads and buildings, while slightly more acreage was being added through the reclamation of land. According to President Carter's widely read *Global 2000 Report*, cropland area seemed unlikely to increase by more than 6.8 percent by the end of the century.[1] Thus, in millions of acres in arable land:

| Years: | 1951–55 | 1961–65 | 1971–75 | 1985 | 2000 |
|---|---|---|---|---|---|
| Acres (M): | 456 | 372 | 495 | 482 | 515 |

So, in the next ten years, arable land may increase by about 7 percent while the population is increasing by 7 or 8 percent. These estimates alone do not portend serious food shortages. However, the *quality* of the land is deteriorating at a frightful rate.

Soil erosion is the greatest threat to cropland. Soil is more than "dirt," it is an ordered, complex tissue which, if formed from parent rock, may have required eons in the making. It is lost in runoff and is lifted by the wind, especially from fine-grained prairie soils that never should have felt the plow. When the prairie vegetation was first broken by man, no roots remained to bind the soil, which dried in summer and was carried away. The Iowa that the First Americans knew carried a natural topsoil about sixteen inches deep; today it measures only eight inches. Farming methods that failed to protect the soil from erosion were responsible for the loss. The Department of Agriculture estimates that over one-third of U.S. croplands are losing annually more than five tons of topsoil per acre. Nationwide, the loss is more than 3 billion tons a year. Moreover, the off-farm impacts are part of the distressing picture. Silt carried in runoff impedes navigation, shortens the life of reservoirs, contributes to flood damage, pollutes drinking water, kills fish and their eggs, and costs the nation about $6 billion a year.[2]

When the basic productivity of their land decreased, farmers compensated by using chemical fertilizers—some synthetic and others mined—at a rate that ultimately reached the equivalent cost of $43 per year for every American. Chemical fertilizers weaken the ability of natural soil-decomposers, such as bacteria and fungi, to do their work, thus gradually leaving the soil ever more dependent on renewed applications of fertilizer. Moreover, because fertilizers are energy costly, the substitution of energy for soil was dismaying to environmentalists. They saw it as Band Aid treatment for a gnawing disease. They questioned its morality. Why, they asked, should we sacrifice our fertile soils—our birthright and source of economic strength since colonial times—merely to buy a few billion barrels of foreign oil? Farmers do not have the right, they said, to engage in the agronomic equivalent of deficit financing.[3]

A Council on Environmental Quality report on desertification in the late 1970s ended with an alarming statement:

> Desertification in the arid United States is flagrant. Groundwater supplies beneath vast stretches of land are dropping precipitously. Whole river systems have dried up; others are choked with sediment washed from denuded land. Hundreds of thousands of acres of previously irrigated

cropland have been abandoned to wind or weeds. Salts are building up steadily in some of the nation's most productive irrigated soils. Several million acres of grassland are, as a result of cultivation or overgrazing, eroding at unnaturally high rates. . . . All total, about 225 million acres of land in the United States are undergoing severe desertification—an area roughly the size of the 13 original states.[4]

•   •   •

Two sprawling agencies—the Bureau of Land Management (BLM) and the Forest Service—manage 318 million acres of rangelands, mostly in the West and Southwest. Encompassing an area as large as Texas, Oklahoma, and California combined, the lands were set aside long ago as watersheds and to provide for livestock grazing, hunting, fishing, camping, mining, and logging. Even the assigned wilderness areas within them were legally open to grazing as long as motorized vehicles were not used. Although the rangelands had been dedicated to multiple use, livestock operators intent on single use gradually gained political control. They paid the government absurdly low grazing fees and they abused the land. Grazing rights were sold, along with private ranch estates, as though they were patrimonial rights. By 1985, the grazing fee charged by the BLM

*Logo of American Farmland Trust*

and the Forest Service would be $1.37 per animal per month, while the fair market value outside the public lands averaged $6.65.[5] Overgrazing led to erosion, impaired the water-storage capacity of the soil, encouraged the spread of weeds, and robbed antelope, deer, elk, and wild sheep of their natural forage. According to the BLM's own assessment in 1975, only 17 percent of its rangelands were in good or excellent condition.[6]

During the mid-fifties I worked at a range and forest experiment station in Colorado where one of my colleagues was a specialist in forage grasses. When we traveled together in the field he would often point to some impoverished rangeland, while fuming at the indifference of the government agency that was allowing it to deteriorate. On one occasion, he placed a golf ball on the ground and photographed it from a distance of ten paces. It stood out clearly above the cropped grass. The photo later served as evidence in the Washington Office that the range had been abused.

Environmentalists were less disturbed by the revenue loss from "rigged" grazing fees than by the destruction of longstanding grassland ecosystems. They complained that the federal stewards of those systems were focusing myopically on grass as a crop, ignoring many other land values. The "chaining" of rangelands to stimulate the growth of forage grasses was particularly obnoxious. Chaining meant connecting six hundred feet of massive chain between two tractors and dragging the chains through the elfin forests of the Southwest: areas which are sparsely covered with brush, pinyon, and juniper. The scalped areas were then seeded to grasses favored by sheep and cattle. Up to 1985, about 3 million acres of semiarid land had been chained. Although chaining helped the livestock owners—at taxpayers' expense—it returned no watershed benefits, destroyed wildlife habitats, rubbed out archaeological sites, and deprived native people of an important winter food (pinyon nuts) and an important source of winter fuel (pinyon branches).

Ecology students learn that the birthplace of American scientific ecology was on the rolling, tallgrass plains of the Midwest in the early years of our century. Although the plains seem monotonous they are, in fact, diversiform in plant and animal communities. They early attracted what one historian has called "the first coherent group of ecologists in the United States."[7] Their names are in the textbooks: Frederic Clements, Homer L. Shantz, Victor E. Shelford, and John E. Weaver. (I knew only Shantz. In the 1950s he often lectured on plant succession, showing paired photographs he had taken at identical sites forty years apart.) Now the third generation of ecologists is studying what remains of the tallgrass cover which is, alas, only one-sixth of one percent of its original area.

• • •

"There is," wrote John Fowles, British poet and essayist, "a spiritual corollary to the way we are currently deforesting and denaturing our planet. In the end what we must defoliate and deprive is ourselves."[8]

During the nineteenth century, the federal government's basic policy for public forested lands had been to dispose of them as quickly as possible for homesteading, logging, and other private uses. But, even as the public domain was vanishing, a few far-sighted citizens were pushing for legislation that would keep the best of the green, unbroken forests in public ownership forever. Out of their concern, the Creative Act of 1891 was born. It gave the president authority to set aside forest reservations. Thus began an experiment in ownership that, by 1984, was to bring one-tenth of the nation's public lands into the National Forest System.

The Forest Service, created in 1905, was empowered to conserve and wisely use the wood, water, and forage of the national forests. The Service managed the forests rather well for the next eighty-five years but—in the view of ecologists—was never quite able to see the forest for the trees; it steadily looked upon its lands as tree farms rather than as intricate systems affecting the welfare of millions of people in manifold ways. With the spread of environmentalism came public demand for a more holistic forest management policy, one that would guarantee the survival of forest products *and* amenity returns *and* jobs for centuries to come. Among the management questions which have troubled the Forest Service for a long time are these:

1. How much of America's ancient forest (with trees over two hundred years old) should be preserved intact as specimen timberlands? While some of these rare lands are now protected, others are not. Ancient (or "virgin," or "old growth") forests are the most stable and diverse of all forest systems. They are vital to the existence of birds such as the spotted owl and marbled murrelet, and mammals such as the marten and fisher.

A recent incident near Portland, Oregon, highlights the persistent hold of corporate business on the people's forests. The Forest Service sold the Millennium Grove, a supreme stand of virgin Douglas fir, to Willamette Industries. The Grove should have been kept as a national shrine where visitors could walk among trees that were young when William took England in 1066. But its amenity value was destroyed in a day. While environmentalists were rushing to get a court injunction, Willamette felled the oldest trees first, thus rendering court action moot. Tragically, the Service had offered Willamette substitute timber, which the company refused "as a matter of principle."[9] (When someone says it's not the money but the principle, it's the money.)

2. Where should timber be harvested by clearcutting and where by selective cutting? There is no easy answer, yet public opinion steadily opposes clearcutting on sites of prime scenic value. A deputy chief of the Service wrote in 1972 that "the Service has been slow and insensitive to the awakening national awareness of our environment. Until recently it has failed to perceive the shocking impact of clearcutting devastation on the public senses. . . . It has failed to understand that clearcutting should be judged not only as a timber harvesting device, but also with respect to its environmental impact. . . ."[10]

3. Where should forests be let stand, uncut, purely because they protect their environment? A federal forester wrote in 1969: "There are many acres of otherwise good timber growing land that should not be logged because of very fragile soils or very steep slopes. Such areas could easily be identified and mapped except that no one has yet been able to specify how much soil movement should be tolerated in individual situations. One of the most pressing tasks in American conservation today, therefore, is the research required to determine the *capacities* [emphasis added] of the land, air, and water resources so that we can retain their quality and productivity under use."[11]

4. How should the Service deal with wildfire? About sixty years ago, managers began to entertain a revolutionary idea: Why not set fires deliberately, though cautiously, to burn accumulated forest litter? That is, set little fires to forestall the big one which would burn more hotly and damage the soil itself. Moreover, under what circumstances should the Service let a fire burn after it has been caused naturally by lightning? And if the fire happens to be in a dedicated roadless area, should roads be built anyway to permit salvage logging?

5. Perhaps the most insistent question put by friends of America's forests is: Can they really be managed on a sustained-yield basis? To the casual observer, particularly in the Pacific Northwest, the acreage of logged-off land appears to be increasing faster than the acreage of young, growing forest.

A forestry professor at the University of California wrote in *Sci-*

*ence* in 1976 that the national forests were "poorly managed and unproductive."[12] Later, the Congressional Research Service reported on a study of government timber sales to private lumber companies. The report created a mild sensation, for it disclosed deficit sales totaling nearly $1.6 billion over the period 1973–83.[13] That is, timber sales did not cover the costs of road building, paperwork in connection with the sales, and other expenses. Environmentalists claimed that the report confirmed what they had long thought: that the Forest Service was in cahoots with the lumber industry at the taxpayers' expense.

Environmentalists will never be satisfied with the management of the green forests they love if the Forest Service keeps a core of authority beyond reach of citizen pressure. As an environmental lawyer has put it, "administrative agencies are inherently undemocratic aberrations in an otherwise democratic society."[14] They germinate and grow because the normal democratic process is unable to cope with complex and often technical management problems.

On the bright side, the Service is now trying to manage its lands for multiple use by partitioning each forest into zones, some dedicated to timber production and others to such uses as recreation and watershed. Whether this objective will ultimately provide (in Pinchot's words) the greatest good for the greatest number for the longest time remains to be seen. Pinchot's goal is attractive in its simplicity but it calls for an impossibility: the maximization of three variables at the same time. "Imagine," says Orris Herfindahl, on the staff of Resources for the Future, "a father trying to distribute a bag of candy to his children so as to maximize the amount of candy received by each child who gets candy *and* the number of children receiving candy *and* the length of time the candy will be visible."[15]

# 4

# *Natural Lands*

*Woe unto them that join house to house, that lay field to field, till there be no place, that they may be placed alone in the midst of the earth!*

Isaiah 5

America's land policy until the middle of the twentieth century was shaped around the conviction that land is for economic use. That policy relaxed under pressure from citizens who insisted that more land be preserved for its contained values in recreation, research, education, and amenity. Thus, in 1972, Congress studied a natural-areas bill (H.R. 13207) based on the premise that "the preservation and protection of such areas, which illustrate the geological and ecological character of the United States, and their appropriate uses including environmental education, scientific research, and public appreciation must be encouraged and assisted." Although the bill did not pass, it signaled a move in public taste. People wanted easier access to nature. Their enthusiasm for adding new natural lands and preserving those already established became a distinctive mark of the environmental age. Today, America's natural lands range in purity or "naturalness" from national parks (older and more disturbed) to national wilderness areas (younger and less disturbed). Let me compare the two extremes.

Conservation was once defined by a distinguished ecologist as a "wise principle of co-existence between man and nature, even if it has to be a modified kind of man and a modified kind of nature."[1] Our national parks are a modified kind of nature. The national park idea, uniquely American, was conceived by men and women who, upon reaching a New World rich in virgin lands not yet privately owned, invented novel ways of zoning them for many uses. (Other nations would follow suit, creating parks in the more nat-

40

ural and scenic parts of their domains.) In 1916, Congress established the National Park Service to improve the administration of parks, historical monuments, and reservations. The Service made plain its intent "to conserve the scenery and the natural and historic objects and the wildlife therein and to provide for the enjoyment of the same in such manner and by such means as will leave them unimpaired for the enjoyment of future generations."[2]

But Park Service administrators soon learned that federal appropriations to protect the parks from the people who used them and wished them well were chronically inadequate. As early as the 1930s, when I spent five summers as a ranger-naturalist in Mount Rainier National Park, I could see erosion spreading across the alpine flower fields under the trampling of people and horses. In 1953, writer Bernard DeVoto, a resolute defender of our public lands, protested in *Harper's*, "Let's Close the National Parks."[3] Because he saw little prospect that Congress would fully support the parks, he advised that the largest one "be closed and sealed, held in trust for a more enlightened future." The staffs and budgets for the closed parks would be diverted to those kept open. The government did not, of course, take his advice.

Thirty years later, an issue of *Life* bore the headline, "National Parks in Peril." The parks were still suffering from neglect. They were reeling under the impact of 300 million visitors a year and were being threatened from all sides by logging, grazing, smelting, power plants, toxic-waste dumps, housing subdivisions, coal mines, oil wells, herbicides, and pesticides. "Unless conservation policies change their emphasis from the maintenance of tourist facilities to the preservation of wilderness," observed a *Life* writer, "the nation's Park Service employees will never be able to defend their beleaguered domains from the trespasses of civilization."[4] The Park Service itself acknowledged in 1981 "the destruction and degradation of the parks."[5] While pleading with Congress for more money, it described over five hundred specific threats to individual parks.

Roderick Nash is a professor of history and environmental studies at the University of California at Santa Barbara. His powerful book, *Wilderness and the American Mind*, described four cultural revolutions that shaped our present wilderness ethic.[6] First, a mature philosophy emerged: "the reasons for wilderness appreciation filtered down from intellectuals to a broader base of acceptance in American society." Second, technological research and development during World War Two left a legacy of new recreational gear. Bulky, heavy materials gave way to fiberglass, nylon, aluminum, and freeze-dried foods. Third, ease of transportation took a quantum leap. "It can be argued," wrote Nash, "that the piece of technology with the most devastating effect on the American wilderness was the family automobile." And fourth, aids to outdoor travel proliferated. Books, guides, films, and maps became available to amateurs as well as professionals. Commercial guide-and-outfitting companies appeared like dandelions in the spring.

We neglected not only our national parklands but our national seashores; we woke belatedly to the need for bringing examples of the best ones into public ownership. A Park Service shoreline survey team returned in 1954 with the dismaying news that, of the 3,700 miles of Atlantic and Gulf Coast beaches, only 6.5 percent were in federal or state ownership for recreational use.[7] Gradually, though, the Park Service designated strips as national seashores, ultimately protecting more than 600,000 acres in the conterminous United States. By 1982, there were ten such strips: In California, Florida, Georgia, Maryland, Massachusetts, Mississippi, New York, North Carolina, and Texas. And three *underwater* parks—in the marine shallows of Florida's Dry Tortugas, the Florida Keys, and the Virgin Islands—protected fragile coral reef communities.

• • •

Some fifty years ago, when the public parks and forests were still fairly natural and wild, a few visionary men were dreaming beyond their time . . . dreaming of scenic retreats even more natural and wild. Each would be "an environment of solitude . . . a natural mental resource having the same basic relation to man's ultimate thought and culture as coal, timber and other physical resources have to his material needs."[8] Those areas would be administered as a *wilderness system*. The dream eventually materialized.

My own glimpse of the dream came in 1937 when, with other members of a biological survey party to the remote Aleutian Islands, led by naturalist/explorer Olaus Murie, I was resting on the lip of an old volcano. We were alone. The islands were unpeopled for two hundred miles in either direction. The clean, awesome beauty of the place reminded Olaus that he had recently helped to create a special wilderness organization. As we ate our lunch he explained. Eight men—a forester, a forest economist, a regional planner, a landscape architect, an editor, a wildlife biologist, a lawyer, and a certified public accountant—in 1935 had organized the Wilderness Society. The forester happened to be Bob Marshall, a wealthy New Yorker who launched the organization with a gift of $1,000 and was later to give it sums totaling about $400,000.

As the young society grew, its goals remained unchanged: to preserve climax examples of wildlands and wildlife, prime forests, parks, rivers, and shorelands. The society spearheaded a citizen campaign that led in 1964 to the creation of the present National Wilderness System, a complex including about 90 million acres within national parks, forests, and wildlife refuges, and within Bureau of Land Management holdings. The campaign succeeded against bitter opposition from commercial interests in mining, gas and oil extraction, lumbering, and grazing. Moreover, it received either lukewarm support or open opposition from the directors of the Park Service and the Forest Service, who foresaw loss of control over their respective domains.[9]

"A river is more than an amenity," declared Oliver Wendell Holmes from the Supreme Court bench in 1931, "it is a treasure. It offers a necessity of life that must be rationed among those who have power over it."[10] The Wilderness Society began in the 1960s to help Congress identify and preserve the last free-flowing reaches of America's finest rivers before they could be "improved" by government engineers. A national Wild and Scenic Rivers Act was signed in 1968, but pork-barrel political pressures to dam or channelize rivers remained incredibly strong. When recreational rafters recently brought suit to prevent the damming of the South Fork of the American River, in California, they were conceded a weekend river only: one that would flow on Saturdays, Sundays, and holidays!

Among men and women ranging from career ecologists to poets, there have always been some who hold for wilderness a respect near reverence. They see in wilderness a Nature unpolluted, ancient, and eternal. The practicing ecologist turns to wilderness for baseline data from which he or she can measure changes inflicted upon adjacent areas by civilization. In the center of the untouched ecosystem he studies energy flow, the recycling of materials, the adaptations of the organism to its habitat, and the succession of species. The poet turns to wilderness for adventures of the mind. Surrounded by models of diversity beyond human grasp, he lets his imagination soar. Though still in the real world he escapes it. Lord Byron, returning from a foot journey through the Alps, wrote in his diary, "I have lately repeopled my mind with Nature."[11]

In the range between the ecologist and the poet are millions who visit wilderness for plain delight. And there are many others who have never set foot in a wilderness and never will, yet cherish the thought that places on earth have been set aside deliberately for the inspiration of generations yet unborn. It has been one of my deep satisfactions to have followed for half a century the evolution of the wilderness idea. Persistently under attack, regarded as elitist by some and impractical by others, it has won a secure place in our national thought. Our wilderness reserves continually remind us that we are a society which, by saving a material heritage, has saved a moral one.

# 5

# *The Ocean*

The world ocean covers 70 percent of the globe. Its plant life yields perhaps 40 billion tons of carbon a year, or more than all the organic carbon produced on land. For centuries we thought of the ocean as a limitless source of seafoods, whales, seals, minerals, and energy; and as a bottomless sink into which we could dump our wastes. We treated it as though its vast size and resilience would protect it forever from insult. We were wrong.

The world seafood harvest reached a temporary peak of 70 million tons a year in 1970; declined; reached the same peak in 1978; and has been rising very slowly since. The *per capita* harvest, though, has been falling since 1970, when it reached 43 pounds.[1] The harvest is unlikely to increase much through artificial farming (aquaculture), for most of the species farmed will be luxury ones. However, certain optimistic estimates based on the productive potential of seawater, the potential of hitherto unused (or "trash") species, and improved methods of harvesting and handling suggest that *maybe* the ocean can yield substantially more seafood than it does. A very big maybe.

The over-hunting of the great whales dramatizes man's abuse of the ocean. Prompted by greed and nationalism, in full knowledge of the consequences, the hunters pursued their prey well into the environmental age. Although the whale population of all species remains at perhaps 25 to 30 percent of its level before commercial whaling, four of the more majestic species are down to less than 10 percent of their original numbers. The hunters were unmoved by a United Nations call in 1972 for a world moratorium on whaling: they continued the chase. (A few nations, however, under pressure of market economics and of world disapproval, quit whaling.)

The Alaska fur seal herd—showpiece of conservationists for half a century—began to decline in numbers in 1956 in spite of efforts to manage it scientifically. By 1984, it had fallen to less than 40

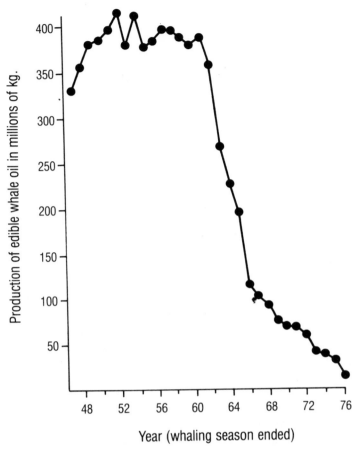

*World Production of Edible Whale Oil, 1947–76*

percent of its 1955 level and was still falling, though less rapidly.[2] The causes of the decline remain mysterious. They may include long-term changes in climate, as well as changes introduced by humans into the oceanic waters where the seals spend two-thirds of the year. Heavy-metal and organic poisons in the foods eaten by seals probably do little harm, although these chemicals have been detected in seal tissues. A leading suspect is the commercial fishery of the Bering Sea and North Pacific, an industry which increased dramatically in the 1960s and 1970s. Seals often become entangled in plastic objects—circular scraps of trawl net, box strapping, polypropylene rope, and the like—which float in the wake of fishing operations. A 1972 estimate placed the total amount of plastic litter lost or dumped into the Bering Sea and North Pacific at 1,833 tons a year.[3] Worldwide, the casualties from plastic litter have been placed at 2 million sea birds and 100,000 mammals. (As I write in 1989, the United States has not ratified the 1973 International Convention for the Prevention of Pollution from Ships, or MARPOL, although in 1987 it ratified Annex V of the Protocol, thus evincing its willingness to cooperate in controlling the ocean dumping of garbage, including plastics.)

The dismal record of man's contamination of the ocean is preserved in the muds of quiet sea basins, in the skeletons of marine organisms held for years in museums, and in the annual layers of long-lived icefields. In Antarctica, scientists have lifted vertical ice cores which represent the snowfalls of 150,000 years. The metallic lead content of Greenland snows, for example, began to rise sharply around 1950 with the use of leaded gasoline and, by 1969, had reached three times its 1950 level.

Many oceanographers have called attention to lumps of crude-oil residue floating on the seas of the world. Three men from the Woods Hole Oceanographic Institution who studied brownish-black particles in plankton hauls in 1969 concluded that "lumps of petroleum exist in surprisingly large amounts on the sea surface and have a complicated history during their residence there. [They] form a chronic type of oil pollution which may significantly affect the marine ecosystem."[4] By rough estimate, 700,000 tons of tar are floating on the world ocean today, their principal source being river runoff.

In the twelve years from 1955 to 1967, the extraction of crude oil from offshore wells rose from 7 million barrels to 222 million. Oil spills, more than any other affront to the marine environment, focused public attention on the hard truths that (a) the petroleum industry had grown very large, powerful, and insensitive, and (b) the average citizen was virtually powerless against it. But photographs of oil-blackened seabirds waiting quietly for death carried a message that even children could read. The message was: ACT! Seashore protection does not simply happen; it starts with citizen anger, followed by personal involvement. When a Union Oil well ruptured off the scenic coast of Santa Barbara, California, in January 1969, it leaked oil for eleven days before it could be capped. It continued to seep and, by mid-May, had poured an estimated 3,250,000 gallons into the sea.

"What obviously angered millions of people," wrote Gladwin Hill, a reporter for the *New York Times*, "was the glaring fact that there was *no* rational answer to the question of why we were drilling for oil in Santa Barbara. There was no pressing need for that particular oil. Foreign countries were clamoring to sell us oil—at considerably cheaper prices than the going rates for oil in the United States."[5] A local group calling itself Get Oil Out (GOO) collected 110,000 signatures on a petition to the government to stop further offshore drilling. The issue went to the Supreme Court, which in 1971 refused to consider it.

And in December 1976, the Liberian-registered tanker *Argo Merchant* broke her back near Nantucket Island, Massachusetts, and leaked over twice the volume of crude oil (7.5 million gallons) that had leaked at Santa Barbara. It was the worst oil spill in American history.

Essayist E. B. White wrote in 1957, "I see by the paper this morning that a steel drum containing radioactive sodium waste is floating at sea, about a hundred and eighty-five miles from here. . . . The Atomic Energy Commission has 'authorized' the dumping of radioactive sodium waste in the ocean. I sometimes wonder about these cool assumptions of authority in areas of sea and sky. The sea doesn't belong to the Atomic Energy Commission, it belongs to me."[6] And when, in 1969, the Army proposed to dump 27,000 tons of nerve gas, liquid mustard, CS riot control agent, and other chemicals in deep Atlantic waters, a National Academy of Sciences panel objected. It referred to the Army's own statement that ". . . we have no information regarding possible deleterious effects of these operations on the ecosphere of the sea." The NAS recommended that the Army build destructive facilities for its poisons rather that dumping them.[7]

Because environmentalism is holistic, its practitioners are concerned for the future of the whole biosphere. Correspondingly, they have encouraged international steps to preserve the health and permanence of the ocean. They have endorsed a Law of the Sea (LOS) as the first step toward that goal. In 1930, the League of Nations first considered the problems posed by certain nations which had begun to stake out territorial claims upon the goods of the ocean, where freedom of the seas had ruled for centuries past. In 1958 and 1960, the United Nations held conferences in Geneva on law of the sea (UNCLOS I and II), each attended by about 70 nations.[8] They focused on the resources of the continental shelf. Many of those nations were former colonies of the great powers of Europe, and they were poor. Then, on August 18, 1967, Arvid Parvo, Ambassador to the United Nations from the tiny state of Malta, made a historic proposal to the General Assembly. The wealth of the ocean bed, he suggested, should be owned as the "common heritage of mankind." The Assembly reacted with surprise and confusion. "Most major powers would have preferred not to discuss this problem, and most other States were not prepared to discuss it."[9] When the Malta proposal was revealed to the U.S. Congress in 1967 it provoked four House resolutions in favor and twenty-three against. As one geographer observed: "It was difficult for Congress to give expression to the commendable but ill-defined values attached to the idea of developing the ocean floor for the benefit of mankind in general."[10]

In 1971, the United Nations overwhelmingly endorsed a treaty banning nuclear weapons from the sea bed (TIAS 7337). Returning to the issue it had first examined in 1958, the UN opened UNCLOS III in 1973 and closed it on December 6, 1982, when representatives of 119 nations signed the Convention on the Law of the Sea.[11] It established four territorial zones of various widths, namely Territorial Sea Zone (12 miles from shore), Contiguous Zone (24 miles), Exclusive Economic Zone (200 miles farther), and Continental Shelf (varying up to 350 miles from shore). Freedom of the seas was to hold sway over the remainder (or 60 percent) of the ocean. "If the gist of this enormous work can be stated in one sentence," wrote political scientist Elisabeth Mann Borghese, "the Convention replaces the traditional laissez-faire system of freedom of the seas with an emerging system of management."[12] (In 1983, President Reagan was to claim for the United States economic control over all ocean resources within 200 miles of the nation's territory. Although his decision was unilateral, it did not conflict with the 1982 Convention.)

A truly workable law of the sea—still many years ahead—will call for the adoption of an *ocean ethic*. It will call for progressively understanding the nature of the ocean and acknowledging its role as the supporter of all life on earth. If peoples diversiform in race, religion, and political loyalties cannot agree on an issue as vital as preserving the world ocean, they are unlikely to agree on the value of preserving civilization itself.

# 6

# *Fresh Water*

Impure water may smell and taste bad yet be harmless to health, or it may seem harmless yet contain toxic chemicals which reveal their presence only after they have caused illness, crippling, or death. The point is important because we Americans use about 150 gallons of water per capita per day from municipal systems alone. Impure water almost always results from environmental mismanagement. It was one of the first signals from the environment during the sixties that we were failing to safeguard an absolutely vital resource.

In November 1963, in the Mississippi where it flows through Louisiana, an estimated 5 million fish floated belly up. Others, still alive, were bleeding and in convulsions. (Lesser kills had been noted in 1961 and 1962.) Biologists tried for months to discover the cause of death, finding it at last in the chemical *endrin,* an organic pesticide widely used to combat the sugarcane borer. It is thirty times more dangerous to fish than is DDT. The source of the endrin was traced to the Velsicol Chemical Corporation's pesticide factory at Memphis, Tennessee, where investigators found endrin mud caked three feet deep at a sewer outfall. Other factories than those of Velsicol were contributing poisons, although when Velsicol was compelled by law to clean up its act, the big fish-kills ended.[1] The Velsicol investigation reinforced a point made by Rachel Carson in *Silent Spring:* that the science of toxicology was woefully behind the times. After World War II, thousands of new organic chemicals had come on the market, the health hazards of which were little known. Public outcry for better testing of drinking water brought major reforms in the 1970s. Today, the National Toxicology Program spends over $75 million a year and is still unable to meet the demands for its technical advice.

When, in the sixties, the Cuyahoga River "burned" and Lake Erie was "dying," environmentalists pointed to those disasters as symptomatic of America's increasingly filthy and careless habits of earthkeeping. The Cuyahoga had, for years, run dirty brown through Cleveland and Akron, Ohio, receiving daily more than a hundred tons of wastes from the production of chemicals, oil, and iron. Domestic sewage added to the river's load. In 1959 the river became so burdened with volatile chemicals that it burned fitfully for eight days. In the summer of 1969 it again caught fire, this time destroying two railroad trestles.

Lake Erie is shallow (only 210 feet deep), and is fed by three other Great Lakes. In 1965, the Public Health Service announced that Erie's waters "are polluted bacteriologically, chemically, physically and biologically, and contain excessive coliform (intestinal) bacteria densities as well as excessive quantities of phenols, iron, ammonia, suspended solids, settleable solids, chlorides, nitrogen compounds, and phosphates."[2] Quite a menu.

*Newsweek* noted in 1970 that "in suburban Detroit, the industrial waste from the massive Ford Motor Co. works has turned the Rouge River into a ribbon of bilge that has contributed measurably to the 'death' of nearby Lake Erie." The main cause of the lake's illness, however, was not industrial poisons but sewage laden with phosphates and detergents from several million washing machines. Between 1956 and 1963, catches of Lake Erie blue pike (now extinct) plummeted from 6.8 million pounds to only 200 pounds. In March 1970, the Canadian government banned all commercial fishing in the lake.[3]

Lake Washington, in Seattle, became another *cause célèbre* in the environmental age. This pleasant body of water covering fifty square miles is wholly surrounded by the city and its suburbs. It was nearly killed by the people who used it. It was on the way to becoming a biological ruin when it was saved by the concerted action of environmentalists: a rescue which won for Seattle the All-America City Award. It had long been used for swimming, boating, fishing, and drinking water. Unfortunately, by 1926 it had also become a repository for the raw sewage of 50,000 people. When public health authorities warned that the lake was becoming a cesspool, the sewage was diverted through tunnels into Puget Sound. Now the metropolitan communities began to pour their *treated* sewage (bacteriologically harmless) from ten treatment plants into the lake— with an unpleasant result: it fertilized the waters. Sewage is rich in phosphates, nitrates, and carbon dioxide, all of which promote the growth of algae. By 1955, Seattleites were complaining of the "fishy" odors rising from the lake and, by 1962, the lake had obviously gone bad. It smelled bad, its once-transparent waters were cloudy, and its deeper strata were lifeless, devoid of oxygen in all seasons of the year. Little wonder, for 20 million gallons of treated sewage were reaching the lake daily.[4]

In 1956, the mayor of Seattle had appointed an advisory committee on metropolitan problems. It soon became the nucleus of an informal cluster of citizen volunteers, including the League of Women Voters, the Municipal League, sportsmen's clubs, and garden clubs, all campaigning for the establishment of a "metro government" whose first mission would be to clean up the lake. It would have legal power and funds not available to any one community. Aroused citizens passed out fact sheets, gave lectures, and debated on TV and radio. Five thousand volunteers passed out 100,000 pamphlets door-to-door before the election. Scientific support, so critical in this as in other environmental disputes, was provided by W. T. (Tommy) Edmondson, a professor of zoology at the University of Washington and a world authority on limnology. "The volunteer Metro Action Committee," he recalled in 1973, "was a remarkable organization, a sort of glorified debating team composed of people of very diverse backgrounds and occupations, united by their concern for environmental quality (and this in 1958!)." Although the proposal to create Metro was attacked as creeping socialism and supergovernment, it was endorsed by popular vote in 1958.

So, in 1963, Metro began to divert treated sewage from the lake into Puget Sound, a restorative job that took five years to complete. By 1975, the lake had reached trophic equilibrium. Its waters were clearing dramatically. By 1977, a standard white plate (Secchi disc) could be seen through thirty feet of water.

In retrospect, the poisoned Mississippi, the burning Cuyahoga, and the dying Lakes Erie and Washington, were indicators of worsening conditions nationwide. At the first dawning of the environmental age, however, there had seemed little cause for alarm. In 1960, President Eisenhower had vetoed a water purification bill which would have increased aid to municipalities from $50 million to $90 million a year. "Because water pollution is a uniquely local blight," he declared, "primary responsibility for solving the problem lies not with the Federal Government but rather must be assumed and exercised, as it has been, by State and local governments."[5] But events were to show that state and local governments were helpless, each alone, to restore the purity of America's waters. These had suffered poisoning for too long by too many chemicals.

Senator Joseph Tydings complained in 1970, justifiably, that Americans had spent in the previous decade $35 billion for space exploration but little more than $4 billion for cleaning up the nation's waters.[6] Perhaps poet Richmond Lattimore was right. Trying to understand the ways of Earthfolk from an observation post on a celestial planet far away, he concluded that

> . . . these people can do anything
> difficult, but nothing easy; catch and tame sight
> and sound out of space; stroll in it; fly tons of
>     steel
> and come down on a handkerchief, yet cannot
>     realize a simple
> covenant. Hundreds of wise men are united by
>     subtle
> communication, to form one mind and talk like a
>     single idiot.[7]

I have touched on surface water contamination. Groundwater contamination—being cumulative, hidden, and difficult to assess in terms of human health—was to become an even more vexing problem. In 1984, the Office of Technology Assessment reported that chemical contamination of underground water had closed more than one thousand wells and was threatening the water supplies of half the nation's population.[8] Groundwater contamination, noted the OTA, is a gradual form of pollution which seldom makes headlines. It is "bad and getting worse because state and federal laws and programs do not adequately protect underground water supplies." (Regrettably, by 1985, because of delays both political and technological, nationwide standards had been set for only eighteen of the more than two hundred contaminants known to exist in groundwater.)

At some time in the 1960s, concurrently with the rise in our national population and our standard of living, we began to use water faster than it was being replenished by rainfall and snowfall. We made up the deficit by tapping subsurface water, much of it "fossil" water thousands of years old. We began to steal from our children's children. While about 150 trillion gallons are accounted for in lakes, streams, and other surface reservoirs, two hundred times that volume repose in aquifers within a half-mile of the surface. Like petroleum, however, the water in the deepest and hardest formations is prohibitively costly to pump. By the 1970s, withdrawal of subsurface water in an average year exceeded recharge by *more than 20 billion gallons a day*. Witness the recent history of the enormous Ogallala Aquifer that underlies six states from Texas to Nebraska and covers 220,000 square miles. In 1950, about *7 million* acre-feet were pumped from it for irrigation; in 1980, about *21 million.* By the year 2000, the practical value of the Ogallala for agriculture will have disappeared. Because of the deficit spending of fresh water, many deep pumps finally reached mineralized waters unfit for use, and wells near the seacoast were invaded by brine. The nation's groundwater problem attained a high level of political interest near that of an earlier and more dramatic one: hazardous waste.[9]

In 1985 the Environmental Protection Agency would tally the main sources of groundwater contamination, showing how carelessly we had been protecting the drinking water of half the nation.[10]

- 19,000 abandoned and uncontrolled hazardous waste sites,
- 93,000 landfills,
- 180,000 surface impoundments (pits, ponds, lagoons, and other holding areas used by cities and industries for disposing of various wastes),
- 10 million underground storage tanks, including 2.3 million gasoline tanks (of which an estimated 3 to 25 percent were leaking), and
- uncounted nonpoint sources, such as pesticides and fertilizers on farms, highway de-icing compounds, and accidental spills of chemicals.

• • •

Some of America's fresh water is stored in *wetlands,* or marshes, ponds, bogs, prairie potholes, seasonally flooded meadows, and bottomland hardwood forests.[11] These provide habitats for fish and wildlife, including one-third of the nation's threatened or endangered species. Wetlands also control floods and erosion, and they purify water by removing silt and by neutralizing certain toxic bacteria and chemicals. Thus wetlands provide ecological services, a generic term for the hard-to-measure contributions of natural ecosystems to human welfare. "The lasting benefits that society derives from wetlands," said President Carter in 1977, "often far exceed the immediate advantage their owners might get from draining or filling them. Their destruction shifts economic and environmental costs to other citizens . . . who have no voice in the decision to alter them."[12]

During the two decades from the mid-1950s to the mid-1970s, ecologists of the Fish and Wildlife Service mapped the nation's wetlands, learning that the average annual rate of loss was 458,000 acres. The rate finally slowed to 200,000–300,000, yet, by 1984, only 45 percent of the wetlands existing in colonial times within the conterminous United States would be left.[13]

Preserving Wetlands 1934 1984 USA 20c

*Preserving Wetlands Stamp*

At this writing, an ecological disaster is building at the Kesterson National Wildlife Refuge, a region of six thousand acres in the San Joaquin Valley of California. Waterfowl chicks without eyes or legs, or with a brain bulging from a malformed skull, are being hatched in the marshlands. The refuge manager is using an incinerator capable of burning 100 pounds of bird bodies an hour. Bass, catfish, and carp have disappeared, while mosquito fish—the only species remaining—contain the highest levels of toxic selenium ever recorded in living fish. The disaster is not unlike others which, across the nation, stem from the mishandling of water over many years. The dying at Kesterson began in 1980 when the Bureau of Reclamation diverted irrigation drainwater—water containing metallic poisons leached from upstream arid lands—into Kesterson. These poisons included selenium, arsenic, boron, cadmium, chromium, and lead. The Environmental Protection Agency's safe limit for selenium in drinking water is ten parts per billion; the concentration in Kesterson water rose to *1,400* parts.[14] Environmentalists now fear that selenium may be descending into the Central Valley Aquifer, a source of water for domestic use and for the growing of crops. The drainwater cannot be diverted into the San Joaquin River below Kesterson, or via canal to San Francisco Bay, for doing so would only move the problem without solving it. The San Joaquin is already in trouble; its salmon population has declined over the past thirty years from 100,000 to between 5,000 and 10,000 (and these mostly hatchery bred). Moreover, residents of the Bay would surely fight any further pollution of their waterfront.

The poisoning of Kesterson has triggered not only an ecological but a political explosion of awesome proportions. At its core are the Bureau of Reclamation (builder of the irrigation system) and the Fish and Wildlife Service (steward of the wildlife habitat). Adding fuel are the farmers of several hundred thousand acres of land surrounding, and south of, Kesterson.[15] Political careers and billions of dollars are at stake. When, and if, the San Joaquin Valley issue is resolved, its case history will surely enter land-use textbooks of the future. Meanwhile, scarecrows stand along the shores of a national bird sanctuary!

One hopes that Kesterson will not suffer the fate of Winnemucca National Wildlife Refuge, in western Nevada. Rich in wetlands and waterfowl, the refuge was created in 1936. Thirty years later it was "deauthorized," for it had become a refuge in name only. It lay baking in the sun with its source of water—the Truckee River—diverted for irrigation. (I recall that a religious service is read when a church is converted to secular use. Perhaps a similar service should be read when the spirit of an ecosystem is withdrawn.)

# 7

# *Air Quality*

Travelers landing at the airports of Los Angeles, Pittsburgh, New York, and other big cities in the 1950s were likely to encounter a dingy, irritating haze. Even from 25,000 miles out in space, the Apollo 10 astronauts could see the brown smudge that was Los Angeles. Public health workers were among the first to suggest that the smudge could be poisonous, as well as irritating to the senses. The editor of the *American Review of Respiratory Diseases* inquired in 1961, "if a substance or mixture of substances present in low concentration can be highly injurious to certain particularly susceptible people after only a few days' exposure, how can one know that two or three decades of exposure to the same low doses will not be injurious to many more people?"[1] He did not, I think, expect an answer.

Air pollution first aroused public concern in the cities. Its sources were, in order of importance: automobiles, households (especially fumes from heating-fuel and burning garbage), and municipal installations (especially fumes from electric generating plants). "Motor vehicles," stated the Public Health Service, "emit carbon monoxide, which reduces man's ability to transplant oxygen to his tissues; lead, which increases man's body burden of this toxic metal; carcinogenic hydrocarbons; and reactive hydrocarbons and nitrogen oxides, which combine with sunlight to produce eye-irritating, plant-damaging, and visibility-obscuring photochemical smog."[2] The California legislature in 1960 adopted the nation's first law with respect to exhaust-emission controls on cars and, by 1966, every new car sold in the state was required to have a catalytic converter. Exhaust pollution was first mentioned in federal legislation in 1955, in the Motor Vehicle Air Pollution Control Act.

From where I sit, I can see the 572–foot stack of the ASARCO copper smelter in Tacoma, Washington. The sight takes me back to the 1920s when, as a Boy Scout, I visited the smelter and saw a hooded workman shoveling a powdery white substance into a small car. It was arsenic trioxide. Fumes containing (I presume) arsenic, lead, and acids were rising in a continuous plume from the stack. The grounds around the smelter appeared to be an attractive green lawn, but were in fact covered with a single species: horsetail rush, a weed notorious for its resistance to poisons. On a foggy night in 1981, activists Jon Hinck and Jeff Peterson secretly climbed the stack to its 500–foot level, where they unfurled a huge banner reading AFTER THE LAST TREE IS CUT, THE LAST RIVER POISONED, THE LAST FISH DEAD, YOU WILL DISCOVER YOU CANNOT EAT MONEY. The pair descended after thirty hours aloft; they were arrested but later released. Jon wrote me the other day that the view of Puget Sound from the smelter was still sharp in his mind. "Thirty hours in crisp autumn weather on the stack was like an ecological vision quest. With our backs to the area's most infamous polluter it was easy to imagine the return of the great salmon runs. All the life that has been in those waters can be there again."

Jon was prophetic. ASARCO, after operating the smelter for ninety-four years, would treat its last batch of ore in March 1985. A spokesman for the company complained that "environmental requirements" had been given more weight than "economic requirements," with the result that federal regulations had threatened the company with commercial extinction. Then he offered a postscript. He had been proud, he said, "to be associated with a company that could invest so much for the next generation."[3]

The kinds of environmental requirements of which he complained were forcing many industrial plants to install air-cleaning devices. By 1983, more than six hundred companies would be manufacturing air-and-water-pollution control equipment, including cooling towers, scrubbers, precipitators, and catalytic converters. Cleaning the public air would become a multibillion-dollar business employing hundreds of thousands of people.

•　•　•

Several years ago I crossed Canada by train, passing for a day through forests along the north shore of the Great Lakes. There I was seldom out of sight of dead spruce trees whose brown skeletons checkered the forest. What plant epidemic, I wondered, could have created a havoc so widespread? Then I remembered . . . acid rain, a damaging form of air pollution.

"Acid rain" is an imprecise term for rain, snow, hail, or fog that carries chemicals in solution or colloidal suspension, along with particles of soot. A product of combustion, acid rain may rise high in the air and travel hundreds or thousands of miles on prevailing winds. It kills fish in lakes, destroys forests and crops, corrodes metal pipes carrying water from acid lakes, and etches metal and limestone buildings and monuments. And (as recently discovered) it releases toxic metals from soil compounds into groundwater, whence they pass into the human food-chain. Its impact on lakes and forests is especially severe on mountain slopes, since these are already stressed by weather extremes.[4]

Oddly, there was little talk about acid rain until the 1980s, when scientists learned *post facto* that its damage had started in the mid-1950s. This they learned by measuring growth layers in trees and annual deposits in glaciers. Starting in 1979, they took core samples from about four thousand trees in the northeastern United States. At some time after 1955—the year varies according to species and site—the layers became thinner. Weather records revealed no episodes of cold or drought that could have depressed tree growth, whereas acidity in rainfall *had* increased.[5] Researchers who analyzed the ice layers deposited from 1870 to 1984 in a Greenland glacier reported that "sulfate concentration has tripled since approximately 1900 to 1910 and the nitrate concentration has doubled since approximately 1955. The increases may be attributable to the deposition of these chemical species from air masses carrying North American and Eurasian anthropogenic emissions."[6] One reason for the time-lag between damaging acid rain events and public awareness thereof is the buffering capacity of bedrocks, soils, and lake muds. These materials can neutralize mild acidity for years, or until their natural defenses are overwhelmed. Some limestone regions have so great a buffering capacity that they may *never* succumb to acid from the skies.

In 1981, the *National Geographic* featured a story, "Acid Rain: How Great a Menace?"[7] The issue had now become a national concern. But what, exactly, *is* acid rain? Those of its components which cause the greatest damage are sulfur dioxide ($SO_2$), nitrogen oxides ($NO_x$), and ozone ($O_3$). In 1981, more than thirty million tons of $SO_2$ and $NO_x$ were spewing annually into the skies over eastern North America. The National Commission on Air Quality estimated that the sources of those acid groups were combustion fumes from: industry (mainly electric utility stacks), 64.2 percent; transportation (auto and truck exhausts), 19.0 percent; and other combustion, 16.8 percent.[8] It is easy to analyze the chemicals in acid rain but difficult to measure their individual and combined (or synergistic) effects on the environment. Clearly, acids of sulfur and nitrogen cause the acidification of lakes, for these compounds can be detected in the water, while their impact on aquatic organisms can be lessened by dumping lime into the lakes. The atmospheric agents responsible for the killing of forests are less clear, but are quite certainly manufactured pollutants.

• • •

The first (1970) report of the Council on Environmental Quality cautioned that "man may be changing his weather. And if he is, the day may come when he will either freeze by his own hand or drown."[9] During the seventies, climatologists learned that man is surely triggering atmospheric changes that will either cool or warm the surface of the earth. The probability that a single organism, *Homo sapiens,* is hastening or delaying the arrival of the next ice age is often cited by environmentalists as evidence of the interlocking nature of the biosphere. This organism is affecting the world's average temperature in three ways:

1. By increasing the carbon dioxide ($CO_2$) content of the atmosphere through burning fuels. The resulting $CO_2$ "roof" admits both the shorter and longer wavelengths of sunlight, then traps the longer ones as they bounce off the earth. The net effect, called the greenhouse effect, is climatic warming.

2. By clouding the atmosphere with dust rising from poorly farmed soils, automobile exhausts, home chimneys, and industrial stacks. These block incoming sunlight and cause climatic cooling.

3. By changing—through citification, agriculture, deforestation, and the building of reservoirs—the ability of the earth's surface to absorb and reflect sunlight. The net effect of these albedo changes is probably climatic cooling. The greenhouse effect is the most worrisome. For more than a century we have been pouring $CO_2$ into the air at an increasing rate, raising its concentration by 20 to 25 percent since the start of the industrial revolution around 1860. The rise has been plotted with great accuracy since 1958 at the Mauna Loa Observatory, Hawaii, where in the rain-washed sky nearly three miles above the ocean, the setting is ideal for air sampling.

The Environmental Protection Agency warned in 1983 that "it is probably too late to prevent the . . . warming expected to result in the next sixty years from rising atmospheric concentrations of carbon dioxide and other 'greenhouse' gases. Even a worldwide ban on coal, shale oil, and synthetic fuels instituted by 2000 would only delay a 2° C warming from 2040 to 2065."[10] One serious consequence of a warming earth will be the melting of polar ice, followed by rising sea levels which will flood coastal cities and croplands and erode shorelines.

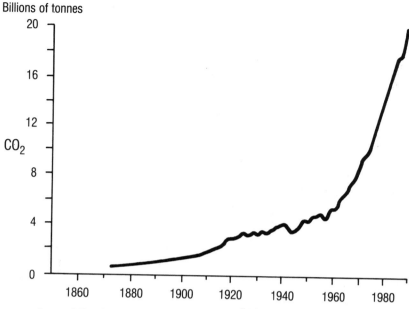

Billions of tonnes

$CO_2$

1860 1880 1900 1920 1940 1960 1980

*Annual Production of Carbon Dioxide by Humans, from 1872*

Although atmospheric $CO_2$ is increasing, and cannot fail to affect world climate, scientists are reluctant to forecast that effect precisely. Never before have they been faced with modeling a system so vast and complex, so full of uncertainties. Among these are the large thermal inertia of the ocean (causing a weather lag of a decade or more), the capacity of the ocean to absorb $CO_2$, the vagaries of sunspots and their effect on weather, future rates of fuel combustion, and future practices in agriculture, deforestation, and reservoir construction. A plausible scenario for the climate of the next century is one of global warming by 2° to 5° F, widespread changes in rainfall patterns (a 40 percent decrease on the American Great Plains), and a rise in sea level (2 to 3 feet). This scenario is based on climatological science, on historical trends in society, and on the observed behavior of celestial bodies. The mean temperature of the surface of the earth has, in fact, been slowly rising throughout the industrial age. Plotted against a straight line since 1861, the rise indicates a warming of about 0.62° C (1.1° F).[11]

Two scientists who published in *Nature* in 1974 aroused public interest by suggesting that the release of chlorofluorocarbons (CFCs) could deplete stratospheric ozone, with harmful effects.[12] CFCs were widely being used as inert propellants in spray-can products, in the manufacture of polyurethane foam as fire retardants, and as coolants in refrigerators and automobile air conditioners. A thinner ozone layer would admit more ultraviolet radiation, with consequent damage to humans, growing crops, and aquatic organisms living in surface waters. Over bitter resistance by DuPont and other CFC producers, the U.S. government in 1978 banned the use of CFCs in spray cans.

But—perhaps because the ban was imposed too late or (more likely) because the use of CFCs in industry persisted—a startling phenomenon would be reported in 1985 by a team of British atmosphere scientists. Since 1957 they had been studying the chemistry of the atmosphere above Antarctica. At first they mistrusted their readings, which showed a steady decline, summer after summer, in ozone content. Eventually they confirmed that ozone *had* decreased by nearly 40 percent, while ultraviolet radiation had increased tenfold. They suggested that inorganic chlorine from the breakdown of $CFCl_3$ and $CF_2Cl_2$ was creating a seasonal "ozone hole" above the Pole.[13] Whether the threat posed by the ozone hole is real cannot be proved or disproved without years of future study, probably into the 1990s. Scientific interest in the subject remains intense; a recent special issue of *Geophysical Research Letters* contained forty-six pages dealing with it![14]

•   •   •

Postwar technology marched to the beat of increasing noise, a form of air pollution. Humanist writer Norman Cousins fumed that

> whether or not they realize it, the American people are waging unremitting war against themselves. The weapons are tranquility smashers, and are fitted out with decibel warheads. They penetrate all known cranial barriers and the innermost core of an individual's privacy, impeding the processes of sequential thought, breaking down the sensibilities, and unhinging the capacity for serenity. The noise level is rising and the level of common sanity is falling.[15]

Noise is the roar of air and surface traffic, the din and hum of construction projects, the snarl of suburban mowers and chainsaws, the spiritless "music" of shopping malls, and a thousand other invasions which interfere with speech, sleep, relaxation, and privacy. These can also damage health. The Council on Environmental Quality estimated in 1979 that cumulative state and federal compensation benefits paid for hearing damage over a decade could easily reach $800 million.[16] Sound levels in America range from zero to 120 decibels (the sound of a jet takeoff at 200 feet). Even 90 decibels (heavy trucks passing at 50 feet) if continued for eight hours will cause hearing damage.

New York in 1965 and California in 1967 were among the first states to limit motor vehicle noise. For unexplained (and, I think, indefensible) reasons, the limits were set higher for trucks and motorcycles than for other vehicles. In 1970, when people were growing daily more aware of ambient noise, Congress authorized the construction of a prototype supersonic transport plane (SST). Traveling at 1800 miles per hour, it would leave an ear-splitting shock in its wake. During transcontinental flight it would produce a cone-shaped boom that would disturb ten million people. The government assured us that the SST would not fly regularly over the United States until the sonic boom problem had been solved. (As well "solve" the problem of gravity.) Due to concerted public protest, and for other reasons, Congress in 1971 killed the SST program. The next year, to widespread disbelief, airman Charles A. Lindbergh spoke out against commercial supersonic flight. "For me," he said, "aviation has value only to the extent that it contributes to the quality of the human life it serves. . . . I believe we should prohibit [supersonic] operations on or above United States territory as long as their effect on our over-all environment remains unsatisfactory."[17]

Senator Gaylord Nelson, one of the founders of Earth Day, has appealed for a ban on pleasure aircraft in America's national parks.[18] The tranquility of Grand Canyon, for example, is shattered by an average of seventy-four flights per day throughout the year. And, near my own home, an ingenious young man who calls himself the Sound Tracker is making and selling tapes of pure outdoor sounds, including the dawn chorus of birds, tumbleweeds brushing a fence, the plopping of pondfish rising to flies, the sleepy drone of summer insects, and the ripple of running brooks. He has found, however, that in the entire state of Washington "there are now only about 20 areas where you can find natural sound uninterrupted for even 15 minutes."[19] (He won't reveal their locations.)

In the wisdom of Herbert Marcuse, "there is no free society without silence, without the internal and external space of solitude in which individual freedom can develop."[20]

# 8

# *Minerals*

The dwindling of America's mineral resources—the ores of iron, copper, aluminum, lead, tin, zinc, cobalt, chromium, mercury, manganese, silver, gold, and other metals—provoked little discussion among environmentalists. What *did* arouse them were the land-abusive methods used to mine the ores and the pollution generated by smelting them. Public concern over environmental damage increased when the minerals industry expanded rapidly during, and after, World War II. A geologist wrote in 1969 that "the entire metal production of the globe before the start of World War II was about equal to what has been consumed since." He expressed the hope that new discoveries and new mining technologies would "develop reserves of mineral resources at an exponential rate until population control and relatively constant or decreasing per capita demand can be achieved—both inevitable requirements of our finite earth."[1]

Until recently, one thorn in the flesh of the environmentalists was the archaic Mining Law of 1872 which gave prospectors the right to search for, and exploit, minerals on most public lands *without fee, lease, or contract.*[2] It was an open invitation to plunder. Searching could be done by bulldozer or drag-bucket regardless of the impact on the environment. I recall a visit to aspen-dotted Grand Mesa, Colorado, in the 1950s, where I learned that a man had legally "mined" the rich, black peat bottom of a lake which had been a favorite of sport fishermen. With the passage of the Federal Land Policy and Management Act of 1976, some (but altogether too few) of the most damaging clauses in the old Mining Law were deleted. The policy of the United States—on paper at least—would henceforth be to manage public lands so as to protect their scenic, scientific, and ecological values.

The Club of Rome, in an impressive study called *The Limits to Growth,* ventured to predict how long the known (1972) global reserves of sixteen critical metals would last in each of three alternative futures.[3] In all futures, gold, silver, and mercury would be-

64

come economically extinct (my term) in less than 50 years; iron and chromium in less than 500 years. The average predicted lifetimes of all reserves were: at the current rate of use, 94.2 years; at an exponential rate based on five times the known reserves, 79.8 years; and at an exponential rate paralleling the current *per capita* use, only 37.3 years.

The Club's prediction was chilling. It gave pause to those who maintained that America could postpone indefinitely a metals crisis by recycling, finding substitutes, adopting new techniques for working poor ores, and discovering new deposits. Even the con-servative Council on Environmental Quality advised that "despite spectacular recent discoveries, there are only a limited number of places left to search for most minerals. Geologists disagree about the prospects for finding large, new, rich ore deposits. Reliance on such discoveries would seem unwise in the long term."[4]

Then, in 1975, the National Academy of Sciences issued a lengthy report on *Mineral Resources and the Environment*. It recognized two increasingly polarized schools of thought championed by the "doomsters," who foresee a time when mineral resources will be exhausted unless we take drastic steps now to reduce economic growth, and by the "cornucopians," who maintain that minerals "are economically and, for any future that may concern us, physi-cally infinite." All panelists concurred on the need for better esti-mates of the earth's extractable metals, the desirability of reaching international agreements for sharing mineral ores, and the need to conserve those metals already extracted. The panelists agreed that the "habits and attitudes sometimes called a 'conservation ethic' should be encouraged."[5]

In 1977, the Brookings Institution prepared a table of life expec-tancies of world mineral reserves that showed how rapidly we were depleting them.[6] It predicted how long the reserves would last un-der alternative postulates of population growth:

### Life Expectancy of Reserves

|  | At 2% Growth | At 5% Growth |
| --- | --- | --- |
| Average (28 minerals) | 53 years | 33 years |
| Shortest (mercury and silver) | 17 years | 14 years |
| Longest (potash, K₂O) | 217 years | 107 years |

The Institution's estimate, derived from a slightly different base from that of the Club of Rome, was even more sobering.

The minerals outlook brightened a little—but only a little—after the exploration of deep sea ores. "Black smokers," or volcanic plumes, on midocean ridges, and the rich metallic sulfide deposits which precipitate around them, were discovered in 1977. Smoker deposits and the previously known manganese nodules remain today virtually unexploited sources of manganese, nickel, cobalt, iron, zinc, and copper.[7] Scientists for a century or more had dreamed of mining the ocean floor. Their dreams took on life in 1968 with the announcement, by President Johnson, of a proposed International Decade of Ocean Exploration (IDOE).[8] In the same year, the United Nations endorsed the IDOE and, by 1973, scientists of more than 35 nations were active in IDOE research. They learned, for example, that the polymetallic nodules lying on the floor of the Pacific may amount to 1.5 trillion tons and hold enough manganese to supply man's needs for 400,000 years.[9] During the 1970s, oceanographers equipped with newly invented devices for "seeing" the bottom of the ocean from submarines, ships, and even satellites produced beautiful, detailed maps of the seabeds of the world. By 1980, the United States was spending nearly $10 billion a year on ocean technology, including research on nodule deposits, offshore phosphorite deposits, metal-rich bedrocks and muds, minerals extractable from seawater, and OTEC (energy from temperature gradients).

Although it is still too early to predict the environmental impact of ocean mining, environmentalists are beginning to worry about the resultant harm to marine mammals, sea turtles, coral reef ecosystems, commercial fisheries, and the food of sea birds. Moreover, if mining *should* prove feasible at the deep sea hydrothermal vents, the question looms: What effect will dredges, drills, and explosives have on the bizarre life forms, as yet barely known, that flourish there? "In its destruction of the environment and its indifferences to the risks to human life," wrote Lewis Mumford in 1970, "mining closely resembles warfare. . . ."[10]

Whatever the future of minerals recovery in the United States was destined to be, experts in 1980 were complaining that the nation had yet no comprehensive minerals policy and was far too dependent on foreign sources. Tony Velocci, writing in *Nation's Business*, pointed out that "the U.S. imports more than 50 percent of 13 strategic minerals needed for our economy and national defense. In the case of eight metals, imports account for more than 80 percent of consumption."[11] Velocci warned, for example, that our imports of chromite and cobalt (each 98 percent of domestic needs) could be cut off overnight by unfriendly nations, much as the OPEC bloc in 1973 cut off petroleum shipments. To forestall a crippling resource crisis he proposed that we increase our stockpiles of strategic minerals—under laws already on the books—and enact new laws designed to stimulate domestic mining.

But these are incomplete, if not flawed, solutions. Conspicuously missing is our need to cut back on the production of military weapons, all of which are frightfully wasteful of metals. Also missing is our need to substitute, wherever possible, commoner metals (e.g., aluminum and silicon) for rarer ones (e.g., copper and chromium). And what about the metals lost to coinage and luxuries? I recall an ad in a Christmas catalogue for a cup-cooler: a cube of silver on a handle which one placed in hot coffee or tea to bring the temperature down! In our insistence that the earth give up its metals to the "now" generation, there's a trace of the grave-robber mentality of Pharaoic times.

• • •

It would be difficult to name a land use more greedy and pursued with less interest in America's future than that of strip mining for minerals and coal. An editor of the *National Geographic* described his shock while visiting a strip mine in the Cumberland Mountains of Tennessee. "I came to realize," he wrote, "just how ugly strip-mining really is. Along once-lovely ridges, bulldozers have chewed away at graceful curves, creating jagged angles on the skyline. They have diminished noble hills into bulbous knobs; choked valleys with overburden; left massive treeless gashes. On one grand sweep I counted seven parallel scars, each a barren face thirty to fifty feet high." [12] And *Newsweek* protested in 1970 that "more than 20,000 strip mines are cutting ugly scars across the landscape at an estimated rate of 153,000 acres annually. By 1980, according to a White House study, more than 5 million acres of America the Beautiful will have been defaced in this way. Before it passed stiff reclamation laws, the lush green state of Kentucky was gouged by strip mines to the extent of 119,000 acres." [13]

Some of the strip-mining machines were monstrous. One operated by the Central Ohio Coal Company stood 20 stories high and used 5-inch steel cables to lift a boom 310 feet into the air. With each bite it could remove 325 tons of overburden to permit "recovery" of the coal underneath. With each bite it could gobble about a dozen heavy truckloads.

One of the strongest voices raised against strip mining was that of Harry Caudill, a small-town Kentucky lawyer who began in the mid-fifties to lobby for government regulation of the industry. He spoke for the welfare of the people as well as for their land. Thousands had, a generation earlier, signed their "X" to a broad-form document offered by the coal companies. It gave the companies title to all "mineral and metallic" substances beneath the signer's land and authorized the companies to do whatever was "convenient or necessary" to extract them. Caudill protested: "as the shortage of open land in this nation grows more and more serious, all this magnificent country is going to have a value far surpassing anything like coal. And we just can't afford to sit back and watch all that be destroyed so a few people can get rich now."[14]

# 9

# *Energy*

On the evening of November 9, 1965, the greatest power failure in history blacked out New York City, parts of eight northeastern states, and parts of Ontario and Quebec. Thirty million people in an area slightly smaller than Great Britain found themselves without electricity: without lights, heaters, refrigerators, radios, television sets, clocks, computers, airport beacons, and traffic signals. Subway trains and elevators froze in their tracks. People trapped in offices and stores spent the night there. Power was restored in New York City at 5:28 the next morning, after twelve hours of darkness. Exactly what triggered the blackout was never learned.[1]

In 1972, America was powered about 40 percent by oil, 35 percent by gas, 20 percent by coal, 4 percent by water (hydro), and 1 percent by other sources including nuclear, geothermal, and wind.[2] Our dependence on fossil fuels had become almost complete. But "the epoch of the fossil fuels," warned M. King Hubbert, of the U.S. Geological Survey, "can only be a transitory and ephemeral event—an event, nonetheless, which has exercised the most dramatic influence experienced by the human species during its entire biological history."[3] A plotted curve of the continuous energy demand per capita by *Homo sapiens* from prehistoric times would touch these points:[4]

1. before the use of fire—energy from food, 100 watts;
2. in the Middle Ages—energy from food, firewood, water, and wind, 500 watts;
3. today—energy from many sources, 1,700 watts

But in the United States, demand is about 10,000 watts, representing a hundredfold increase since primitive times. Thus each one of us is now attended by a hundred energy "slaves."[5]

Hubbert predicted that world production of oil and gas would level off around the year 2000. "The imminent culmination and decline in the annual supplies of these fuels poses problems of immediate concern." Coal, he said, might last a century or two.

And he made a point which is often overlooked—that *the earth's remaining fossil hydrocarbons have far greater value as organic chemicals than as substances to be burned for their heat.*[6] Fifteen years later his words would seem as true as ever. In 1984, the Congressional Research Service projected a 17–29 percent decline in U.S. oil production by the year 2000, a projection based upon estimates of oil still undiscovered and upon the past performance of geologists in finding oil.[7]

Environmentalists deplored our reckless draining of finite energy sources. With but 6 percent of the world's population in 1973, the United States was guzzling 35 percent of its energy. Power demands were doubling every eight years. "When we compare the energy consumption in the United States with that of the rest of the world," wrote biophysicist Arthur R. Tamplin in 1971, "the fact that we are facing an energy crisis is a national disgrace. . . . Do enough individuals who could do something about it really give a damn?"[8]

Energy was deceptively cheap because it did not take into account important social costs, including aesthetic losses and damage to public health. Environmentalists insisted that we should turn from a traditional or "hard energy" path to a "soft" one. As defined by Amory Lovins, British physicist, a soft energy path is one that combines a serious commitment to efficient use of energy with the use of renewable resources. Following the soft path means accepting conservation as a working ethic and it means pressing for alternative sources of energy that promise to endure as long as humankind itself. Moreover, following the soft path means inflicting less damage upon land, water, air, and wildlife. Lovins argued that "debating which [fossil-fuel powered] electric power station to build is like shopping for brandy to burn in your car or Chippendales to burn in your stove. Compared with efficiency improvements, any new power station is so uneconomical that we would save money by never operating it!"[9] His message, among others like it, seems to have been heeded. After 1979, energy consumption in the United States began to decline.

Environmentalists who were campaigning for conservation of energy and for energy alternatives were given unexpected support by a fuel crisis in the mid-1970s. The oil producing and exporting countries (OPEC) of the Persian Gulf quadrupled the price of oil between 1972 and 1974 and, late in 1973, banned oil exports to the United States in retaliation for our having supported Israel during an Arab-Israeli war. Shock waves of indignation here at home were

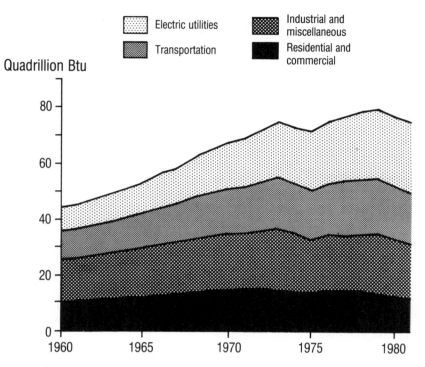

*Energy Consumption in the United States by Sector, 1960–81*

followed by long lines at gasoline pumps, and even plans—never carried out—to ration gasoline. Energy experts began more diligently than ever to study the potential of six kinds of renewable energy: solar (including biomass), wind, ocean tidal, ocean wave, ocean thermal energy conversion, and geothermal.[10]

**Solar.** The energy in sunlight reaching the earth is about ten thousand times greater than the energy in all fossil fuels being used by man (6,500 x $10^{20}$ cal/yr versus 0.6 x $10^{20}$ cal/yr).[11] The sun's energy has of course been used for centuries through the burning of biomass which, in the form of wood, peat, crop residues, and dung, is a product of photosynthesis. Biomass is still the primary source of energy in the lesser developed countries. Its energy is released either through burning or through distillation (or fermentation) to yield methane gas, alcohols, and other combustibles. In the final analysis, however, biomass energy from agriculture can never meet more than a tiny fraction of U.S. needs. If *all* of our farmlands were

71

devoted to producing biomass fuel in amounts equivalent to forty gallons of gasoline per acre per year, the nation could support only 23 million people.[12]

"The time has come for . . . an upsurge in public demand for a shining new cause, solar energy," declared Russell E. Train, president of the World Wildlife Fund-US, in 1978.[13] The Worldwatch Institute agreed. "Solar voltaic cells may become one of the most rapidly expanding energy sources . . . of the next 20 years."[14] When Jimmy Carter visited the Solar Energy Research Institute (SERI), established in 1977 in the clear sunlight of Golden, Colorado, he announced that he had asked for an additional $100 million to be diverted to solar and other renewable energy projects. A national Sun Day was celebrated on May 3, 1978.

The thirty-year struggle of activists for support of solar energy development remains the story of a good idea ignored, or censored, or fought against by long-established power interests, especially those associated with fossil fuel and nuclear sources of energy. But solar power will surely win recognition in America's future. As I write, a solar plant in the Mojave Desert is turning out 194 megawatts of power, and its corporate builder is planning a $1.2 billion expansion.[15]

**Wind.** Although very large wind turbines were designed in the 1970s, they behaved uncertainly in full-scale tests. Little was known about how turbines—especially giant ones built with novel materials such as glass fiber—would behave in a real storm on a real hilltop. Some blew over, others burned out, and still others exploded. Wind can change speed in less than a second, and when it doubles in speed (say, 10 to 20 mph) it becomes eight times more forceful. Wind turbine engineering in the seventies was roughly at the stage where aircraft engineering had been fifty years earlier, when such parameters as metal fatigue, load limits, and airflow efficiency were first being measured.

The world's first commercial "wind farm," or cluster of turbines linked to an electrical grid, would begin delivering current in New Hampshire in 1981. From 1981 to 1984, in California alone, more than nine thousand turbines were installed, most having outputs of 30 to 100 kilowatts. According to the Worldwatch Institute, wind power may become, by 1990, California's second least expensive power source—right behind water power. Some limited wind farming has begun in the states of Hawaii, Montana, New York, Washington, and Oregon, as well as the New England states.[16] "Large-scale assembly line production of wind machines should begin soon, putting wind power about where the automobile industry was when Henry Ford introduced the Model T," reported the Institute in 1984.[17]

**Ocean Tidal Power.** Considering the tremendous energy contained in the tides, it may seem odd that the first tidal power generator in North America began to deliver electricity as recently as 1984, in the Bay of Fundy, Nova Scotia. It was only a pilot plant producing about 20,000 kilowatts. The estimated potential of all tidal power sites in North America is about 10 million times the output of that prototype.[18] But perhaps our delay in harnessing the rhythmic motion of the sea is not so very odd after all, for the ocean will sink the greatest ships and relentlessly corrode the steel machines with which we try to convert its energy to useful work. Plans for a joint U.S.-Canadian tidal plant at Passamaquoddy Bay, near the Bay of Fundy, were drawn during the Franklin D. Roosevelt administration. They were placed on hold, revived during the Kennedy administration, then dropped when it seemed that the tides could not compete economically with conventional sources of energy. But tidal power will doubtless have its day, for it is based on an inexhaustible resource, is nonpolluting, and causes little disturbance to the ecological and scenic environment.

**Ocean Thermal Energy Conversion (OTEC).** The principle here is evaporation of warm surface seawater (or other working fluid) through a turbine wheel. The evaporate passes next to a chamber where it is reliquified by cold deep sea water. The system can run continuously; in many tropical seas there is a vertical temperature difference of 36°F or more throughout the year. If the power plant is near shore, the electricity generated can be delivered via submarine cable to the shore, while if it is floating far from shore, the electricity can be used to electrolyze seawater. Electrolysis yields hydrogen (a fuel) and oxygen. In a second-stage process, hydrogen can be combined with nitrogen from the air to produce ammonia, a widely used chemical.[19] The Department of Energy believes that OTEC systems sited in American waters could be producing 10,000 megawatts by the end of the century.[20] The technology has already been demonstrated off Hawaii in the floating plants Mini-OTEC (1979) and OTEC-1 (1981).

On a much smaller scale, thermal gradient solar ponds began to turn out electricity in the late seventies in Ohio, New Mexico, Nevada, and Virginia. A solar pond is an engineered basin containing a bottom layer of heavy brine and a top layer of fresh water. Sunlight passes through the top layer, is converted to heat in the bottom one, and is trapped here in the heavier water. As in the OTEC process, electricity is generated by taking advantage of the thermal difference between layers. At a solar plant in Ohio in February sunshine, the temperature of the deep layer reached 83°F while ice floated on the surface![21]

**Geothermal.** "A vast supply of natural steam, produced by heat within the Earth itself, exists in the United States as an energy source for generating electric power. Geothermal energy is clean and cheap. In the western United States, the geothermal energy potential is estimated at 0.1 to 10 million megawatts [100 million to 10 billion kilowatts]."[22] Thus wrote geologist Robert W. Rex in 1971. The internal heat of the earth is generated by nuclear decay and by pressure upon, and friction between, layers of rock. It manifests itself in geysers, hot springs, and volcanic flows. It can be tapped by wells drilled into fields of superheated water or dry steam. In the United States, hot water fields are believed to outnumber steam fields by 20 to 1.

Geothermal energy was virtually ignored before the environmental age. Then, in 1960, steam fields at The Geysers, in northern California, were tapped. By 1983, seventeen power plants would be delivering 1,000 megawatts, some at costs as low as five cents per kilowatt hour. The future of geothermal energy seems assured, not only in the volcanic regions of the Pacific Coast, Alaska, and Hawaii but also in the Gulf states, the Appalachians, the Ozarks, and other regions. It would be rash, however, to suppose that geothermal power can be tapped forever as cheaply as now. The richest near-surface fields will eventually peter out. M. King Hubbert concluded, "while geothermal energy is capable of sustaining a large number of small power plants in a limited number of localities, it still represents only a small fraction of the world's total energy requirements, and this for only a limited period of time."[23]

• • •

In 1971, as public interest in the environment was nearing its peak, economist Bruce N. Netschert expressed concern over the danger of a monopoly trend in the energy industry. The ten largest petroleum companies, with total assets of $70 billion, had stakes not only in oil but in oil shale, tar sands, coal, and uranium. Their diversification was a phenomenon so complex and tortuous as to have shielded them from antitrust prosecution. "It must be alarming," wrote Netschert, "when antitrust policy falters in the preservation of . . . vital competition."[24] The monopoly trend in the energy industry continues even now to hamper the efforts of environmentalists to win support for alternative sources of energy.

In the 1970s, two lawyers and an economist—David Roe, Tom Graff, and Zach Willey—sponsored by the Environmental Defense Fund, challenged California's giant Pacific Gas and Electric Company (PG&E).[25] It was a David and Goliath confrontation. PG&E had applied in 1975 for the first of a series of rate increases which would enable it to quadruple its construction of new power plants. But PG&E had ignored the clear mandate of the state's Public Utilities Commission that unchecked proliferation of power plants must not continue. Utilities must first explore opportunities in both *conservation* and *alternative sources* of energy. The David team won its case primarily on economic arguments and, late in 1979, PG&E was fined $14.4 million for having failed to consider the public good. A writer for the *New York Times* observed that the case was "an assault on the longstanding assumption that steady growth in coal- and nuclear-generating capacity was the only solution to the nation's energy needs. The surprise in the Fund's approach was that it relied not on appeals to environmental conscience but on economic analysis aimed at showing that a shift to energy conservation and alternative energy sources alone could slake the thirst for electricity."[26]

The U.S. Committee for Energy Awareness is (its name notwithstanding) a nongovernmental body. It promotes the electrification of America and is funded by about 150 organizations which produce or use electricity. It recently predicted America's energy future, as follows:[27]

### Electrical Utility Energy Consumption (quadrillion BTUs per year)

|                              | 1982 | 1990 | 2000 |
| ---------------------------- | ---- | ---- | ---- |
| Coal                         | 12.7 | 17.3 | 23.0 |
| Nuclear                      | 3.0  | 6.5  | 7.9  |
| Hydropower and geothermal    | 3.5  | 3.4  | 4.1  |
| Natural gas                  | 3.3  | 2.6  | 1.8  |
| Oil                          | 1.5  | 2.0  | 1.3  |
| Wood                         | —    | 0.1  | 0.3  |
| Solar and wind               | —    | —    | 0.8  |

These predictions suggest that we are still far from willing to give up our mined sources of energy for renewable ones. And we are still ravenous for energy. United Nations statistics for 1983 show "the commercial energy consumption in kg coal equivalents per capita per year" for various nations. That value for the United States was 9,304; for the world, 1,820; and for Ethiopia, 24. The average American was demanding the energy used by 384 Ethiopians.[28]

# 10

# *Control of the Atom*

*The bones of a human hand fused within the glass which melted when the plutonium bomb exploded over Nagasaki can be taken as the symbol of a wholly new distrust in the beneficence of science and the certainty of progress.*[1]

Barbara Ward (1982)

Men split the atom by imitating an event in Creation itself. Dazzled by their cleverness, they dreamed of limitless energy to be won with little cost from ordinary rocks containing uranium and its chemical relatives. But, while the power contained in every atomic nucleus is indeed a form of energy, thoughtful persons began forty years ago to insist that it should never be regarded as simply another kind of energy to replace combustibles like petroleum and dynamite. Albert Schweitzer was one such person. He perceived that man is now living in the most dangerous period of human history because he "has learned how to control elemental forces of nature—before he has learned to control himself."[2] (This truth cannot be too strongly emphasized.)

The potential of nuclear energy was first measured under field conditions near Alamogordo, New Mexico, in 1945. At daybreak on July 16 an elemental flame with the light of a hundred suns lit the desert sky, followed by a shock equal to the explosion of 20,000 tons of TNT. How mighty the human creature had become! The nuclear power industry in the United States began in December 1956, when a small experimental 5,000–kilowatt plant produced electricity for the Argonne National Laboratory near Chicago. The first full-scale plant, rated at 60,000 kilowatts, produced electricity in 1958 at Shippingport, Pennsylvania.

Harrison Brown, a brilliant geochemist, was one of the first to estimate the total size of nuclear fuel reserves in the United States.

In his 1954 book, *The Challenge of Man's Future*, he surmised that the uranium and thorium in conventional ore deposits could supply our power requirements for more than a thousand years. If, in addition, methods of extracting uranium and thorium from average granites were to be perfected, all of the granites of the earth's crust would be at our disposal. "[The] reserves in ordinary rocks," he wrote, "should certainly last for tens of thousands of years, and more probably for millions of years."[3]

Many of us recall the heady years from 1945 to 1965 when various schemes for using nuclear fission as a controlled explosive were being designed. Captain Eddie Rickenbacker, wartime hero and (later) aviation executive, even proposed in 1946 that Antarctica be atom-bombed. The U.S. military, he said, should select "sites for bombing the ice-shelf that extends for millions of square miles beyond the South Polar plateau as well as bombing of the South Polar plateau itself." That creative act would "unlock the icy doors that withhold from human knowledge the potential riches of the Antarctic Continent."[4] (Better poetry than sense.) Stewart Udall recalled the prevailing optimism, in the years when he had been Secretary of the Interior (1961–69), toward the future of nuclear energy. "Everyone, it seemed, had an eye-catching act. The physicists and engineers at the Atomic Energy Commission spent hundreds of millions of dollars working on pet 'Plowshare' schemes to use atomic explosions to dig harbors, to increase the output of natural gas fields, and to prepare for the excavation of a new Panama Canal."[5]

Department of Defense technicians supervised 126 open-air tests of nuclear bombs in Nevada between 1951 and 1961. "The military aspects provided a wondrous cloak of cover for any stupidity, rashness, and lack of concern for human health and safety that could occur in this overall activity [the development of nuclear weapons]. Criticism of direction, of goals, of errors was easily silenced through the use of security classification and secrecy, and it is still so silenced."[6] Those were the 1971 comments of John W. Gofman and Arthur R. Tamplin, scientists at the Lawrence Radiation Laboratory at Livermore, California. But eventually the Department of Defense would be called to account. In 1984, a federal judge in Salt Lake City awarded the families of ten cancer victims $2.6 million. All had lived downwind of the fallout from the Nevada explosions. The judge wrote in his opinion: "This case is concerned with atoms, with government, with people, with legal relationships, and with social values."[7] Sadly, a U.S. Court of Appeals and the Supreme Court would later reject all the damage claims on narrow procedural grounds.

In the four decades after Alamogordo we have learned that the atom can, in theory, be controlled but at a price which may prove too costly. Built into that price are high social and economic costs. Thus:

1. Nuclear plants will never be safe, for they must be built and run by humans born with human fallibility (the Chernobyl factor). Recognizing the danger inherent in atomic power generation, the federal government gained legal protection in 1957 through the Price-Anderson Amendment to the Atomic Energy Act of 1954. The 1957 version stated that "the aggregate indemnity [by government] for all persons indemnified in connection with each nuclear incident [i.e., accident] shall not exceed $500,000,000. . . ." (But, if nuclear power is truly safe, should not industry be willing to underwrite its own insurance?)

2. No safe places for storing radwastes are likely to be found, for the earth's crust is a membrane of restless liquids and solids, some explosively hot, many leaking, and all subject to transgression by adjacent materials.

3. If one counts the dollar costs of building nuclear plants *and dismantling them* at the end of their useful life, they become very expensive. One energy expert has estimated an average dismantling cost of $3 billion apiece (in 1984 dollars), or about the same cost as building the plant in the first place.[8]

4. Nuclear plants are large and centralized. In their performance to date they have shown no more regard for their impact on the local environment than have older utilities such as coal, oil, gas, and hydropower.

5. Certain fissionable materials used in power generation can also be used in atomic bombs. If world religious, racial, and patriotic tensions mount—as they surely will if the earth's population continues to grow—some fanatic may trigger the Last World War.

So, by the 1970s, the nuclear industry seemed to be expanding too fast for its own good. Stark figures show its rise and fall in public favor: 153 plants were ordered from 1970 to 1978; 103 orders were canceled from 1974 to 1984.[9] At the time of writing, no nuclear plants have been ordered in the United States in ten years.

The nuclear industry suffered a grave setback in 1979 when a reactor at the Three Mile Island plant (in the Susquehanna River, Pennsylvania) failed through human inexperience and error. The core of Unit 2 melted and very nearly breached its container vessel.

The situation remained critical—and was reported on television screens throughout America—for twelve days. It was the nation's worst commercial nuclear energy accident and it cost us at least one billion dollars. "It left the industry's public image in tatters and prompted a sheaf of costly new regulations that further depressed the industry's already sinking economic fortunes."[10] Organized opposition to nuclear power increased after Three Mile Island. The *Los Angeles Times* estimated in late 1979 that there were more than 400 "antinuke" groups in the West alone and perhaps 1,000 in the United States.[11] Their ranks included some old social activists from the sixties: Tom Hayden, Jane Fonda, and Daniel Ellsberg.

The story of the Washington Public Power Supply System (WPPSS, nicknamed WHOOPS!) is another tale of nuclear trouble.[12] WPPSS drew plans for five nuclear plants in the state and broke ground for the first one (No. 2) at Hanford, on August 12, 1972. The cost of the plant was to be $450 million, but by the time it began to generate electricity on May 27, 1984, the cost had risen to $3.2 billion. Alarmed by rising costs, WPPSS "mothballed" plants Nos. 1 and 3, abandoned Nos. 4 and 5, and faced a legal default of $2.25 billion in bonds. Utilities owning almost 70 percent of the two plants eventually learned that they had possessed no legal authority in the first place to become involved with the project and thus did not have to pay a share of the debt. Behind the years of incompetent management by WPPSS was the fatal assumption that future power demands in the Northwest would call for more than one or two nuclear plants.[13]

A spokesman for the Environmental Defense Fund, looking back on the history of nuclear power, singled out for attack its dubious economics. "Environmentalists," he wrote, "would not need to oppose nuclear power if the utility industry were to bear the full economic risks of constructing, operating, and decommissioning . . . nuclear plants, and of disposing of nuclear waste. Methods to reach this end are simple: nuclear plant owners should be paid, at fair market rates, for the electricity their plants generate, and only for that power." If nuclear power follows the discipline of the marketplace (he continued) "we can enjoy economic benefits. If it fails it will be because better alternatives have succeeded."[14]

Is atomic energy a promise or a peril? *The answer rides almost entirely on one's faith in the ability of scientists and politicians to reduce the health hazards of radwastes.*[15] These byproducts of power generation are both continuous and residual; they must be dealt with during the daily operation of the nuclear plant and during its final dismantling. One year's operation of a 1,000–megawatt plant produces—in addition to tens of thousands of cubic yards of radioactive uranium tailings at the mine—hundreds of cubic yards of low-level radwastes and tens of cubic yards of extremely high-level radwastes. And the plant itself is radioactive when its life comes to an end. Three decades have now passed since the first civilian nuclear plant in the United States began to operate, yet geologists have still found no radwaste burial sites which are both technically suitable and politically acceptable. "The situation," wrote Dean Abrahamson, professor of Public Affairs at the University of Michigan in 1983, "is a major embarrassment for the industry and a potential public health disaster."[16]

Low-level—though still very poisonous—radwastes contain more than twenty isotopes having half-lives which range from 74 hours to 4.46 billion years. Moreover, the wastes and the engineered structures surrounding them give off heat while they chemically decay. Radwaste slurries generate heat at rates as high as 200 watts per gallon. The fuel rods in a 1,000–megawatt plant continue to generate more than 200 megawatts of heat even after their useful life is spent. High-level wastes were first buried in liquid state in steel tanks at the Hanford Reservation. By 1979, an estimated 500,000 gallons had accidentally seeped into the soil and had permanently contaminated it. One large leak in 1973, which went unnoticed for fifty-five days, lost 115,000 gallons.[17] Many ways of disposing of radwastes have been considered. Here are five:

1. Bombard them in an atomic pile to transmute their elements into others having shorter lives. This solution remains theoretical.

2. Rocket them into the sun.

3. Encase them in a ceramic container, the melting point of which is higher than that of ordinary rocks. Each container then acts as a hot "mole" slowly settling into the earth.

4. Drop them into an ocean trench where a downward moving tectonic plate would carry them eventually (but temporarily) far under the seabed.

5. Bury them in salt mines or in bedrocks thought to be stable. The very existence of salt deposits shows that they have not been in contact with moving water for long geological periods.

Knowing that radwastes hold for millennia their power to sicken or kill, how can we store them through a future time as long as the past of human civilization? And how can we warn coming generations to keep away from our radwaste cemeteries? One proposal has been made seriously by Thomas A. Sebeok, of the Research

Center for Language and Semiotics at Indiana University.[18] It is to establish an "atomic priesthood." Its priests would be the keepers of document vaults and Stonehenge-like monuments located in parks above burial sites. An atomic priesthood might, for example, discourage Earthling geologists generations hence from prospecting for potash or gypsum in salt deposits where a long-vanished race had dumped its radioactive garbage.

Not until 1984 would the nuclear industry need to practice the complex, sensitive, and experimental operation of dismantling a wornout nuclear plant. The Shippingport plant, which had been dedicated by President Eisenhower, ran for twenty-five years and was silenced in 1982. It was suffering metal fatigue and had become so radioactive that repairmen could no longer reach its critical parts. After a two-year wait while the uranium was cooling, decommissioning of the plant itself began in late 1984. Plans called for shipping the hot core—the 770–ton reactor vessel encased in concrete—down the Ohio River to the sea and eventually up the Columbia River to a 30–foot-deep grave on the Hanford Reservation. (It did reach its burial site, after traveling 8,100 miles, on April 14, 1989.)

A nuclear plant at Humboldt Bay, northern California, had earlier been shut down (in 1976) after only thirteen years of service, mainly because its operator, Pacific Gas and Electric Company, could not afford to make it earthquake-proof. "No money for decommissioning was collected from consumers during the power plant's lifetime, so the costs will be reflected in the rates charged consumers who never received its power," wrote Carole Douglis, a Tufts University major in public policy.[19] Someone said of the Humboldt plant that, although its life was thirteen years, its afterlife could be eternity.

The future of atomic energy is perceived in two different lights by the pronukes and the antinukes. Hannes Alfven, among other pronukes, has placed his faith in fusion (as against fission) energy. A Nobel laureate in physics, he drafted in 1971 the Alfven Memorandum:

> In the long run, fossil fuels cannot satisfy the rising energy demand in the world. There are only three sources of energy known which are sufficiently powerful: solar energy, fusion energy, and fission energy. The first one is completely pollution-free, the second one almost pollution-free. The third one is necessarily combined with production of

large quantities of radioactive poisonous elements. . . . If solar energy or fusion energy were available now at comparable cost no one would use fission energy (for peaceful purposes). . . . In my opinion a solution of the fusion problem is less distant today than the Moon was when the Apollo project started. This means that if a national effort of the same kind as the Apollo program were made, fusion energy would be available in a comparable time. If this is achieved, the fission reactor, especially the breeder, will be of interest only as a danger which must be eliminated as soon as possible.[20]

But a respected environmentalist, Norman Myers, has written that "the nuclear industry is sick. Far from providing a cheap and plentiful supply of energy that would satisfy world demand for the foreseeable future, it has provided us with an expensive energy source fraught with intractable technical problems and unacceptable environmental risks. Long-lived radioactive wastes cast a shadow which reaches across the generations."[21]

The conclusions of the Investor Responsibility Research Center (IRRC) rest between those of the pronukes and the antinukes. The IRRC was created in 1972 as a coalition of universities and foundations within whose walls questions of corporate social responsibility and public policy were to be studied. Soon the IRRC was providing research reports to more than 150 institutional investors.

In 1981 it released a sobering statement, *The Nuclear Power Debate,* which ended with these words:

> What was viewed several years ago as a primary energy source is viewed increasingly as an energy source of last resort. Increasingly, energy planners, politicians, investors and consumers are emphasizing energy conservation before energy growth; coal and renewables before nuclear. The development of nuclear power will be limited to that which is necessary, and vast efforts are underway to limit that necessity.[22]

# 11

# Society's Wastes and Poisons

*Ours is the greatest* discarding *century in history.* . . .
*[We] define ourselves in what we discard as much as in what we create.*[1]

Anatole Broyard (1985)

Our wastes include garbage, trash, and treated sewage from homes; commercial refuse; industrial scrap; the rubbish from construction and demolition; agricultural waste; and mining debris. By 1960, waste disposal had become a problem growing faster than its solution. Urban waste (consumer solid waste) rose from 2.6 pounds per person per day in 1960 to 3.7 pounds in 1978 and was projected to reach 4.4 pounds by 1990.[2] We had become, as zoologist Garrett De Bell put it, "a nation knee-deep in garbage, firing rockets at the moon."[3] The waste crisis was essentially economic, a sudden convergence of three curves representing rising waste, dwindling disposal sites, and rising haulage costs. Waste was rapidly becoming our second national debt.

Although waste disposal was not a crisis that aroused deep passion in the breasts of environmentalists, it troubled them, for it was a symptom of America's delayed progression toward a conserver society. As our vision cleared and we saw that the earth is indeed a closed system, and that most "waste" is simply unused material, we began to design a society in which more waste would be recycled and less would be generated in the first place. In that better society:

1. At the industrial level, producers would depend more on recycled, and less on virgin, materials; would turn out products having less built-in obsolescence; and would sell separated, classified wastes and byproducts originating in their own factories.

2. At the commercial level, handlers would replace many packages with reusable containers.

3. At the domestic level, consumers would recycle glass, metal, paper and organic wastes such as kitchen scraps, garden debris, and sewage.[4]

The recycling of sewage was soon being tested. The City of Milwaukee began in 1978 to compost sludge and sell it as "Milorganite." By 1984, the city would be distributing 60,000 tons a year throughout the United States. Near my own home, about 200 tons of sludge were being hauled daily in 1984 from Metro Seattle to nearby forest plantations. Other cities were experimenting with compost-fermentation or compost-distillation to produce methane and alcohol.

So-called "clean burning" at high temperatures was promoted as a means of reducing the volume of solid waste while generating useful products. However, a 1,500-ton-per-day clean burner leaves 500 tons of ash in the pit and throws 1,000 tons of emissions into the air, emissions that include carbon dioxide, nitrogen oxides, and submicron-size particles, or fly ash. Some of these, such as dioxin, are mutagenic. An argument in favor of burning is that waste heat can be used for steam-electric generation. Albany, New York, pioneered a refuse-derived-fuels (RDF) technology in which the city garbage was shredded after its metals were removed. The shredded fuel, about 150,000 tons per year, was burned to heat the entire State Capitol and the Empire State Plaza.

The disposal of ordinary garbage and junk, however, posed less of a threat than the disposal of *hazardous* wastes. By the early 1960s, many Americans found that they were living in a world of new poisons—unfamiliar chemicals in the soil they handled, the water they drank, the air they breathed, and the food they ate. When they protested through action, they gave the environmental movement its single most powerful shove. Even those who were playing merely spectator roles in the early movement were stung into action when they realized that their surroundings had become not only noisy, smelly, and unsightly but downright unhealthy. The menace of anthropogenic poisons was to become a continuing theme in the message of environmentalism.

During the industrial expansion that followed World War II, more than 4 million "unnatural" chemicals were synthesized for the first time.[5] Of these, 60,000–70,000 were subsequently manufactured for sale and 10,000 became commercially important. Most of the 4 million were organic (carbon compound) substances; all were foreign to human culture. By 1984, the UN General Assembly would be listing 1,500 chemicals "whose consumption and/or sale have been banned, withdrawn, severely restricted or not approved by governments."[6]

We wondered, at what concentration would this or that new chemical be injurious to wildlife, or to humans and their crops and their livestock? Although not toxic, might it (like thalidomide) be mutagenic or (like benzidine) be carcinogenic? Would it enter and contaminate the environment after having served its purpose? Would it accumulate at the end of natural food chains? If dangerous, how long would it remain so? And finally, who could be trusted to regulate its manufacture, distribution, and use? Scarcely any answers were forthcoming and many of these were inconclusive. In the meanwhile, the news media began to report new cases of poisoning from the mishandling—innocent or malicious—of modern chemicals. Thousands of cases. Tens of thousands. Some like Love Canal, Seveso, and Bhopal became notorious. The National Audubon Society likened the chemical threat to a violent wind twisting overhead, touching the ground now and then to make headline news. "Management of toxic chemicals in our society," concluded Audubon's president, "can only take place within a structure carefully designed by the federal government. This government has not embraced the task. Focusing on the chemical disaster of the day will not tame the toxic tornado."[7]

Hazardous waste was defined in federal law in 1976 as a solid waste which may contribute to serious illness or death, or pose a threat when improperly managed.[8] Congressman Albert Gore, Jr., stated in 1978 that hazardous waste "may be the single most significant health issue of this decade."[9] More recent estimates of the magnitude of the issue are that about 290 million tons of hazardous waste are generated in the United States each year and that, since 1950, about *6 billion tons* have been dumped at 2,500 or more sites which may require fifty years to clean up, at a cost of several hundred billion dollars.[10] Even more alarming, the Comptroller General reported to Congress in 1985 that "the full size and extent of the hazardous waste site problem in the United States is not fully known."[11] There may exist 400,000 hazardous dumps, while as many as 1.3 million dumps may have to be mapped and evaluated to determine whether they *are* problem sites.

Most hazardous waste is generated by the chemical and petroleum industries (71 percent) and the metal-related industries (22 percent).[12] The major categories of waste are flammables, heavy metals, asbestos, corrosive acids and bases, and synthetic organic chemicals. In 1980, investigators from the EPA sampled 350 hazardous waste dumps and found these toxic chemicals, in order of frequency: chlorine and its compounds, benzene, ethylene, acetylene, toluene, methane, sodium hydroxide, sulfuric acid, antimony, chromium, xylene, mercury, phosphorous, propylene, lead, zinc, and arsenic. These were only half the chemicals; others were present but scarcer.[13]

Hazardous-waste management was not a serious issue in the early environmental movement. It was out of sight, out of mind. In 1965, a lengthy report by President Johnson's Environmental Pollution Panel barely mentioned it. But in 1970, mercury was discovered in dangerous concentrations in food fish. Canada banned commercial fishing in lakes St. Clair and Erie, while the U.S. Food and Drug Administration ordered about one million cans of tuna and two million pounds of frozen swordfish withdrawn from the supermarkets. Repeatedly during the early seventies, ecologist Barry Commoner focused on mercury in food as an example of a hazardous waste deserving far more attention from the government than it was getting. More than half the mercury used by industry between 1945 and 1958 was still "missing." Where and how soon would it surface?

As *Silent Spring* in 1962 had jolted Americans into thinking about the hazards of biocides, so Love Canal sixteen years later jolted them into thinking about hazardous wastes. The partly dug Love Canal, in the city of Niagara Falls, New York, had been used as an industrial dump from the 1920s to the early 1950s, when the city bought it, covered it with dirt, and let it be developed for housing.[14] By the mid-1970s, the surface was sinking and stinking. Poisonous chemicals were seeping into basements. "Gradually," reported Wanda Veraska, "families in the neighborhood began experiencing an abnormally large number of physical problems. Four mentally retarded children were born to families on one block. Pregnant women miscarried at a rate far above normal. Several children in the area were born with serious birth defects, such as abnormal hearts and kidneys; or they grew double sets of teeth. Cases of epilepsy, liver diseases, nervous disorders [and] rectal bleeding were all above the normal rate." (The link between these physical problems and Love Canal proved later, in some cases, to have been imagined, yet the hysteria generated was real.) In 1978, President Carter declared Love Canal a disaster area, and in 1980 authorized the immediate evacuation of 719 families. When the Hooker Chemical Company abandoned the dump in 1953, it could have cleaned up its waste for about $4 million. It left the task to others—a task which will cost $200 million before it is finished in the late 1980s. "Landfills do not solve the problem," writes Peter Borrelli, editor of the *Amicus Journal,* "they *store* it."[15]

The most disquieting threat of environmental poisons is that they may subtly interfere with human reproduction and early development. They may depress sperm and egg production, cause genital cancers, provoke spontaneous abortion, cripple the fetus, or harm the brain cells of the growing child. Medical reporter Michael Castleman has written that "the catalogue of known genotoxins [substances which interfere with reproduction] includes pesticides, herbicides, and many common industrial chemicals, as well as a number of substances whose effects on genetic health are less well understood: alcohol, tobacco and marijuana smoke, certain antibiotics, diethylstilbestrol (DES), lead, X-rays, plutonium, and possibly video-display terminals."[16]

The effects of environmental poisons on human reproduction and early growth were little studied until the 1960s. They are still being studied. Sperm counts in U.S. males declined significantly over a thirty-year period, from about 106 million per milliliter in the 1950s to 70 million in the 1970s. Six chemists who reported the decline suggested that changing patterns in sexual behavior, increased use of drugs, and increased stress could have contributed to it. They did find, however, in a recent study of the semen of Florida State University students, a strong correlation between a high level of PCBs and a low sperm count.[17] Moreover, during the forty-year period up to 1976 in the United States, the age-adjusted incidence of testicular cancer among whites doubled.[18] Cancer in various other forms may also have increased, if two researchers who published in the *New England Journal of Medicine* in 1986 have rightly interpreted their data. "We are losing the war against cancer," they flatly declared, "notwithstanding progress against several uncommon forms of the disease, improvements in palliation, and extension of the productive years of life."[19]

Although neuropsychologists have long known that lead (Pb) in high concentrations will damage the brain of a growing child, they did not learn until 1979 that a concentration as low as 20 parts per million can have the same effect; it can depress the IQ score of the child.[20] (Concentrations were measured in milk teeth shed by the children after exposure to environmental lead.) But the picture is not altogether dark. Environmental lead pollution is diminishing; the measured amounts carried to the mud of the Mississippi River delta in 1982 and 1983 were only 60 percent of those carried a decade earlier.[21] The scientific team that hit upon this ingenious measure of lead content noted that the Clean Air Act of 1970 had brought catalytic converters and the use of unleaded gasoline in new 1975 automobiles.

• • •

Besides the environmental poisons distributed in hazardous waste, another large class of poisons known as biocides—or chemicals deliberately designed to kill plants, animals, and microorganisms—began to challenge our management skills even before the dawning of the environmental age. The first members of a new family of biocides—the chlorinated hydrocarbons, including aldrin, dieldrin, and endrin—were first applied to America's fields, forests, and wetlands in 1945.[22] Another new family, the organic phosphorous compounds, including parathion, malathion, and phosdrin, followed in the early 1950s. Sales of biocides throughout the world grew rapidly and, by 1983, would add up to $13.7 billion, of which the U.S. share would be $4.6 billion, or 34 percent.[23] Among the world's most widely used biocides today is carbaryl, made with the help of methyl isocyanate, the choking gas that gave Bhopal a place in history. There, in 1984, gas pouring into the air from a factory accident killed 1,757 people within a few days and sent more than 200,000 to the hospital.

The threat posed by biocides to nontarget species, including wildlife and people, first captured public attention in 1962 with the publication of *Silent Spring.* The main arguments in Miss Carson's book were these:

1. Biocides must be applied repeatedly, whereas biocontrols—such as the release of ladybeetles to control aphids—may need to be applied only once.

2. Biocides, by their very design, cause harmful and unexpected side effects on humans, farm crops, forests, and wildlife.

3. Plant and insect pests change genetically under prolonged assault by poisons. They become "fast" to the poisons and thus provoke an endless war which calls unceasingly for new counterweapons. Ecologist Garrett Hardin once remarked that every pesticide selects for its own failure. *Between 1970 and 1980, the number of resistant pest insects and mites nearly doubled, from 224 to 428.*[24]

4. Certain chemicals are stable and persistent. They accumulate in food chains. Here they are biologically magnified as they pass unchanged from (for example) lake mud through plankton and fish to waterfowl, where they may concentrate at levels up to 10 million times their level in the mud.

A more recent comment on the illusory value of pesticides came from Robert L. Metcalf, an entomologist at the University of Illinois Center for Advanced Study. Farmers, he wrote in 1985, use more than twice as much pesticide as they need and still get poor results. "We now suffer about a 20 percent crop loss to insects, the same as we did in 1900. We've won some individual battles along the way but we're losing the war." [25] These are strong words.

By far the most controversial of the biocides was DDT. By 1964, DDT or its impurities and breakdown products had been found in the body fat of humans and wild animals throughout the world. The Fish and Wildlife Service pointed out that only one part DDT in a billion parts of water would kill blue crabs. (That concentration is about the same as an ounce of chocolate syrup in one thousand railroad tank cars of milk.) A shocking side effect of the widespread use of DDT up to 1972—when its use was banned—was a decline in the number of insectivorous, raptorial, and fish-eating birds. Among the victims were quail, eagles, falcons, grebes, pelicans, cormorants, and ospreys. The decline was unmistakable. The familiar brown pelican of southern waterfronts almost disappeared. For reasons that long defied understanding, pelicans either failed to lay eggs or crushed the ones they were brooding. Scientists eventually learned that when DDT circulates in the blood of laying birds it disturbs the calcium metabolism and causes the birds to produce thin, easily broken eggshells. This cause-and-effect relationship was elegantly revealed by biochemist Robert Risebrough and his contemporaries through research that began in the late 1960s. [26] Any lingering doubt as to the cause of broken shells was dispelled by a study sponsored by the American Poultry and Hatchery Federation in the early 1970s. The eggshells of chickens fed for ten weeks on a diet containing only one part DDT per 10 million were significantly thinner than those of a control group. [27]

Rachel Carson devoted a chapter in *Silent Spring* to the unpleasant side effects of chemical weed killers, or herbicides, especially 2,4–D and 2,4,5–T. Her words affected me strongly, for I had just visited a Colorado mesa where I had seen the devastation worked upon aspen, willow, sage, and evergreen trees by weed killers dropped from aircraft. The Forest Service was "opening up" rangelands to provide more grass for cattle. The damage to herbaceous plants, shrubs, and trees was starkly evident. The damage to a myriad lesser, unseen species supporting the mesa community was not. By 1959, more than 100 million acres in America, including rangelands, croplands, roadsides, utility corridors, parks, golf courses, and private lawns had been treated with herbicides. "The chemical weed killers," wrote Carson, "are a bright new toy. They work in a spectacular way; they give a giddy sense of power over nature to those who wield them, and as for the long-range and less obvious effects—these are the baseless imaginings of pessimists."[28]

In the late 1960s, 2,4,5–T (and its contaminant, dioxin, one of the most toxic substances known) was shown to cause birth defects in laboratory mice. And if in mice, why not humans?[29] The discovery came when military forces were exposing thousands of Vietnamese to Agent Orange. It came when President Nixon wanted to hear no talk about the public-health hazard of weed killers; he wanted no publicity which might slow the pace of the war or annoy the nation's chemical manufacturers. "Nader's Raiders" offered, in a 1972 book *Sowing the Wind,* a lively history of bureaucratic efforts to suppress the truth about weed killers. One government official, commenting on birth defects in laboratory mice exposed to 2,4,5–T, complained: "Six mice in a cage! Twenty-five years of use without hurting anybody and it all counts for nothing against six mice in a cage."[30]

Public fear that weed killers were causing nervous disorders, genetic mutations, miscarriages, and cancer spread in the 1970s and 1980s. Citizens brought lawsuits against manufacturers of dioxin-laced compounds and against federal agencies using herbicides on public lands. In 1983, the Dow Chemical Corporation, principal source of 2,4,5–T, would stop producing it. In 1984, a federal judge would ban the use of herbicides on Forest Service and Bureau of Land Management holdings in Oregon and Washington. And the Forest Service would voluntarily halt aerial spraying (but not ground spraying) on all the national forests.

•   •   •

The poisoning of America by chemicals did more, I think, to galvanize the environmental movement than any other demonstration of man's failure to understand, accept, and work within, the natural order. People soon learned to fear both known and unknown chemicals. They were told by the federal government that 3,500 chemicals in daily use were definitely or potentially hazardous to health. They were told that these poisons can appear without warning in food, water, and air. They wondered what fraction of our everyday ailments and anxieties might subtly derive from poisons in our surroundings. And they wondered about the future. Would their children's children inherit a poisoned earth which they would be forced to inhabit, though blameless for its condition? *Time* magazine warned in 1980, "The society that created the plethora of new chemicals that so enhanced human life must now use its scientific genius to make sure that these creations work safely for mankind."[31]

# 12

# Endangered Species

*When Daniel Boone goes by, at night,*
*The phantom deer arise*
*And all lost, wild America*
*Is burning in their eyes.*[1]

Stephen Vincent Benét (1933)

In 1963, about forty California condors were alive in the wild; in 1988, none. Now these great soaring birds can see the sky from cages only . . . and condors behind bars are not condors. The shy black-footed ferret is also teetering on the edge of extinction. The world population in 1986 was estimated at ten or fewer.

America's vanishing wildlife was high on the list of concerns that sparked the environmental movement. Environmentalists campaigned for the preservation of the condor, ferret, whale, wolf, sea otter, grizzly, eagle, falcon, and indeed, all forms of life whose long genetic lines were suddenly at the mercy of mankind. They knew that extinction is shocking in its absolute finality, and that the wild things are "miner's canaries" warning of a human future which will be forever diminished if these vanish. Environmentalists struggled to find the right words to alert the public to the escalating rate of plant and animal extinction. They compared it to the rate at the end of the Cretaceous Period (the Time of the Great Dying). They offered estimates such as "175,000 species become extinct each year" and "100 a day by the year 2000." Norman Myers argued that, "from a biological standpoint it ranks as one of the greatest, if not the greatest, of all episodes in the history of life's four billion years on Earth."[2]

It is rare to find a life scientist who is not appalled by extinction, yet one of them recently protested, "Let us not be disturbed at the loss of some species. Extinction is normal and necessary." He was quickly challenged by five biologists who replied, substantially: Must we evaluate every species according to its present utilitarian value, ignoring its potential contributions? One affirmed that "perhaps the only possible answer to the question, 'What good is a species?' is another question, 'What good is a newborn child?'"[3]

Zoologist Vincenz Zisweiler summarized in his book, *Extinct and Vanishing Animals*, the causes of extinction for which mankind has been responsible.[4] These include:

1. Habitat destruction through the logging of forests, the draining of wetlands, and "civilization or monoculture" (i.e., urban encroachment and farming).

2. "Denaturalization" through the introduction of goats, sheep, rabbits, dogs, cats, pigs, rats, foxes, mongoose varieties, and mustelids such as the weasel and polecat. These become either predators upon, or competitors with, native species.

3. Hunted for meat, fat, hides, feathers, trophies, or souvenirs (witness the extinction of the dodo, the Steller sea cow, and probably the kouprey, or Indochinese wild cow).

4. Combatted as alleged pests (witness eagles, wolves, and bears).

5. Hunted for sheer sport (Arabian ostrich and rufous gazelle).

6. Captured for the live-animal trade (parrots and macaws).

7. Destroyed by introduced diseases (Hawaiian thrushes and New Zealand quail).

8. Eggs and young collected (spectacled cormorant and great auk).

9. Hunted because of superstitious belief in the medicinal or other beneficial powers of the body parts (Schomburgk's deer in Siam).

While conservationists of an earlier day spoke of "protecting" species, and subsequently promoted laws against hunting them, they later understood the complete dependence of every species upon its *habitat*. The American sporting fraternity, for example, saw the critical relationship between waterfowl abundance and wetlands. In 1934, sportsmen persuaded Congress to enact the "Duck Stamp Law," requiring every waterfowl hunter sixteen years old or older to buy a one-dollar stamp. The revenue from the sale of stamps was used to buy and lease wetlands, mainly in the four great north-south flyways. By 1984, more than 285 million duck stamp dollars would have been spent to save 3.5 million acres of wetland. "In the past," observed science writer Boyce Rensberger, "many conservationists focused heavily on a few, popularly appealing endangered species such as bald eagles and leopards. By contrast, the new [environmental] movement looks at whole ecosystems, noting that soil bacteria and insects usually are more ecologically important than the showier species. . . . [At] its most fundamental level, the movement now sees its mission as preserving life's genetic diversity."[5]

My own favorite example of species diversity is the microcommunity discovered by Harvard biologist E. O. Wilson in a single tropical tree. It contained more than forty-three species of ants!

Contrary to popular belief, sport hunting has not, in the United States during the present century, threatened any wild animal species with extinction. Whatever ideological stand one may take for or against hunting, it *does* help keep populations of game animals within the carrying capacity of their ranges, especially where the ranges have been perturbed by the killing of predators, such as wolves, or the introduction of competitors, such as domestic sheep. (Possible exceptions are the hunting of black ducks in the central and eastern states. But acid rain, which destroys the critical food organisms needed by egg-laying females and their ducklings, may be more to blame than gunfire for the 60 percent decline of the black duck population in recent years.) Hunters may have hastened the demise of the California condor; the issue is not clear. Blood samples taken from birds found dead or held for study have shown elevated levels of lead. One bird "had so much lead in its blood that it couldn't have walked a straight line," reported a biologist.[6] He suggested that condors ingest bullets by feeding on deer that have been mortally wounded and abandoned by hunters.

According to Zisweiler, only one full species of North American animal was hunted to extinction because of its injurious feeding habits—the Carolina parakeet, a bird of the cypress swamps that resorted to eating plantation fruit when its natural haunts were converted to orchards. However, a number of animal *subspecies* were exterminated, including local races of the grizzly, wolf, and cougar. The California grizzly can be seen on the State Seal but not, since 1922, in the forest. And the last Washington State wolf may have been trapped in 1920; its skull is now in the National Museum.

The reduction or "control" of wild animal populations thought to be harmful to human interests was under criticism long before the dawning of the environmental age. Control operations were directed for years against individuals or species called nuisance animals, pests, varmints, destructive rodents, or predators. The federal government had in 1915 launched a campaign against predatory animals which was later to meet resistance from citizens who claimed that it was cruel, nonselective (killing nontarget species), wasteful (not really effective), and politically dominated. Growing public resistance during the 1950s caused the government to back off. The federal kill of bobcats, bears, and cougars tapered off in the early 1960s.

One of my childhood memories is of watching my father poison prairie dogs on rangelands near Flagstaff, Arizona, in 1912 or thereabouts. He was hired by the old Bureau of Biological Survey to scatter strychnine-coated oats over "dog towns" to kill the prairie dogs and any other rodents competing with livestock for native vegetation. Today, the sight of prairie dogs in the wild can be enjoyed only in scattered enclaves, such as the one in Wind Cave National Park, South Dakota. Whereas in the mid-1800s there had been billions of prairie dogs, now fewer than 1 percent survive. They were destroyed, not only by poison and gun but by the conversion of prairie lands to agriculture and residential or industrial use. Tragically, the black-footed ferret, which depended on prairie dogs for food and which denned in dog burrows, went down with its prey.

Eastern and Rocky Mountain wolves were historically thought to be serious threats to wildlife, livestock, and humans. For over a century they were relentlessly shot, poisoned, gassed, and trapped. Now only 1,250 remain in the East and a few score in the Rockies. Grizzly bears in the United States outside of Alaska have been reduced to about a thousand individuals roaming over less than 2 percent of their ancestral range. They are especially vulnerable because their populations are small and fragmented. They are shot by poachers, stockmen, outfitters, campers, and hunters (mistaken for black bears). A "rogue" grizzly is apt to be shot if it approaches a garbage dump and poses a threat to human safety.

Kenneth E. F. Watt, an ecologist at the University of California, recently analyzed the voluminous literature on coyote control on Western sheep pastures and demonstrated the economic futility of trying to poison them. "At kill rates up to 60 percent," he wrote, "the result of control is to raise the coyote population to a higher level than it would have attained in the absence of control. . . . One must kill over 70 percent of the pups and adults each year to achieve significant reduction in coyotes."[7] If, however, the rancher is determined to kill coyotes he can succeed, at the penalty of increasing the number of herbivores—such as mice, voles, rabbits, hares, gophers, and grasshoppers—which compete with sheep and which are controlled naturally by coyotes.

The introduction of foreign animals, once an important cause of extinction, declined in importance as governments regulated commerce in live animals. Moreover, governments corrected past mistakes whenever they could. In the United States, they removed foxes from Aleutian seabird islands, feral goats and burros from the Channel Islands of California, and feral goats and pigs from Hawaiian national parks. Removing them was resisted by sport hunters and trappers claiming historical right-of-use and by some animal liberationists opposed on principle to *any* killing of wildlife. At the close of 1983 the list of endangered and threatened native U.S. species totaled 297:[8]

|           | Endangered | Threatened |
|-----------|:----------:|:----------:|
| Animals   | 183        | 45         |
| Plants    | 58         | 11         |

But these were only the ones listed under the Endangered Species Act; an additional 3,827 species—including the rare Western yellow-bellied cuckoo, desert tortoise, and lynx—had been merely *proposed* for listing. The listing process, according to Defenders of Wildlife, is "the cornerstone of the Endangered Species Act, critically important because it sets in motion all the other provisions of the Act, including protective regulations, consultation requirements, and recovery funding."[9]

• • •

Until the sixties, the average American—if he or she gave any thought at all to wild animals—would have arranged them in some taxonomy such as "game, fur animals, fish, pests, songbirds, and crawly kinds." Not until the environmental age did the message penetrate that countless quintillions of living things are individuals, no two alike, each playing a role in the transmutation of lifeless matter into living, each part of a population evolving at random yet guided by the common laws of natural selection, each touching upon human life in ways that are real though widely unperceived. (Consider the tiny coral secreting its limy shell in the Devonian Period and now revealing, through the banding of its growth-layers, that its ancient calendar year had four hundred days.) With the coming of the environmental age, many of us began to see wild animals as they had been seen by primitive folk: as other persons—distant cousins—traveling with us through time and space.

Wild animals became, in the environmental age, symbolic of the world that gave birth to our species: a world that we cannot leave, a world that we must study continuously if we are to keep our bearings. Only if we care for the animals with which we coevolved will we care for the species which we ourselves represent.

# 13

# *The Human Population*

Biologically, the nature of individual men changes on the
100,000 year scale of organic evolution. Our reproductive
systems are appropriate for the environmental demands of
the Old Stone Age.[1]

Paul K. Anderson (1971)

If the world's population continues to grow as it has since the birth
of Christ it will, on Friday, November 13, 2026, fill infinite space.[2]
The scientists at the University of Illinois who made that unlikely
extrapolation were dramatizing the unprecedented rate at which
the human race is doubling its numbers. There's another way to
look at the population explosion. If one assumes (1) that *Homo sapiens* originated in 300,000 B.C. at the beginning of the Old Stone
Age, (2) that the average life span gradually lengthened from twenty
years to fifty years, and (3) that population growth was exceed-
ingly slow until about 1650, when the printed word became influential in human affairs and growth became rapid (at times exponential) thereafter, then about *9 percent of all the people who have ever
lived are now alive.* Or if one starts from a base of 2.5 million years
ago when *Homo habilis* emerged, the number of people now alive
is still an impressive 4 percent.[3]

The population of the United States has already tripled in my
lifetime. Its increase did not, however, until the 1960s receive the
media attention it deserved, primarily because it is a politically
sensitive issue. To discuss population growth is to bring in contraception, abortion, and the right of society to legislate private reproductive behavior. But the issue was nonetheless there, smoldering,
notably from 1916 when social activist Margaret Sanger opened the
nation's first birth control clinic.[4] (She later served thirty days in
Queens County Penitentiary for her bravery.) Birth control slowly

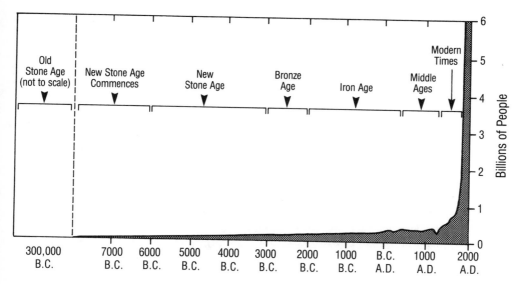

*World Population Growth through History*

won support from social workers, public health nurses, and humanitarians in many walks of life. In 1938, *Fortune* magazine declared that birth control was a yearly business worth $250 million.[5] The term "birth control," with its overtone of compulsion, evolved semantically into family planning, child spacing, and planned parenthood. Today's influential Planned Parenthood Federation of America adopted its name in 1942 after the restructuring of antecedent groups filling similar roles.

Birth control won semiofficial sanction in 1964–65 when the American Public Health Association and the National Academy of Sciences and National Research Council declared that "family-planning discussion and instructions must be regarded as an essential part of all pregnancy and post-delivery care; birth-control advice must be included."[6] But in 1968, when Pope Paul VI, spiritual advisor to millions, might have used his enormous leverage to encourage birth control, he issued the encyclical *Humanae Vitae* which forbade all contraception except by natural methods: the rhythm method and abstinence. (Many Americans regard these as *un*natural.) The Pope's edict was the more tragic in that it put a stop, temporarily at least, to a dialogue that had grown in the preceding years between popes and bishops, one that seemed destined to liberalize the Church's absolute ban on artificial contraception. Significantly, 76 percent of American Catholics polled in August

1968 *after* the Pope's encyclical thought that contraceptive information should be available to anyone who wanted it.[7]

As late as 1969, many Americans doubted that a population problem existed. A Gallup poll posed the question: Do you think it will be necessary at some time to limit the human population if our present living standards are to be maintained?[8] Incredibly, 43 percent answered no. Evidently Joe and Jane Citizen still had faith in some new blend of laws, controls, inventions, and applications of technology that would maintain forever the free status of the individual within the tightening crowd. This attitude prevailed in spite of the appearance, in the late sixties, of popular books calling attention to the world's runaway population growth. They carried such titles as *Famine—1975, The Silent Explosion, Too Many Americans, Hungry Nations,* and *Standing Room Only.* Paul Ehrlich's *The Population Bomb* (1968) sold over 3 million copies.[9] Ehrlich warned that "the battle to feed all of humanity is over. In the 1970s the world will undergo famines—hundreds of millions of people are going to starve in spite of any crash programs embarked upon now."[10] Although his projection may have overshot the mark, it did emphasize the relationship between population size and the environmental base. Although the United States was home to 5.7 percent of the world's population, its people were consuming 40 percent of the world's production of natural resources. "Each American child," Ehrlich wrote, "is 50 times more of a burden on the environment than each Indian child."[11]

When thirty-one professors, foundation leaders, and civil servants met in Boston in 1969 to ponder the question, "Is there an optimum level of population?" their inquiry foundered on the hard rock of reality.[12] It did, however, evoke several interesting comments. Lester R. Brown, a research institute executive, concluded that "we have already, at some time in the past, exceeded our optimum population level in the United States."[13] We reached that date, he continued, when our vaunted levels of productivity began to damage the environment and when we refused to foot the bill for repairing it. Barry Commoner defined optimum level as "that size to which population is likely to have grown by the time humane methods of population control have achieved their ends."[14]

The National Academy of Sciences approached the looming population crisis by asking seven authorities on natural resources and one demographer to estimate how quickly we were moving toward Doomsday and how we might reverse our course. Their unsettling report, *Resources and Man* (1969) became a textbook for students of sociology, economics, geography, and ecology. Its final words were: "It now appears that the period of rapid population and industrial growth that has prevailed during the last few centuries, instead of being the normal order of things . . . is actually one of the most abnormal phases of human history."[15]

Computer capabilities in the sixties were growing unbelievably fast. In 1968, thirty men and women from ten countries gathered in Rome to discuss the present and future predicament of mankind. Out of the meeting grew the Club of Rome, an elite research group composed of scientists, educators, economists, humanists, and industrialists. With essential support from a computer team at the Massachusetts Institute of Technology (MIT), the Club generated models of twelve future "worlds." Each differed from the others according to the variables introduced into its program. One model gave an optimistic picture of a world essentially in equilibrium by the year 2000—a visionary world based on profound changes both technological and cultural that could have been, but were not, initiated in 1975.[16]

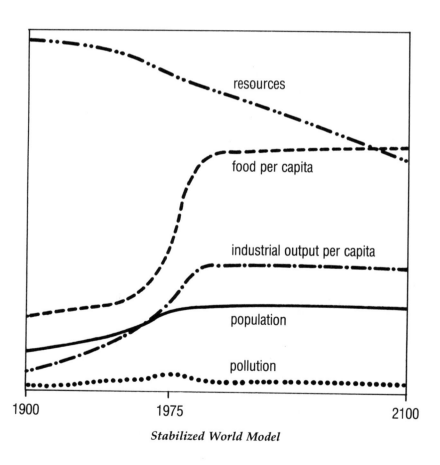

*Stabilized World Model*

In this visionary world:

1. Population is stable at about 5 billion and the average desired family size is two children; the average lifetime is seventy years.

2. Nonrenewable resources are still dwindling, though at a rate per unit of industrial output one-fourth its 1975 value.

3. Industrial output per capita is well above 1975 levels, and per capita services—such as education and health facilities—have tripled. The average lifetime of industrial capital has lengthened through better design for durability of products.

4. Pollution per unit of industrial and agricultural output is one-fourth its 1975 level.

5. Food per capita is very much higher as a result of diverting capital to agriculture even though such investment seems "uneconomic." Soil enrichment and preservation have high priority.

This rosy future, along with others darker, were described to over 3 million readers of *The Limits to Growth*. Paul Ehrlich praised the book at once, writing that "the Meadows and the MIT team have done a great service in constructing a preliminary model of the world in which all the assumptions and parameters are explicit and thus open to criticism and modification. Those who object to the characteristics of the model are challenged to help improve it; those who dislike the characteristics of the system it simulates might consider working for changes in the real world."[17] But economist Gunnar Myrdal called the book "pretentious nonsense."

Not all national leaders in America during the sixties acknowledged the link between rising population and declining environmental quality. Buckminster ("Bucky") Fuller, developer of the geodesic dome, insisted in 1968 that "the population explosion is a myth. As we industrialize down goes the annual birth rate and by 1985, if we survive, the whole world will be industrialized and . . . the birth rate will be dwindling and the bulge in population will be recognized as accounted for exclusively by those who are living longer."[18] Other pundits assured us that advances in science and technology would keep pace with the increase in population. Newfound materials and methods would forever satisfy the demands of growing numbers.

Among the more influential voices raised on the population issue during the sixties and seventies were those of three scientists: Barry Commoner, Paul Ehrlich, and Garrett Hardin. Agreeing that population growth was indeed a factor in the ecological crisis, they disagreed as to its importance. Commoner, called by *Time* magazine "the Paul Revere of ecology," was convinced that the dominant factor in environmental degradation was the impact per unit of production due to technological changes. That is, the nature of the technology, not the size of the population, was the prime factor. He blamed postwar decisions in which the public had had no input. "These decisions—to replace cotton and wool by synthetic fibers, soap by detergents, manure by artificial fertilizers, railroads by trucks—called for heavy use of petroleum stocks and energy, and produced goods that do not degrade when thrown away."[19]

Ecologist Paul Ehrlich, with engineer John Holdren, blasted Commoner's work as representing "assiduous selection of data . . . and studious disregard of the cause-and-effect relation between the size of a population and the nature of the technology needed to support it." They declared that postwar increases in energy use and in the production of environmentally harmful materials (as detailed by Commoner) "have been the combined result of population growth (meaningfully defined to include amenities as well as necessities), and the misuses of technology that both we and Commoner deplore. These factors are multiplicative, not additive, and none is unimportant." In other words, population growth causes *disproportionate* harm to the environment.[20]

Garrett Hardin has been called a biologist turned moralist. He has lectured tirelessly on our duty to save civilization even though the saving may entail suffering for millions. "Cherishing individual lives in the short run diminishes the number of lives in the long run," he wrote in 1980. "It also diminishes the quality of life and increases the pain of living it."[21] He was both praised and attacked for two bold metaphors that he coined in 1968 and 1973—"the tragedy of the commons" and "living on a lifeboat."

> The tragedy of the commons develops in this way. Picture a pasture open to all. It is to be expected that each herdsman will try to keep as many cattle as possible on the commons. Such an arrangement may work reasonably satisfactorily for centuries because tribal wars, poaching, and disease keep the numbers of both man and beast well below the carrying capacity of the land. Finally, however, comes the day of reckoning, that is, the day when the long-desired goal of social stability becomes a reality. At this point, the inherent logic of the commons remorselessly generates tragedy.[22]

How can we forestall the tragedy of the commons whenever it looms in modern society? By mutual coercion, says Hardin, mutually agreed upon by the majority of the people affected.

Hardin developed the lifeboat theme around his belief that chronic starvation among the poor and overcrowded can best be solved by letting millions die. Ultimately, the population in each poor country will decline to the carrying capacity of that country. In the meanwhile, its government—without hope of food transfusions from richer nations—will be forced to develop a policy calculated to prevent future overpopulations and misery. He wrote:

> Metaphorically, each rich nation amounts to a lifeboat full of comparatively rich people. The poor of the world are in other, much more crowded lifeboats. Continuously . . . the poor fall out of their lifeboats and swim for a while in the water outside, hoping to be admitted to a rich lifeboat, or in some other way to benefit from the "goodies" on board. What should the passengers on a rich lifeboat do? This is the central problem of "the ethics of a lifeboat."[23]

He argued that the rich passengers should let the others drown. He made clear, however, that he was *not* against feeding people if their government had adopted a tough birth control policy and if the food offering was accompanied by tools and expertise calculated to help restore the carrying capacity of the needy land.

Many humanitarians were shocked by Hardin's lifeboat metaphor. Ecologist Ronald Carroll called it obscene. Rajni Kothari, a member of the Centre for the Study of Developing Societies, Delhi, attacked it as "eco-imperialism." Others protested that it failed to consider two points: that rich nations have arrived at prosperity, not by foresight but by accidents of climate and geography, or by having exploited poorer nations, and that cooperation among nations has now become essential to human survival.

Distress over population growth—the proliferation of human bodies—was a conspicuous mark of the environmental awakening. During the decade preceding 1974, about two hundred major articles on population were submitted to *Science.* Meanwhile, however, population growth rate in the United States was slowly declining:[24]

### *Average Annual Rate of Growth, 1950–1984, Percent*

| 1950 to 1954 | 1955 to 1959 | 1960 to 1964 | 1965 to 1969 | 1970 to 1974 | 1975 to 1979 | 1980 to 1984 |
|---|---|---|---|---|---|---|
| 2.1 | 2.3 | 2.2 | 1.6 | 1.7 | 1.8 | 1.7 |

I shall not guess what fraction of the decline stemmed from environmental enlightenment and what from tightening economic pressure upon families. There would have been other factors also: social, religious, and political. Certainly the *fertility rate* (births per woman) has been declining since 1820, except for the war-induced baby boom between 1947 and 1964.[25]

As environmental wisdom spread during the sixties, the federal government began openly to discuss the problem of runaway populations. John F. Kennedy—a Catholic—may have been the first American President to endorse family planning. At a press conference in April 1963, he said that research on human reproduction is "very useful and should be continued. If your question is, Can we do more, should we know more, about the whole reproductive cycle and should this information be made more available to the world so that everyone can make their own judgment, I would think that it would be a matter which we could certainly support."[26] (Within months, the successor to the assassinated Kennedy would sign a bill approving population control: the Foreign Assistance Act of 1963.) In 1964, the Office of Economic Opportunity granted $8,000 for a family planning program in Corpus Christi, Texas; the first open birth control aid within the United States provided by a federal agency.[27] In 1965, Stewart L. Udall issued a directive to the Bureau of Indian Affairs and the Office of Territories. He explained, "What I have requested is that information and services for family planning be available on Indian reservations and wherever we [Interior] have responsibilities for people programs. The use of these services is to be strictly on a voluntary basis."[28] Most of the families affected would be non-Caucasians, that is, American Indians on continental lands and the Virgin Islands, and Micronesians on tropical Pacific Islands under U.S. jurisdiction.

In 1967, the Agency for International Development began supporting population control programs abroad through grants to the International Planned Parenthood Foundation, the Population Council, and the Pathfinder Fund.[29] In the same year, Congress identified family planning as "a special emphasis" project and specified that no less than 6 percent of federal appropriations for maternal and child health be spent in promoting it. Late in 1968, Congress authorized matching funds to local health agencies for family planning. "Never before has the government taken such positive action on this urgent issue," editorialized the *Christian Century*. "Aimed at helping families keep off welfare rolls, the program is intended for all disadvantaged families, not merely for those now on welfare."[30] Despite *Humanae Vitae* in 1968, Congress that year gave to the National Institutes of Health $2.5 million for contract research on new contraceptives and for population research by behavioral scientists. The researchers were told to deal with the relation of fertility to social factors such as unemployment, divorce rate, sexual habits, family income, and city crowding.

In 1969, President Nixon addressed a long message to Congress on the looming population crisis. How, he asked, will we house the next hundred million expected by the year 2000? How will we educate and employ them? What impact will they have on the environment and its natural resources? He pointed to the sad consequences of "involuntary childbearing."[31] And in a talk to the General Assembly of the United Nations in 1970 he said that "one of the greatest threats to the well being of mankind is the burden of excessive population growth. . . . The world is already experiencing a population explosion of unprecedented dimensions. We are, in short, in a rush toward a Malthusian nightmare."[32]

At his request, Congress in 1970 established a twenty-member Commission on Population Growth and the American Future. Its mandate was to study "the various means [including, implicitly, family planning] appropriate to the ethical values and principles of this society by which our Nation can achieve a population level properly suited for its environmental, natural resources, and other needs." The Commission was chaired by John D. Rockefeller III. Carrying that name, he might have been thought an ultraconservative, yet he called for a liberal change in American values. He wrote that we are "living in a way that is inconsistent with our finite environment and fragile ecological structure. . . . What I do want to urge is that we can move toward reproductive habits that eventually will be consistent with a balance of births and deaths." Having worked within the Commission, he recognized that "concern over the effects of population growth has been mounting. Two-thirds of the general public interviewed in the survey conducted by [our commission] felt that the growth of the U.S. population was a serious problem. Half or more expressed concern over the impact of population growth on the use of natural resources, on air and water pollution, and on social unrest and dissatisfaction."[33]

By 1970, such had been the gains in respectability of the "women's libbers" and the environmental activists, that Congress found courage to meet the population issue head-on. It passed the Family Planning Services and Population Research Act of 1970. One of the act's purposes was "to assist in making voluntary family planning services readily available to all persons desiring such services." Another was to establish in the Department of Health, Education, and Welfare an Office of Population Affairs. And by 1975, observed social writer James Reed, "contraception, once shunned as a vice practiced by the selfish, had become a public virtue, a moral imperative in a crowded world."[34] Meanwhile, the population of the United States was increasing. Between 1960 and 1980 it grew by 26 percent.

# A Revelation
# Becomes a Revolution

# 14

# *The Citizens Organize*

A typical advance in society begins with a change in personal values, then follows a route like this: Those holding similar views on the need for improvement band together in organizations. To reinforce their group belief and to build persuasive arguments for it they engage in fact finding. To publicize it outside the organization they engage in promotion and education. Having attained political strength, they persuade legislators and judges to install in law the desired improvement.

Will Rogers once said that Americans will join anything but their families. The strength of the environmental movement derived from the enthusiasm of citizens acting alone ("bearing witness") but its power came from those acting in organized groups. Some groups recruited members from the lay public; others from educators, lawyers, foundation managers, and similar professionals. The movement gave rise to an astonishing number of new organizations. The speed with which they multiplied and the variety they displayed give insight into the revolutionary nature of the movement. From 1901 to 1960, an average of only *three* new public-interest conservation groups per year had appeared on the American scene; from 1961 to 1980, *eighteen* per year.

How are we to interpret this skyrocket trajectory? After many years blessed with ample resources and clean skies and waters, Americans began in the 1930s to recognize the early symptoms of environmental abuse. Those were the Dust Bowl years. Environmental groups began to increase, and to push for remedial legislation. Franklin D. Roosevelt gave us the Civilian Conservation Corps and the Tennessee Valley Authority in 1933, the Taylor Grazing Act in 1934, the Soil Conservation Service in 1935, the Pittman-Robertson Wildlife Restoration Act in 1937, and the National Resources Planning Board in 1939. Newly formed departments of fish and game in the states attracted satellite citizen clubs. The Wil-

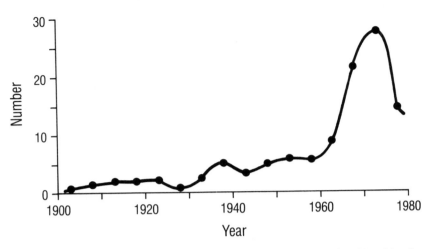

*Number of Environmental Organizations and Periodicals (Combined) Founded in the United States from 1901 to 1980, and Still in Existence in 1983*

derness Society was founded in 1935 and the Wildlife Society in 1937.

From 1939 to 1945—or shortly before and during World War II— military concerns displaced environmental ones, and the number of new organizations declined. During the postwar period through 1965, citizen interest in the environment slowly revived. Suddenly, more organizations came into being in the next decade (1966–75) than in all the preceding years of the twentieth century. After the peak years 1971–75, the trend declined, showing that the national need for new organizations had largely been met. By 1979 (according to a *New York Times* estimate), the organizations claimed more than four million members and were enjoying an aggregate income of about $1.5 million a week.

Public interest in air and water pollution gave the movement its strongest push. According to indices applied by conservationist J. Clarence Davies, that interest peaked in 1970, or slightly ahead of the peak in new organizations.[1]

The early years of the environmental movement were distinctly experimental. Max Nicholson, a leader of scientific conservation, wrote in 1970 that the movement "continues to be a mass of inconsistencies and contradictions—passionately upheld yet constantly let down or repudiated, rich in public spirit and often aggressively sectional, massively manned by trained professionals and yet often amateurish and unsure of itself, deeply concerned over the future and yet too often hag-ridden by the legacy of the past."[2] It could not have been other than experimental, for the majority of its activists were untrained volunteers. Alexander Adams, former president of The Nature Conservancy, wrote in 1970, "I would be surprised if the number of full-time conservationists employed by national private organizations amounts to more than a thousand, and the number is probably lower."[3] If we compare this total to the hundreds of thousands employed in 1970 by corporations that were lukewarm toward, or openly hostile to, environmentalism, we can better appreciate the accomplishments of the volunteers who won for it a place in American thought.

Philosopher and teacher Joseph W. Meeker is editor of a periodical describing itself as a "thinly disguised journal of environmental ethics." He concludes that dedicated citizens on the point of founding an environmental organization are apt to choose from three possibilities, the selection of which depends on the background of the founders.[4] That is to say:

*If business:* Found a corporation, enlist big names for the letterhead, publish a newsletter, plan media projects, raise funds, build a constituency, create events of high visibility.

*If academic:* Identify a special area of inquiry, define it so as to exclude all others, prove that all prior studies have missed the point, found a department, then proceed as businesses do (see above).

*If religious:* Identify the enemy, preach a simple and clear message of good and evil, practice virtues and oppose vices, promise distant rewards, and proceed as businesses do (see above).

Meeker implies that, when an environmental organization comes of age, it becomes a business. Not a bad formula . . . unless the organization forgets that its reason for existence is stewardship, not profit making.

Membership in environmental organizations across the United States has remained distinctly regional. Geographer Kathleen A. Ferguson recently scored the fifty states and the District of Columbia on "the percentage of the population who were members of ten major environmental organizations primarily in 1984."[5] She has kindly let me condense and rearrange these scores. The membership of the sampled organizations totaled 3.9 million. "The lower third of the population of each state who were environmental organization members were assigned a score of 0; middle third 1; and upper third 2. The scores were then added together for a cumulative state score." Concern for the environment has been strong in the West and Northeast, moderate in the Central States, and weak in the South. Two reasons for strong concern come to mind: better outdoor-recreational opportunities (as provided by forests, ski slopes, and marine beaches) and a tradition of intellectual discussion of environmental problems. For example, Alaska (with a score of 20) and the District of Columbia (with a score of 19) rate highest among the fifty-one regions. Alaska is not only blessed with incomparable outdoor values but with a high proportion of men and women who are determined to save them. The District is peopled with many educated professionals who (one may suppose) endorse environmentalism.

### State Scores on Environmental Organization Memberships, 1982–84*

| Lowest Third Score 0–2 | Middle Third Score 3–9 | Highest Third Score 10–20 |
| --- | --- | --- |
| Alabama | Arizona | Alaska |
| Arkansas | Delaware | California |
| Georgia | Florida | Colorado |
| Kentucky | Hawaii | Connecticut |
| Louisiana | Idaho | Maine |
| Mississippi | Illinois | Maryland |
| Missouri | Indiana | Massachusetts |
| North Carolina | Iowa | Montana |
| North Dakota | Kansas | New Hampshire |
| Ohio | Michigan | New Mexico |
| Oklahoma | Minnesota | New York |
| South Carolina | Nebraska | Oregon |
| Tennessee | Nevada | Vermont |
| Texas | New Jersey | Washington |
| Utah | Pennsylvania | Wisconsin |
| West Virginia | Rhode Island | Wyoming |
|  | South Dakota | Washington D.C. |
|  | Virginia |  |

* After Kathleen A. Ferguson.

The campaign methods employed by the environmentalists were defined in a Sierra Club handbook as "ecotactics . . . the science of arranging and maneuvering all available forces in action against the enemies of earth."[6] They consisted mainly of *education, litigation,* and *political action.* The three can be thought of as major fronts in the campaign. Fronts of lesser importance—though still very important—were: acquiring natural lands as model ecosystems, exploring ways to maintain career professionalism, and analyzing environmental history as it was being made.

# 15

# *The Educational Front*

The early environmental movement attracted a number of influential writers. Some were natural scientists, while others were simply lay persons who had learned to appreciate nature through intimate contact with the outdoors. Their writings in popular books and journals lent credibility to a movement which, at the time, was widely thought to be a passing fad.

Bernard DeVoto wrote for *Redbook,* the *Saturday Evening Post, Colliers, Harper's, The Saturday Review, Atlantic, Holiday, Fortune, Woman's Day,* and scores of other magazines. He was a vigorous writer. His "inward sky," wrote one historian, was "an undulating terrain that kept him bucking and plunging throughout his life."[1] Some of us remember him as the man who, in the mid-1950s, helped battle the Bureau of Reclamation and the Army Corps of Engineers to a standstill to prevent the flooding of Echo Park, in Dinosaur National Monument. During the battle, Congressman Wayne Aspinall of Colorado sputtered that "if we let them [the conservationists] knock out Echo Park Dam, we'll hand them a tool they'll use for the next hundred years." But they did knock out the dam and, in the process, learned to appreciate the political power of an angry public—especially one aroused by a DeVoto.

The Dinosaur fight is important to students of environmental history because it shows how keenly men and women were beginning to feel, as early as the 1950s, about protecting wilderness. I've mentioned DeVoto, but others equally persuasive and politically effective were drawn into the fight. A beautiful book of essays and photographs, *This Is Dinosaur,* edited by Wallace Stegner, was distributed in 1955 to all members of Congress.[2] It appeared at a strategic time; on April 11, 1956, President Eisenhower signed an act which banned dam or reservoir construction within any national park or monument.

E. B. White began in 1959 to write editorials for *The New Yorker* under the heading, "These Precious Days." "Because the slaughter of the innocents continues here and abroad," he declared, "and the contamination of air, sea, and soil proceeds apace, *The New Yorker* will undertake to assemble bulletins tracing Man's progress in making the planet uninhabitable. This is Bulletin No. 1."[3] Who among us today would try to measure the influence of such a wise and compassionate man?

Joseph Wood Krutch had labored for thirty years in the city as drama critic, author, philosopher, and teacher. Suddenly in the 1950s he fell in love with a sun-filled cactus desert in Arizona, moved there, and began a new career as a literary naturalist. "I found something more than merely a relief from the pressures of city life," he wrote in his autobiography, "that there was something very positive in a consoling, indeed a quasi-mystical sense, of being a part of something larger than myself or my society. I took pleasure in knowing that living things, in various forms both like and unlike me, were sharing the world with me."[4] Krutch is remembered with affection as one who could make living with the land seem so very civilized.

William O. Douglas, Supreme Court Justice for thirty-six years, was a mountain climber, civil libertarian, lover of the earth, and missionary for wildland preservation. Among his many books were *A Wilderness Bill of Rights* (1965) and *The Three Hundred Year War: A Chronicle of Ecological Disaster* (1972).[5] Although his writing did not impress the literati, it was factual and forceful. "Wherever we turn," he concluded in 1972, "whether it be to air, water, radiation, strip mining, estuaries, wildlife, forests and wilderness, transportation, or land use—we are worse off than we were a decade ago. . . . Whether we can make a religion out of conservation or give that cause a messianic mission is the critical issue of this day."[6]

Anthropologist Loren Eiseley's *Immense Journey* traced human-kind's lonely ascent.[7] The book was an immediate success. A new Eiseley book appeared almost yearly until 1979 (the last two post-humous). Eiseley gently, though persistently, called our attention to environmental abuses. He explained in 1970 that we had become "world eaters." And "if I term humanity a slime mold organism it is because our present environment suggests it. . . . Western man's ethic is not directed toward the preservation of the earth that fathered him. A devouring frenzy is mounting as his numbers mount. It is like the final movement in the spore palaces of the slime molds. Man is now only a creature of anticipation feeding upon events."[8]

As measured by her influence, Rachel Carson was the greatest of the environmental writers. It was *Silent Spring*'s literary quality, as well as its scientific content and popular influence, that earned it a place among the great books of the twentieth century. Paul Sears, pioneer ecologist, recognized its importance at once. "The result, over and above [Carson's] usual clarity of structure and presentation, is a brief of which any attorney might well be proud. If anything can convince the court of public opinion, this should do so."[9] Another ecologist, Frank Fraser Darling, confessed that, although he himself would not have liked to write the book, he was very glad that it had been written. He explained that scientists prefer reasoned statements to emotion when they set out to change people's minds. In real life, he conceded, the publicist usually precedes the scientist in arousing attention.[10]

But, from other quarters, *Silent Spring* met a storm of abuse. "Perhaps not since the classic controversy over Darwin's *The Origin of Species* . . . had a single book been more bitterly attacked by those who felt their interests threatened," wrote Paul Brooks, Miss Carson's biographer.[11] *Time* magazine attacked it in a long review which claimed that "scientists, physicians, and other technically informed people" consider her case "unfair, one-sided, and hysterically overemphatic. . . . Chemical insecticides are now a necessary part of modern U.S. agriculture, whose near-miraculous efficiency has turned the ancient tragedy of recurrent famine into the biologically happy problem of what to do with food surpluses."[12] A softer rebuke came from I. L. Baldwin, chairman of the Committee on Pest Control and Wildlife of the National Academy of Sciences. Openly pro-chemical himself, he ended a review of *Silent Spring* with these words: "It is my hope that some equally gifted writer will be willing to do the necessary research and to write the even more dramatic story of the values conferred on mankind by the chemical revolution of the last two decades."[13] But of course Carson had not set out to retell a story already publicized over and over again by an industry which was grossing $300 million a year from the sale of biocides. The attackers of *Silent Spring* eventually retreated. The book was translated into fifteen languages, including Icelandic. Rachel Carson was proved right, though she did not live to enjoy her fame; she died of cancer in 1964.

A few environmentalists chose to publicize the dependence of humankind on the health and permanence of agricultural soils. These few demonstrated that croplands can be farmed "naturally" and still at a profit. They experimented with land uses midway between traditional peasant farming and modern agribusiness. The peasant has always understood, they said, without exactly knowing why, that soils are sensitive, responsive, interacting systems.

*Rachel Carson Stamp*

The peasant has used small plots separated by other uses, has grown many compatible species together, and has rotated crops. He has encouraged natural selection, not necessarily for high yields but for year-in, year-out resistance to local diseases, pests, and the vagaries of weather.

So now we have the examples of the New Alchemy Institute and the Land Institute. In 1969, biologists John Todd and William McLarney founded the New Alchemy Institute near Falmouth, Cape Cod. They described their venture as a "small, not-for-profit research and educational organization dedicated to the belief that humanity can and must live in a more gentle, environmentally sound manner. Our goal is to devise new productive ways to provide food, energy, shelter, and community design."[14] New Alchemy developed an impressive complex of experimental projects in wind power, solar power, fish farming, organic gardening, agricultural research, and recycling. In line with its goal of promoting ecologically derived, low cost energy, food production, and waste recycling, it published a study of crop-pest insects, a fish cookbook, a guide to midge (fish food) culture, designs for methane (biogas) converters, and other reports.

And in 1974, Wes Jackson, holding a doctoral degree in genetics and a college professorship in California, chucked his job and returned to his homeland on the Kansas plains. There he and his wife, Dana, started an experimental farm to demonstrate that agriculture can be profitable and socially rewarding without being ruinous to the land. Poet Wendell Berry praised their attempt to set agriculture back on its biological feet. Within a decade, the farm had become a $200,000–a-year research center and school: the Land Institute.[15]

Concern for the Good Earth had another spinoff effect: renewed interest in organic gardening and natural foods. The term "organic gardening" had been coined in the early 1940s by J. I. Rodale, a Pennsylvania farmer, as a synonym for the raising of food crops untouched by any of the chemicals used in modern food production. No synthetic fertilizers; no pesticides; no bleaches, antioxidants, or ripeners; no artificial colors, flavors, sweeteners, or taste enhancers; and no preservatives such as saltpeter, sulfur dioxide, or benzoate of soda. Rodale (1898–1971) was the messianic leader of the organic gardeners until his death from heart arrest on a national television show. By 1983, the family-owned Rodale Press would be grossing more than $100 million a year from the sale of numerous books and brochures on gardening, nutrition, and doctorless medicine. Some of Rodale's notions, such as the value of sitting under a short-wave radio each day to replenish the body's supply of electricity, were simply nutty. Others, such as eating seventy food-supplement tablets a day were probably useless, if not mildly harmful.[16]

How much the modern popularity of natural foods owes to Rodale's rousing appeals during four decades can hardly be measured, though the debt is substantial. These foods quickly became available everywhere—in supermarkets, consumer cooperatives, and specialty stores. Gross sales for 1983 amounted to more than $2 billion, or tenfold their 1973 level.[17] Some skeptics, however, maintained that the natural food industry never did answer two important legal questions: Exactly what are natural foods? And are they any more wholesome than other foods? These questions will doubtless be addressed some day in the courts.

• • •

In the late 1960s, the conceptual change from an older "resource conservation" to a newer "environmentalism" was felt in academia. "There is even the suggestion that a new science of environment is emerging," predicted geographer Ian Burton in 1968, "[one] which will eventually develop professional loyalties of its own and be accorded departmental status in the universities."[18] The dawning of the environmental age began to color a great many university courses, including biology, civil engineering, geology, geography, public relations, resource economics, rural and urban sociology, soils, and statistics. Jurist Russell E. Train told a Berkeley audience in 1967: "It may be that we should be considering throughout the university a new environmental approach to total education. . . . I wonder if our students are not ready for this. I wonder if our institutional arrangements are not lagging behind the real wants of the new generation of citizens."[19] And in the same year, a Cornell professor declared that "to write an essay on education for environmental management is to write an essay on the future of the university. . . . Almost without exception, the separate parts of a modern American university's curriculum yield some angle of perspective on the environment."[20] Both men were prophetic; by 1972, at least fifteen colleges and universities were offering environmental education programs.

Harvard's Ernst Mayr recognized that *student demand* was partly responsible for the changeover. "[It] was in the year of unrest (1968)," he wrote, "that student interest rather suddenly began to veer away from molecular biology, toward ecology, behavior, and evolution. The visible evidence for this change was a petition of two-thirds of the biology concentrators [majors] for more faculty appointments in the nonmolecular branches of biology. . . . Although molecular biology continued to flourish, its monopoly was broken."[21] In 1970, William Murdoch, a biology professor at the University of California in Santa Barbara, asked five hundred students which of twenty-five topics they would like to see included in a general biology course for nonmajors. The top favorites were human population problems, 85 percent; genetics, 71 percent; and ecology, 66 percent.[22]

It was logical that environmentalism should have been explained best by persons who understood its genesis and its richer meanings. One such was Clay Schoenfeld, now professor of journalism and mass communication at the University of Wisconsin. He began in 1967 to train students in two related skills which he called environmental *education* (mainly directed toward students and teachers) and environmental *communication* (directed toward the public). These skills evolved from antecedents in nature writing, outdoor recreation and travel writing, science writing, public-affairs reporting (as of the "death" of Lake Erie), and persuasion (as employed by the first environmental crusaders). The Center for Environmental Communication and Education Studies, founded at the University of Wisconsin in January 1968, was a pioneer among those which were to appear in the sixties and seventies across the nation.[23] They faced immediate problems (many still unsolved). For example: Where might be found biology teachers who could see beyond the confines of traditional conservation and nature study to the new domain of environmentalism? If found, how might they be induced to work together; to orchestrate their individual skills; to solve "turf" problems? How might teachers of the humanities be encouraged to explain the myriad links between man's natural environment and his arts, language, literature, philosophy, and history?[24]

In Congress in 1970, Senator Warren G. Magnuson, of Washington, and thirty-six colleagues offered a resolution to create a World Environmental Institute which "would act as a global research center [to] disseminate knowledge of environmental problems and their solutions to all nations of the world. . . ."[25] Although the Institute died unborn, its central idea signaled the educational euphoria of the times. In the same year, Congress enacted the Environmental Education Act of 1970, designed to spread environmental literacy. It was nobly conceived but, by 1982, would be in trouble. As *Audubon's* Peter Steinhart wrote, "[the act] had lapsed with virtually no teachers trained or curricula disseminated. He explained that "the schools have never been the cutting edge of social reform. They did not bring us racial harmony or sexual equality or stand up against the denigration of rural people. In the end, they seem unlikely to solve our environmental problems." The reason many teachers deserted the environmental ranks—or never joined them in the first place—is quite possibly, as Steinhart puts it, that they are so uncertain about discussing values that they prefer not to teach about the environment at all.[26]

Environmental education should lead to an understanding of humankind's place in nature and of the abiding ethic necessary to safeguard that place through time. Environmental responsibility should be taught exactly as honesty, courage, and selflessness are taught: at home as well as in the classroom.

Virtually all the national environmental organizations were educational in the sense that they spent money to publicize environmental abuses and to propose ways of ending them. One of their more dazzling and effective educational ploys was the "teach-in," conceived during planning sessions for the first Earth Day on April 22, 1970.[27] A typical teach-in would be held at a university, high school, or community center. It might feature a convocation, songfest, dance, and smorgasbord, along with panel discussions, symposiums, and talks by environmental evangelists. The agenda might include the drafting of legislation, the reporting of pollution-law violators, the filing of environmental lawsuits, and active campaigning for elective candidates holding sound positions on environmental issues. On the University of Washington campus, twenty-two-year-old naturalist Bob Pyle organized and directed a "plant-in" at the Union Bay site of what had been a wetland biology preserve . . . until the university let it be filled as a dump. Pyle and nearly four hundred students, faculty members, housewives, and business people marched to the dump to plant pines, firs, willows, and natives shrubs. In a mood both festive and ceremonial, they finished the job by dinnertime.

The nationwide celebrations of Earth Day were held at an eminently teachable moment in history. Nearly 20 million Americans took part in that broad communion: that exchange of thoughts and ideas about ways to reverse humankind's rush toward cultural extinction. Experts and concerned lay people spoke about rising problems of pollution, overpopulation, slums, wasted resources, planned obsolescence, and military overkill. Congress recessed for the day. Environmental Action described it as the largest, cleanest, most peaceful demonstration in America's history. Aging René Dubos regretted that he could not march with the students, who, he thought, were

> vigorous, informed and still uncommitted to vested interests; they constitute one of the few groups in our society that can act as a spearhead of this movement. I wish that I were young enough to be a really effective participant in the "Environmental Teach-in." I would proclaim in action rather than just in words my faith that gross national product and technological efficiency are far less important for a truly human life than the quality of the organic world and the suitability of the environment.[28]

Earth Day reminded us that in a democratic society we, the people, can solve our problems through the legislatures, in courts, in community hearings, in stockholders' meetings, and in the streets. Denis Hayes, summarizing Earth Day, spoke hotly: "We will not appeal any more to the conscience of institutions because institutions have no conscience. If we want them to do what is right, we must make them do what is right. We will use proxy fights, lawsuits, demonstrations, research, boycotts, ballots—whatever it takes. This may be our last chance. If environment is a fad, it's going to be our last fad."[29] But it was not to be a fad. It was to gain a permanent place among America's credos.

•  •  •

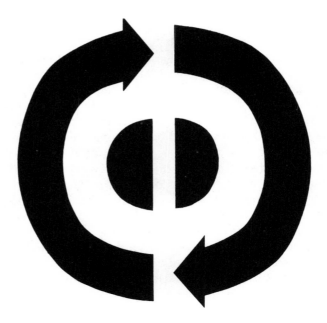

*Logo of Earth Day, 1970*

By no means all the demonstrations in the early 1970s were passive. Hundreds were active, if not violent. At the University of Oregon an *ad hoc* group calling itself Nature's Conspiracy organized a march of 1,500 demonstrators wearing green armbands to oppose a government sale of timber in scenic French Pete Valley. At the University of California, students staged a sit-in where recruiters from Olin Corporation, Monsanto, and Ford Motor Company were holding job interviews. The students were spotlighting corporation contributions to the national pesticide menace and to auto-exhaust pollution. At the University of Texas, scores of students perched in campus trees to save them from the axe. (We can see them now, touched by moving sunlight.) Twenty-six were arrested, but a few days later the faculty voted to impeach the university's president. In San Francisco, the Environmental Vigilantes poured oil on a reflecting pool in front of the Standard Oil Building to protest against recurring oil spills at sea. Small acts, to be sure, though significant. Like the Boston Tea Party, they were skirmishes in a campaign which was to have lasting impact.

The colorful history of the Greenpeace (GP) organization illustrates the progress of a group which set out in 1970 to confront by direct and often dangerous methods the perceived enemies of earth.

Thereafter it rode a wave of popular support. Among its campaign records are the following.[30]

In 1971, a GP attempt to block the underground testing of a nuclear bomb in the Aleutian Islands National Wildlife Refuge ended when one of its ships sailed into the test zone and was seized by the Coast Guard. In 1972, a GP ship at Mururoa Atoll, South Pacific, tried to stop the French from testing nuclear weapons in the atmosphere (which belongs to all peoples). French commandos boarded the ship and beat two crew members with clubs, partially blinding one. In 1974, GP activists in rubber boats confronted a Soviet whaling fleet off the California coast, where several of the boaters were nearly struck by a 250–pound harpoon fired at a sperm whale. In 1976, GP called attention to the annual killing of newborn harp seal "whitecoats." Blocked by Canadian officers from spraying the pups with harmless green dye to destroy the value of the pelts, GP members bodily shielded pups from the spiked clubs of the sealers. From 1977 to 1984, GP carried out repeated demonstrations against whaling and sealing. Incredibly, one protest at St. Johns, Newfoundland, took place while the local minister was blessing the sealing fleet.

Greenpeace members have picketed at proposed sites of nuclear power plants and radwaste dumps throughout the United States, often suffering arrest in the process. They have crawled under fences and over barriers, and have parachuted into KEEP OUT zones. In 1981, on Lopez Island, I talked with a group of Greenpeacers who were building plywood boats for one-time use (before they would be sunk) to block the trial run of a supertanker into the narrow marine waterways of Washington. Environmentalism grew out of ecology and scientific conservation; it grew also out of passion and self-sacrifice.

In extreme contrast to Greenpeace, the Conservation Foundation (1948) was created by businessmen primarily concerned with prevailing national shortages of strategic goods.[31] The Foundation later explored a wide range of environmental issues. It continued to maintain a low profile. It still does not lobby, litigate, or buy and sell land. It emphasizes "action-oriented research to influence policy," and describes itself as "an advocate characterized by reason and balance." It was the brainchild of Fairfield Osborn while he was president of the New York Zoological Society. His 1948 book, *Our Plundered Planet,* was one of the seminal works like *A Sand County Almanac* and *Silent Spring* which introduced millions to the true condition of Mother Earth.[32] He was ahead of his time. Keenly aware that the human population was outracing its resource base, he insisted that the Zoological Society do more than simply manage the Bronx Zoo, so he and a few friends created the Foundation. It began to turn out books, films, and special reports on underground water resources, pesticides, fire ants, flood control, population pressure, Alaska's resources, vanishing bighorn sheep and prairie dogs, and other environmental matters. The Foundation grew to such size and national importance that, in 1965, it moved to Washington, D.C., where its influence continued to grow under the presidency of Russell E. Train.

The Foundation directors heard the faint, early sounds of the environmental revolution and, in 1965, sponsored a weighty conference on the Future Environments of North America. Thirty-four ecologists, regional planners, economists, jurists, and conservationists probed the nature of human pressures on the North American Continent and discussed possibilities of easing them. At the conference, young men and women destined to become leaders in the environmental movement mingled with, and caught fire from, older conservationists such as Osborn and Train.[33]

The Foundation, observed one political reporter, "had enough throw weight intellectually to influence national policy in a quiet way."[34] However, because of its manifest links with capitalism, it was accused of using "conservation" as a ploy to ensure future profits. A pair of writers in left-wing *Ramparts* magazine—fearing that the environmentalists were about to upstage the antiwar and civil rights activists—took aim in 1970 at what they called "the eco-establishment." Ecology, they claimed, was in the ascendancy "because such stewards of the nation's wealth as the Ford Foundation with its Resources for the Future . . . and Laurance Rockefeller's Conservation Foundation needed a grass-roots movement to help consolidate their control over national policy making, bolster their hold over world resources, and escalate further cycles of useless economic growth."[35] But the record of the Foundation in the subsequent three decades proved its commitment to environmental durability and its contribution toward preserving that durability.

The National Wildlife Federation (1936) was another old-line conservation organization which grasped the import of the environmental revolution. In 1969 it came up with an educational ploy—the environmental quality index (EQI)—designed to be roughly analogous to such national indices as gross national product, cost of living, and unemployment.[36] The EQI was based on interviews with government and private experts and academic researchers, and on current news reports. It was admittedly subjective, based on the collective thinking of Federation staff. It was designed (I suppose) to be less scientific than educational. Its message reached thousands or even millions, but an index comparable to GNP it never became.

•   •   •

Environmental activists spread their message in other ways. They founded special educational organizations and journals, and set up intern programs offering hands-on experience in environmental fields.[37] The Scientists' Institute for Public Information (SIPI) was created in 1963 by Barry Commoner and associates. Its magazine, *Environment*, is today one of the most useful and readable journals in the field. When news of the Three Mile Island disaster broke in 1979, SIPI was overwhelmed by inquiries such as "Exactly what went wrong?" And "Do scientists share the explanation offered by the government?" SIPI's experience on that occasion led it to form the Media Resources Service, a listing of 15,000 scientists and engineers who agreed to provide advice and comment to the media.

A private publisher in Madison, Wisconsin, launched the *Journal of Environmental Education* (at first called *Environmental Education*) in the fall of 1969. Billed as "a new journal of research and development in conservation communications," it was the first important journal in its field. The Educational Resource Information Center (ERIC), well known to American teachers, is a national system of sixteen clearinghouses, each responsible for a specific area of education. ERIC is funded by the National Institute of Education, a federal agency. In 1970, the Clearinghouse for Science, Mathematics, and Environmental Education was established, thus bringing ERIC into the environmental age.

The American Society for Environmental Education (1971) serves about eight hundred teachers at all educational levels through workshops, conferences, and literature. It publishes the *Environmental Education Report and Newsletter* and other aids to teachers.

The North American (formerly National) Association for Environmental Education (1971) plays a similar role. It "promotes the analysis and understanding of environmental issues . . . as the basis for effective education, problem-solving, policy-making, and management." In 1984, it sponsored a review of public instruction in awareness of environmental issues, 1971–82.[38]

The Center for Environmental Education was created in 1972 when the Marine Mammal Protection Act was signed. The Center has focused on "maintaining the quality of our marine environment and conserving marine resources." It has produced research reports and teaching aids on whales, seals, and sea turtles.

129

The Alliance for Environmental Education (1973) brought together about thirty organizations as disparate in their primary goals as the Girl Scouts, the Humane Society of the United States, the American Gas Association, the United Auto Workers, and Zero Population Growth. The Alliance was designed to represent "the diverse interests of youth, physical fitness enthusiasts, naturalists, educators, labor unions and research institutions." It specializes in bringing environmental news to key decision-makers inside and outside government.

Two organizations—Earthwatch (1971) and the Worldwatch Institute (1974)—flourish in the field of *experiential education*. Earthwatch reported in 1984 that "since 1971 we have sent more than 11,000 volunteers ages 16 to 80 on 658 projects in 68 countries." Participants (called volunteers) pay their own expenses to study and work in many regions of the Free World. They dig for fossils and the remains of ancient villages, watch the behavior of seals and dolphins, assist in marine aquaculture experiments, examine pre-Columbian art, and engage in scores of other projects. The Worldwatch Institute was established "to alert policy makers and the general public to emerging global trends in the availability and management of resources—both human and natural. The research program is designed to fill the gap left by traditional analyses in today's rapidly changing and interdependent world. Worldwatch is tax-exempt and is funded by personal contributions, private foundations, and United Nations organizations." Among the wide-ranging issues dealt with in its *Worldwatch Papers* are the politics of North American agriculture, population control, nuclear dangers, equal education for women, solar energy, the health hazard of tobacco, disappearing species, acid rain, and the geopolitics of peace.

The highly successful Center for Environmental Intern Programs (CEIP) was founded in 1972 on the premise that a college student who majors in a traditional disciplinary field will go farther than one who majors in the new and untested "environmental studies." As the premise was phrased by a geography professor:

> Whatever the virtues of US undergraduate interdisciplinary environmental studies programmes may be, graduates of these programmes have not fared well in the job market. Entry-level positions in government and the private sector are almost always pigeon-holed, in the sense that they are defined in terms of a disciplinary background with an associated set of skills. Employers often have a specific need, and seek applicants to fill that need: botanists for vegetation inventories, chemists for monitoring, engineers for techni-

cal work, historians for preservation projects, geographers for urban planning, and lawyers for regulatory affairs. Seldom do they seek environmental studies majors for their integrated problem-solving skills. . . ."[39]

CEIP is the parent of four regional EIPs. Each places students having at least college junior year standing in short-term positions (12–24 weeks) with private industry, government, and nonprofit organizations. CEIP's budget in 1984 was $1.8 million, and it placed 222 interns or "EIP Associates" in that year.

• • •

Paul Shepard taught ecology as a liberal art at Knox College, Smith College, and Williams College. He had this to say in 1969:

> If the ecological crisis were merely a matter of alternative techniques, the issue would belong among the technicians and developers (where most schools and departments of conservation have put it). Truly ecological thinking need not be incompatible with our place and time. It does have an element of humility which is foreign to our thought, which moves us to silent wonder and glad affirmation. But it offers an essential factor, like a necessary vitamin, to all our engineering and social planning, to our poetry and our understanding. There is only one ecology, not a human ecology on one hand and another for the subhuman. No one school or theory or project or agency controls it.[40]

# 16

# *The Litigational Front*

The environmental dawn revealed a host of abuses, either accomplished or predictable, against outdoor America. Here an oil spill had reduced "without due process" the value of a waterfront property. There a developer was planning to scar a green hillside which had offered its beauty to three generations, or a corporation was proposing to build a power plant, submitting with its plans a cost-benefit analysis which studiously avoided all social costs. In these and similar ways were environmental crises precipitated. The people turned to the courts for help. Citizen action at the litigational front was spearheaded by lawyers, law students, and professors of law. Collectively they worked for new statutes and case precedents which, in the 1970s, would become *environmental law*. Although that corpus was mainly a regrouping of older laws, it soon earned a name of its own and became the most effective tool of the environmentalists.[1]

Among the handful of men and women who have chronicled the growth of environmental law, Joseph L. Sax, professor of law at the University of Michigan, has been notably productive. His many articles and books show insight into developments which one may call (in evolutionary terms) speciation, adaptive radiation, and extinction. New laws appeared while old ones underwent change or disappeared. One of Sax's favorite themes was

> the need to reassert citizen initiative in the management of our environment. . . . [An] essential format for reasserting participation in the governmental process is in the courtroom—not because judges are thought wiser or because the processes of litigation are particularly rapid, but because the court preeminently is a forum where the individual citizen or community group can obtain a hearing on equal terms with the highly organized and experienced interests that have learned so skillfully to manipulate legislative and adminis-

trative institutions. . . . The citizen, as a member of the
public, must be recognized as having rights enforceable at
law, equal in dignity and status to those of private property
owners.[2]

The courts, declared Sax, can make special contributions to the
resolution of environmental disputes. Judges are beyond ordinary
political pressures. They have the duty, and the time, to listen to
citizen complaints. As they weigh complex issues—such as those
involving the use of public resources—they often frame new policies. And, by remanding cases to the legislative branch, they call
attention to the need for new laws.

Ecologist Kenneth E. F. Watt studied the various ways in which
citizens can obtain environmental justice through the courts. He
concluded that two offer the greatest leverage:[3]

1. *The class action suit* brought against a defendant in cases where
(for example) "the members of the class might all have become
sick, lost their jobs, or had their business or homes ruined or decreased in value because of a chemical pollutant, noise adjacent to
an airfield, or some other environmental problem."

2. *The suit against government* on grounds that an agency, or
agencies, is not enforcing the law. Tuna fishermen in 1973 in the
tropical Pacific were "incidentally" (a euphemism for deliberately)
killing about 300,000 porpoises a year in defiance of the Marine
Mammal Protection Act of 1972. Eleven public-interest organizations brought suit and, in 1977, won a federal ruling that the kill
must be cut to one-half by 1980. By 1978, in fact, the kill was down
to 15,000.

Federal judges, drawing support from the general welfare provisions of the Constitution, began to deal with a host of issues
undreamed of by the Framers. Even the basic question of an American *right* to a decent environment was called into question. Environmental jurists in the sixties and seventies gradually discovered
in the Constitution specific guarantees or powers which they could
employ for the good of a space-age people. For example:[4]

1. The power "to regulate commerce . . . among the several
States" enabled the government to control air pollution and noise,
and surface and subsurface water pollution: effects which commonly extend beyond state lines.

2. The power over federal property gave the government authority to police and manage its vast parks, forests, grasslands,
and other public regions.

3. The treaty power enabled the government to execute interna-

tional agreements for the protection of species—such as migratory birds and mammals—that cross national boundaries.

4. The taxing power could force industries to pay prohibitive fees for discharging pollutants.

5. The "admiralty and maritime" power gave authority for controlling oil spills, oil transportation at sea, and the dumping of contaminants in marine waters.

6. Among miscellaneous powers, that of preserving the "common defense and security" enabled the government to take control of peacetime use, in addition to military use, of atomic energy. The Constitution specified that Congress must approve interstate compacts, thereby giving the federal government a handle on river diversion schemes. And some jurists argued broadly that the "equal protection" clause could—in the absence of clearer authority—be used to guarantee a person's right to a healthy environment. Thus a state could not offer less protection from arsenic fallout to people living *near* a smelter than to those living *far* from it.

The famous Storm King controversy which alternately blazed and smoldered from 1962 to 1980 is often cited as a pivotal case in the evolution of environmental law. In 1962 the Consolidated Edison Company (Con Ed) obtained a license from the Federal Power Commission to carve out of Storm King Mountain, on the Hudson River, room for an electric generating system. Dismayed conservationists banded together as the Scenic Hudson Preservation Conference to fight the plan. Con Ed's public relations men identified the Conference people as "birdwatchers, nature fakers, and militant adversaries of progress." But a spokesman for the preservation team testified that "[Storm King] rises like a brown bear out of the river, a dome of living granite, swelling with animal power. It is not picturesque in the softer sense of the word but awesome, a primitive embodiment of the energies of the earth. It makes the character of wild nature physically visible in monumental form."[5] After long-drawn proceedings, a Court of Appeals judge handed down a decision on December 28, 1965. Himself reluctant to substitute judicial decision for the findings of a federal commission, he remanded the case to the Commission.

His decision, however, was hailed as "one of the great modern conservation victories,"[6] for it established two precedents: (1) that citizen groups, even though they foresee no direct economic injury to themselves, have standing to challenge construction which threatens an aesthetic environment, and (2) that every agency such as the Power Commission must be prepared to defend its decisions with its *own*—not the applicant's—environmental impact statement. A member of the preservation team recalled that "the whole body of later environmental legislation began with that single decision, which had demonstrated the capacity of judges to weigh in the scales of justice such questions as ecological balance, preservation of species, and potential pollution."[7] (Not to mention the beauty of granite mountains.) The Storm King case was finally settled in December 1980, when the "peace treaty of the Hudson" was signed. Perhaps the most important legacy of the case was its contribution to the rapidly evolving concept of *standing:* the right of any citizen or group to bring action to court.[8]

Another legal precedent was established as a consequence of the misuse of a biocide by a public agency. In the spring of 1966, the Suffolk County Mosquito Commission, in New York State, authorized the spraying of Yaphank Lake with DDT to kill mosquitoes. The mosquitoes died; and so did the lake's fish. Victor J. Yannacone, a brilliant, scrappy New York attorney, filed suit to restrain the commission from further spraying. He obtained a temporary injunction.[9] His reasons—as he told reporter Frank Graham—were, first, to put scientific evidence about the unwanted effects of DDT on the open record and, second, to force environmental abusers to stand up in court and defend their behavior. On Yannacone's legal team were such experts as Charles Wurster, of New York State University at Stony Brook, and George Woodwell, of the Atomic Energy Commission's Brookhaven National Laboratory. The most telling evidence they offered was that DDT had reduced the average number of Eastern osprey chicks from 2.0 per nest in 1948 to 0.07 in 1967. (Ospreys would later return to nearly their pre-DDT numbers to rear 1.32 chicks per nest in 1985.)

Yannacone based his argument on the fundamental, unenumerated rights specified in the Fifth and Ninth Amendments and summed up in the Fourteenth: "No State shall make or enforce any law which shall abridge the privileges or immunities of citizens of the United States; nor shall any State deprive any person of life, liberty or property, without due process of law; nor deny to any person within its jurisdiction the equal protection of the laws." "Property," argued Yannacone, means not only a citizen's possessions but the air and water on which he or she depends for life.

"Yannacone lost the battle but won the war," Frank Graham wrote in 1970. "At the end of the trial the judge ruled that the prohibition of DDT is a matter not for the courts but for the state legislature to decide. [But] the resulting public pressure brought about the policy changes that Yannacone went to court for in the first place."[10] And precedent had been set; a court had confirmed the right of citizens and groups to sue for relief against environmental pollution. They could now bring class-action suits against corporate or government offenders.

Yannacone's clear vision into the future of environmental law was demonstrated in a second case. Not far from where I once lived in eastern Colorado, the Florissant Fossil Beds display some of the finest specimens of Eocene plants in the world. When, in 1969, land developers were about to bulldoze a road through the beds, an *ad hoc* group calling itself Defenders of Florissant sought an injunction. They hired Yannacone to present their case. The judge was puzzled. "What statute does this [proposed] excavation violate? . . . What right have we to control the use of private land unless there's a nuisance perpetrated by the owners?" "Your honor," Yannacone replied, "if someone had found the original U.S. Constitution buried on his land, and wanted to use it to mop up a stain on the floor, is there any doubt in the mind of this court that they could be prevented?" The injunction was granted, and in the same year, Florissant was designated a national monument.[11]

Other lawsuits brought answers to old questions newly raised in the environmental age: Who really owns America? Who decides how it shall be used? When, in 1966, the Bureau of Reclamation proposed to flood the lower Grand Canyon for water storage, environmentalists rushed to the ramparts. The Sierra Club risked (and lost) its tax exempt status to lobby against the proposal. The dam was never built. In 1967 the Supreme Court rebuked the Federal Power Commission for having given a private power company license to flood the Snake River in scenic Hell's Canyon (Idaho-Oregon). The court told the FPC to hold further public hearings and to consider other values of the Snake than merely water storage. That dam, too, was never built. In 1970, President Nixon and Florida authorities, under pressure from conservationists, halted the construction of a mammoth jetport near the Everglades which would have imperiled the wildlife of a national park. And in 1971 Nixon ordered the Corps of Engineers to stop work on the Cross-Florida Barge Canal (authorized in 1942 to protect American ships from Nazi submarines). Completion of the canal, into which $50 million had already been sunk, would have destroyed a priceless wetland. Nixon's hand was forced by the Environmental Defense Fund, which successfully sued to stop the construction. In the Mineral King decision of 1972, the Supreme Court ruled that the Sierra Club did not have sufficient personal stake in the outcome to prevent Walt Disney Enterprises from building a ski village in a national forest. Nonetheless, by the year 1972, the political muscle of the Sierra

Club and its sympathizers had grown so impressive that Disney volunteered to drop its ambitious plan.

I don't wish to leave the impression that the first environmental lawyers won justice easily. As late as 1970, wrote Professor Sax, most citizen suits were lost, or were won on procedural grounds rather than on their merits. Many were summarily dismissed with the claim that the plaintiffs had no right to sue, or that some indispensable party was not present in the courtroom.

As the need to improve environmental law grew ever more urgent, judges pondered questions for which the Constitution, code, and precedent offered few answers. They wondered whether, in fact, it should be their responsibility to concede "emotional injury" arising from the threatened abuse of scenic environments such as Storm King. Perhaps they should disavow responsibility on the ground that aesthetic standards ought to be established by lawmakers, not by the courts. But, assuming that they did choose to accept responsibility, could they then use common law nuisance doctrine to support their decisions? Those were some of the touchy questions that Richard R. Smardon, a New York professor of landscape architecture, examined in a discourse entitled "The Interface of Legal and Aesthetic Considerations." As a case in point, he observed that courts have traditionally been less willing to declare a property unsightly than to declare it smelly or noisy. A visual aesthetic is, of course, harder to define than is one of smell or sound.[12]

And what judge previous to the seventies could have imagined himself or herself being asked to decide an environmental issue revolving around the American Indian Religious Freedom Act? The Forest Service had proposed to build a road, and to cut timber, in the high country of the Blue Creek Unit of Six Rivers National Forest, California. The site was sacred to Karok, Yurok, and Tolowa Indians living nearby. For generations, they had visited it for prayer and to prepare themselves for religious and medicinal rites. In 1982, the tribes sought to enjoin the Forest Service from carrying out its plan. They won in district court and again in circuit court. Because of its importance, however, the issue was slated to end up in the Supreme Court.[13]

• • •

The first environmental law organizations and periodicals took root in the sixties from the soil of Pinchot conservation. The initial pages of the *Natural Resources Journal*, launched by the New Mexico School of Law in 1961, acknowledged its origin (in part) in the Paley Commission's report of 1952. (William S. Paley, broadcasting executive, had headed President Truman's Materials Policy Commission.) That report, *Resources for Freedom*, was a shocking account of how rapidly the United States was using its reserves.[14]

The Conservation Law Society of America began in 1963 "to assist conservation groups with the many legal problems encountered in the course of their activities, and to protect . . . the public interest in lands and natural resources." It later joined amenity issues such as the proposed dams in Hell's Canyon and in Grand Canyon National Park, roads in dedicated wilderness areas, and commercial developments along seashores.

The Environmental Defense Fund (EDF), founded in 1967, was the first member-supported professional group to challenge government giants like the Environmental Protection Agency and the Office of Management and Budget. It would achieve by 1984 a membership of 50,000, a staff of 45, and a budget of more than $3 million. One of its staff, attorney Michael Bean, wrote *The Evolution of National Wildlife Law*, the best book (in my opinion) ever written on that subject.[15] Another staffer, David Roe, wrote *Dynamos and Virgins*, a personal account of EDF's surprising victory over the Pacific Gas and Electric Company on the issue of nuclear plant construction (mentioned earlier).

The American Bar Association's Natural Resources Law Section began in 1968 to publish the *Natural Resources Lawyer* (later titled *Natural Resources and Environment*). As the environmental movement gathered speed in 1969, three groups stepped to the litigational front. The Center for Law and Social Policy was the first foundation-funded public interest law firm. Although its staff remained small, its interests gradually broadened to include civil rights, health, poverty, legal services, and (oddly) the protection of marine environments in Antarctica. The Washington-based Environmental Law Institute specialized in "multidisciplinary analysis of issues concerning the design, implementation and effectiveness" of environmental programs. In 1971 it began to publish the *Environmental Law Reporter* and in 1982 the *Environmental Forum*. The National (later the Stanford) Environmental Law Society set out to sponsor original student research in environmental law. As one of its bright young founders wrote at the time, "Experts abound in the fields of tax dodge, corporate merger, and labor law. Everyone has heard of oil and gas law, tort law and criminal law. But whoever heard of environmental law? How many students have been supplied the tools with which to win court battles over environmental polluters?"[16] The Society became known for its *Environmental Law*

*Annual* and its *Handbook* dealing with such matters as land planning, energy, water, and hazardous wastes.

When the University of California began publishing the *Ecology Law Quarterly* in 1971, its editor provided a rationale. The law's resistance to change, he observed, had become an impediment to creative thought in an era when environmental problems were calling for exactly that kind of thought. Moreover, there seemed to be general ignorance among his legal associates of the true nature and complexity of the problems.

Environmental Action organized in 1970 to coordinate the celebrations of the first Earth Day. It later grew into a vigorous body, known (and cursed by some) for its annual naming of the "Dirty Dozen" political figures whose votes during the previous year had brought the greatest harm to the environment. The League of Conservation Voters (1970) adopted a similar strategy. Marion Edey, one of its founders, started with the premise that "we must stop acting like a small pressure group and become more like an unofficial political party that brings people together to elect better legislators." She observed that "a Congressman can give a speech warmly endorsing a bill, then turn around and vote for an amendment that cripples it entirely."[17] In 1970, the League began to analyze the voting and absentee records of members of Congress, subsequently grading them by points. During the years 1972 to 1985, the average grade given to House Democrats was about 60; to House Republicans, about 33. Conceding the possibility of bias, the conclusion is inescapable that one political party is more sympathetic than the other to the needs of the ecosphere.

The Natural Resources Defense Council began life in 1970 with one lawyer and a secretary working out of a one-room office in New York. Its dream was to forge a nonprofit law office "which would vigorously implement environmental and health laws passed by Congress." By 1984 it would be rated the topmost of forty Washington organizations engaged in lobbying for pollution control. It publishes the *Amicus Journal* and other literature, trains annually about fifty law interns, and takes legal action against abusers of the environment.

After Earth Day 1970, some of the national environmental organizations began to create in-house legal branches, such as the Sierra Club Legal Defense Fund, which began to operate in 1971 and, by 1983, would be operating offices in San Francisco, Denver, Washington, D.C., Juneau, and New York. It joined with American Indians to win the California "sacred peaks" case.

The preceding list of organizations and periodicals is not a *catalog raisonné*. It simply indicates the diversity of effort spent by the early environmentalists in sharpening their best weapon: litigation. Had not the environmental revolution won for ordinary Americans new standing in the courts, it would have been little more than a brief discursion in history.

# 17

# *The Political Front: Congress*

*Congress, in its twenty-year course [1960–80] dropped one bomb burst after another on the nation—and then left it to the courts and the regulators to clean up in [its] wake. . . .*[1]

Theodore H. White (1982)

The early environmentalists fought their cause both in the courts and, through their elected representatives, in the halls of Congress. True, Congress was a bit slow in reacting to citizen pressure. The lawmakers needed time to grasp the meaning of environmentalism. They had been called upon suddenly to deal with new and unfamiliar issues. They had been obliged to learn a dialect bristling with terms such as ecosystem stability, optimum sustainable population, carrying capacity, faunal diversity, and environmental impact. Political scientist Lynton Caldwell wrote in 1963:

> In the evolution of American political institutions thus far there appears to be no clear doctrine of public responsibility for the human environment as such. It therefore follows that concern for the environment is the business of almost no one in our public life. . . . At the higher political levels of government, environment is seldom recognized in other than the vague and generalized sense of "good living conditions" or "safeguarding our national heritage."[2]

The Constitution Framers could not have imagined an environmental crisis, for they lived on a continent free of oil spills, pesticides, atomic wastes, and sonic booms. America's forests were home to 3 billion passenger pigeons and her plains to 60 million bison. Two centuries later, evidence of environmental abuse had become overwhelming. Now the citizens called for federal help in restoring

141

the health and beauty of their surroundings. Democratic and Republican lawmakers alike scurried to comply.

When Congress ventured into the unexplored territory of environmental law it routinely looked back for bearings. Insofar as possible, it based new laws on older ones which had been tested in the courts and found constitutional. Witness the Refuse Act of 1899 which banned the discharge of "any refuse matter . . . other than that flowing from streets and sewers and passing therefrom in a liquid state" into any navigable water of the United States, except by permit from the Secretary of the Army. The Lacey Act of 1900 authorized the Secretary of Agriculture to assist the states in managing local wildlife. The feds, by that act, crossed a legal boundary long jealously guarded by the states; the Lacey Act stuck; it became precedent for expanded federal wildlife legislation in later years. The Insecticide Act of 1910 and the Federal Food, Drug, and Cosmetic Act of 1938 served as grounds for subsequent legislation in the broad field of environmental contamination.

The political front was joined at just the right time by a powerful ally when, in 1961, young and visionary Stewart L. Udall was appointed Secretary of the Interior. An attorney who understood that knowledge of history can confer political power, he prepared himself for his new responsibilities by researching and writing a book on conservation: *The Quiet Crisis*. It was a popular history of land stewardship from colonial times to 1960, and opened with these words:

> America today stands poised on a pinnacle of wealth and power, yet we live in a land of vanishing beauty, of increasing ugliness, of shrinking open space, and of an over-all environment that is diminished daily by pollution and noise and blight. This, in brief, is the quiet conservation crisis of the 1960's.[3]

Few cabinet members have tried as responsibly to understand both the duties of high office and its potential for good as did Udall of Arizona. He was to serve for eight years, through the administrations of John F. Kennedy and Lyndon B. Johnson. The Department of the Interior, prodded by Udall, renamed its annual report the *Conservation Yearbook*, and began calling itself "the conservation agency." (What effect this claim had upon sister departments, especially Agriculture—a longtime conserver of grasslands and forests—and Commerce—a conserver of marine fisheries—is not recorded.)

**NEPA, CEQ, and EPA.** The political front can be divided into three salients: public health, outdoor values, and material and energy sources. But, before I deal with these, I should like to describe a daring venture by Congress into a new field which was to become *environmental administration.* That venture produced in 1970 the most important body of conservation law ever created: the National Environmental Policy Act of 1969 (NEPA), the Council on Environmental Quality (CEQ), and the Environmental Protection Agency (EPA). Many of the federal acts signed earlier, between 1960 and 1970, can be seen in hindsight as experimental steps toward that body of law. During the second half of 1968 and the first half of 1969, more than 140 environmental bills were introduced in Congress. Although most were doomed, they nonetheless sharpened congressional thought about the proper design of a lasting, comprehensive environmental policy. So, NEPA sailed easily through Congress and was signed by Nixon on New Year's day, 1970. It was clean and simple, barely five pages long. It declared "a national policy which will encourage productive and enjoyable harmony between man and his environment [and] enrich the understanding of the ecological systems and natural resources important to the Nation." It brought two important innovations.

1. It required each federal agency to prepare an estimate of environmental impact before taking major action which might significantly harm the environment. It did not *forbid* harmful acts, it simply demanded prediction of their ultimate costs and benefits, both economic and social.

2. It established in the Executive Branch a Council on Environmental Quality, a powerful body which was to set long-term policy, advise the president, and monitor the environmental impact statement (EIS) process.

Political scientist Geoffrey Wandesford-Smith identified two important reasons behind NEPA. First, environmental management had grown too complex to be held in the compartmented and largely economic framework of the Congress and federal agencies. Second, the federal government carries ethical responsibility "as the agent of the people to manage the environment in the role of steward or protective custodian for posterity. [This] requires the abandonment of government's role as umpire among conflicting and competing resource interests and the adoption of the total environment as a focus for public policy."[4]

Six months after Nixon signed NEPA, he established the huge Environmental Protection Agency (EPA). It started life with a staff of 6,673 and an annual budget of $1.28 billion.[5] (By 1980, the budget would reach $5.60 billion.) It took over most of the environmental responsibilities of existing agencies, sixty-three in total, located within ten of the thirteen cabinet departments, plus sixteen independent agencies of the Executive Branch. As though to underline the principal role of EPA as an enforcer of antipollution laws, Nixon named William D. Ruckelshaus its first administrator. Here was a thirty-eight-year-old attorney carrying a good record as director of the civil law division of the Department of Justice.

Environmentalists followed with great interest the test runs of NEPA during its early years. It was primarily a full-disclosure act. It forced the manager of each government agency to write an EIS, an exercise which often brought to light environmental considerations previously ignored. But NEPA was abused. Political scientist Lettie McSpadden Wenner analyzed 1,100 court cases brought under its provisions during its first ten years.[6] About 40 percent were won by the people and 60 percent by the government. She estimated that 11 percent of all plaintiffs took unfair advantage of the act, thus evading its real intent. She classified these misuses as:

1. *Competing for the pork barrel.* "In 1975 [for example] two local government units in New Jersey competed over ownership of a former private airstrip. Both a county and borough wished to take over the operation of the airstrip, but the Federal Aviation Administration favored the county and made its grant to it. The borough then sued the FAA arguing that it must write an EIS before transferring ownership. The court . . . dismissed the case because nothing was to be built."

2. *NEPA as a full employment act.* "These cases are initiated by people who feel their jobs are threatened or the economy of their area endangered by the transfer of a federal facility from their area. They attempt to prevent the change by arguing that an EIS should be written about the proposed move."

3. *Harassing the economic competition.* "In 1972 a group of Alabama businesses (including several gasoline stations) challenged the EIS for a public highway built with federal funds. The plaintiff's motive was their potential loss of business along an older road whose traffic would be reduced when the new road was completed. . . . The district court characterized the action as 'spurious' because the plaintiff's primary goal was to avert a loss of business."

4. *Evading regulation.* "In 1975 sheep ranchers and the state of Wyoming complained against EPA's cancellation of the use of toxic substances to kill predators. Although the district court issued an injunction preventing the EPA's action, the U.S. Court of Appeals . . . reversed, citing all those cases that had demonstrated

that EPA was exempt from writing EISs while performing its environmental protection duties." The score for business versus government in the cases studied by Wenner was 82 to 18 for the government. The courts usually found that a plaintiff's eyes were fixed, not on the beauties of nature nor the public good, but on the dollar sign.

By its fourth year, the CEQ had received 4,140 impact statements, each requiring study. (More than 80 percent came from the Federal Highway Administration and the Corps of Engineers.) Because every EIS must be circulated for comment by every agency which has jurisdiction by law or special expertise with respect to it, the amount of paperwork became staggering. And because different agencies—for example, the Forest Service and the Park Service—had different ideas about proper land use, they often disagreed on the relative importance of the impacts predicted by an EIS. Interagency bickering gave comfort to those environmental organizations which had been fighting the proposed land change all along.[7] Impact-statement law provided for public hearings. As the law went into effect, community folk began to show up in force at agency meetings and to soften the formal relationship between themselves and agency managers. One Forest Service officer described the change this way: "Five years ago, my membership in (a local organization) would have been considered a conflict of interest. In this particular case, I was 'encouraged' to join."[8]

Sociologist William Catton concluded that NEPA was foredoomed to fall short of its goal. He wrote:

> American Congressmen in 1969 were too new to ecological thinking to realize that what they were trying to do when they enacted NEPA was to halt by legislative command the man-caused succession overtaking man. They certainly had little comprehension of succession's inexorability. . . . [Before] long the filing of EIS's tended to become defined as a pro forma nuisance, after which habitat exploitation as usual was to remain the norm. But we had tried, and this needs to be remembered.[9]

I respectfully disagree. While I served on the Marine Mammal Commission from 1973 to 1976 I learned that every EIS, however imperfect, is evidence that an agency has at least studied the problem and has accepted accountability for its solution. And I believe that NEPA was a solemn promise to the American people that the government would assume, for the protection of the environment, a responsibility like those it had accepted two centuries earlier for the protection of civil liberties, commerce, health, education, welfare, and public defense. I must admit that drafting an EIS can be arduous and exasperating. (A recent case in point: writing the EIS on the proposed Two Forks Dam, southwest of Denver, took the time of about four hundred people working two and a half years at a cost of $36.6 million!)[10]

•   •   •

In 1972, the young Environmental Protection Agency, hoping to learn how it could better serve the people, staged a symposium on the "quality of life concept." It wished to generate "some sense of whether a potential mechanism exists for systematically incorporating the inputs of the public into the decision-making processes that affect the quality of their lives."[11] Quality of life (QOL) was defined as "an individual's overall perceived satisfaction of his needs over a period of time." But those at the symposium—including psychologists, sociologists, economists, and environmentalists—could not agree on how to measure QOL. (How indeed quantify feelings and attitudes, hopes and fears?) Psychologist Kenneth W. Terhune thought that answers to the simple question, How happy are you? might serve as a crude index. In one series of national polls, respondents had answered that they were:[12]

| In Year | Very Happy | Not Too Happy |
|---------|------------|---------------|
| 1946 | 39 percent | 9 percent |
| 1947 | 38 | 4 |
| 1949 | 43 | 12 |
| 1957 | 35 | 11 |
| 1963 | 32 | 16 |
| 1965 | 30 | 17 |

These returns suggest that the quality of life worsened during two decades. If so, we may reasonably ask, What share of the blame should be placed on a worsening environment?

146

**Public Health.** The responsibility for maintaining a healthy environment was at first seen as one for engineers and medical technicians. Only later was the role of ecologists acknowledged. Consequently, some of the early efforts in environmental research and practice were called "public health engineering." But, in 1961, the Surgeon General appointed a twenty-member Committee on Environmental Health Problems which duly recommended the creation of a new Office of Environmental Health Sciences and called for serious study of five national problems: air pollution; water pollution by industrial wastes, including radionuclides; urban crowding, "a form of creeping paralysis which, if not recognized and corrected, can lead to urban stagnation and death as surely as the most violent epidemic"; food contamination by, for example, new strains of *Salmonella,* and by pesticides and herbicides; and problems in occupational health created by, for example, lead, mercury, phosphorus, silica dust, and cancer-producing tars.[13]

The committee mentioned only briefly the hazard of atomic radiation. Looking back, it is hard to understand why we condoned the military testing of nuclear bombs in air and space as late as 1963. A bomb that exploded in the tropical Pacific in 1954 killed four unlucky Japanese fishermen caught in its fallout. Barry Commoner made headlines in 1958 when he disclosed that children's milk contained strontium-90. Another test bomb, in 1962, created electromagnetic effects that disrupted street lighting and tripped burglar alarms in Hawaii. In 1962, without foreknowledge of the consequences, the military exploded a 1.4 megaton bomb in the Van Allen belts of space which circle the earth at such distance as to shield us from cosmic rays. Not until 1963, eighteen years after its founding, did the Atomic Energy Commission undertake what John W. Gofman called "a long-range program to evaluate the impact of its activities—weapons testing, the peaceful uses of nuclear explosive; in fact, every aspect of atomic energy—on man and the biosphere."[14] (Gofman was an authority on medical physics who had contributed to the original Manhattan Project.) In 1963, the Senate ratified the Treaty Banning Nuclear Weapon Tests in the Atmosphere, in Outer Space, and Under Water, banning further testing except underground.

When Congress took up the task of drafting environmental health laws it faced not only the questions, Who will enforce them? and Who will fund the programs? but the more pressing one: Who will set the standards? The establishment of tolerance levels in the human body for all the man-made chemicals in our surroundings was to become one of the most difficult obligations of the government. Consider the "Delaney Amendment" of 1958, often cited as a well-meant regulation which remained to haunt law enforcers in later years. An amendment to the Federal Food, Drug, and Cosmetic Act, it stipulated that "no additive shall be deemed safe if it is found to induce cancer when ingested by man or animal." But safe in what amounts? And how does science prove the *absence* of something? Garrett Hardin suggested that the amendment was adopted because Congress was stacked with older men having "an immoderate fear of cancer, which led these otherwise intelligent men to abandon rationality."[15] In 1976 and 1977, the Food and Drug Administration, following the letter of the law, banned the use in foods of two popular chemicals: the colorant Red No. 2 and saccharin.

In 1966, the Secretary of the Department of Health, Education, and Welfare (HEW) appointed a civilian Task Force on Environmental Health and Related Problems, charged with recommending "goals, priorities, and a Departmental strategy to cope with environmental threats." In its report the following year, the task force warned that "American affluence today contaminates the Nation's air, water, and land faster than nature and man's present efforts can cleanse them. . . . As the facts become clear, the public will be shocked at the price it is paying for its affluence."[16] The task force proposed ten action goals which, in the context of their time, were quite farsighted. Stripped to essentials, they called upon HEW:

1. to push for an Air Quality Restoration Act, especially one that would reduce factory-stack and auto-exhaust emissions;

2. to formulate and enforce compliance with standards for public drinking water quality;

3. to step up research on the disposal of wastes, including radio-nuclides;

4. to decide the scope of its responsibility "with respect to family planning and population dynamics";

5. to undertake research on human levels of tolerance for crowding, congestion, noise, and odor;

6. to establish safety levels for synthetics, trace metals, and chemicals currently in use, and to prohibit after 1970 any use of new ones until approved by HEW.

These goals were followed by recommendations for action on consumer protection, occupational diseases and hazards, urban housing, and transportation. The signing of the Clean Air Act in 1963 greatly expanded the authority of the Public Health Service to control air pollution. PHS authority was extended, however, only to interstate air pollution. *Newsweek* commented in 1970: "If the smell of boiling chicken offal had not wafted across the nearby Delaware line from Maryland, the first prosecution under the Federal Clean Air Act of 1963 never would have gone to trial."[17] The act was significantly amended in 1970 and 1977.

The Noise Pollution and Abatement Act of 1970 tackled the growing problem of noise. It called for cooperation between the EPA and the National Bureau of Standards in setting standards for safe exposure to noise. Two years later, Congress was ready to pass the strong Noise Control Act of 1972 which defined those standards in relation to noise source. But the act had a loophole: it assigned responsibility for regulating aircraft noise to the Federal Aviation Administration, a promoter of air transportation. (Conflict of interest?) In the Quiet Communities Act of 1978 Congress amended earlier noise control measures and authorized a broad attack—through education, monitoring, regional planning, and federal grants—against noise. The authors of the act were concerned about the psychological and physiological effects (and even the "nonauditory" effects) of noise upon humans, other animals, and property.

The acid rain phenomenon, which had drawn little attention for two decades, exploded in a political bombshell in the late 1970s. Some harmful agent (but what?) was devastating forests of Eastern spruce, balsam fir, and sugar maple, and was killing the life in lakes. While ecologists believed that the cause was factory smoke, representatives of the chemical, steel, coal, electrical, and automobile industries professed to disbelieve; they refused to accept blame. The Acid Precipitation Act of 1980, signed by President Reagan, admitted only that acid rain *"could* [emphasis added] contribute to the increasing pollution of natural and man-made water systems" and *"could* affect areas distant from sources and thus involve issues of national and international policy."

•  •  •

The shocking degree of aquifer, lake, and stream contamination from many sources in America was not fully recognized until the 1980s, although Congress, as early as 1899, had begun to enact legislation touching on water purity.[18] The Water Pollution Control Act Amendments of 1956 became the legal backbone for a modern water-cleanup campaign. Chief responsibility was transferred by stages from the Public Health Service to the Department of the Interior and to the EPA (signifying, I suggest, a widening understanding of ecology). Congress expanded the scope of the 1956 act and strengthened federal enforcement powers through the Water Quality Act of 1965, which sent a clear message to the states that if they did not establish water quality standards by mid-1967 the federal government would do so for them. It was controversial, for it "involved Federal authorities in the field of water-quality management, traditionally a state and local preserve, far deeper than ever before. Consequently, it was the subject of lengthy, acrimonious congressional debate, raising anew the old issue of the balance of power between the Federal government and the states." [19]

Other water legislation followed: the Clean Water Restoration Act of 1966, the Water Quality Improvement Act of 1970, and the Federal Water Pollution Control Act Amendments of 1972. Nixon vetoed the last because of its nearly $25 billion price tag, but Congress, on the following day, overrode his veto. This important act became known as the Clean Water Act and was termed by the Natural Resources Defense Council "one of the strongest environmental laws ever written." It spoke not only for pure water but for ecological integrity. It placed obstacles in the path of developers bent on "reclaiming" wetlands. It assigned supervisory authority over wetlands to the Army Corps of Engineers and the EPA. Developers thenceforth had to prepare impact statements and to obtain permits before undertaking to dredge-and-fill or drain wetlands. The 1972 Clean Water Act was credited with saving Americans up to $1 billion a year from the absence of waterborne disease and up to $9.4 billion in increased recreational and property values.

The Safe Drinking Water Act of 1974 set health standards for toxic contaminants in finished drinking water. President Gerald Ford signed it after protesting that it would cost too much and would give EPA too much power over state governments. The "Kepone Lawsuit," settled in 1976, made national news when a federal judge fined the Allied Chemical Corporation more than $13 million for contaminating the James River, Virginia, with the chemical Kepone, used in insecticides. Grounds for the judgment were that employees of the Allied plant suffered neurological disorders, while fishermen along the lower James lost their livelihood when the river was closed to fishing.

Shortly after President Carter took office in 1977 he addressed a strong message to Congress on the environment. On his "want list" was authority to spend $4.5 billion in each of the next ten years for municipal waste water treatment. On December 27 he signed the Federal Water Pollution Control Act of 1977, which tackled the problem of sewage disposal by requiring most cities to build treatment plants and by offering federal grants for plant construction. As a result, many of us are now able to swim in, and catch fish in, lakes and streams that had been unsafe for years.

A weighty, 317–page report, *Restoring the Quality of Our Environment*, appeared in 1965 as the work of the President's Science Advisory Committee (PSAC). It dealt mainly with pollution. "The public," it stated, "should come to recognize individual rights to quality of living, as expressed by the absence of pollution, as it has come to recognize rights to education, to economic advance, and to public recreation." The PSAC report is of historic interest because it outlined early efforts to *monitor changes in environmental quality* and to *set threshold limits (tolerance levels) for poisons affecting human health.* "With some pollutants there is no Federal authority to act until a problem exists," concluded the authors of the report. "With some pollutants there is no Federal authority to act at all."[20]

The Insecticide Act of 1910 had offered some protection from the hazards of biocides. After World War II, when thousands of new synthetic poisons came into general use, Congress increased its protective role. In 1964, remembering *Silent Spring*, it amended the Federal Insecticide, Fungicide, and Rodenticide Act (FIFRA). When President Johnson signed the act he remarked, "I am sorry that one voice which spoke so often and so eloquently for measures like this—the voice of Rachel Carson—is still today. She would have been proud of this bill and this moment."[21] One signal effect of the bill—which amended a weak 1947 version—was that it shifted from the government to the manufacturer the burden of proving a chemical safe. The stronger Federal Environmental Pesticide Control Act of 1972 required all producers of pesticides to register their products with the EPA on the basis of submitted safety data, and it prohibited the sale of pesticides which did not bear registered labels. The Federal Pesticide Act of 1978 extended and tightened loopholes in FIFRA. It obliged the government to release, on demand, industry data on pesticide safety. Industry fought this provision until the Supreme Court demolished the last of its arguments. Justice Harry Blackmun said, in effect, that the right of the people to health outweighs the proprietary right of the chemical manufacturer.[22]

The Toxic Substances Control Act of 1976 was called by *Science* magazine "the first comprehensive regulation of the chemical industry."[23] (It exempted pesticides, tobacco, nuclear material, ammunition, foods, drugs, cosmetics, and other substances already regulated under older laws.) While protecting industrial trade and financial secrets, it opened to public scrutiny information such as the manufacturer's test data on the health and environmental effects of a suspected chemical. Eight months before the act was passed, Russell E. Train (then administrator of EPA) had announced that "It is time we started putting chemicals to the test, not people. It is time we gave the people of this country some reason to believe that, every time they breathe or eat or drink or touch, they are not taking their life into their own hands."[24] It was the strongest act thus far to prevent carcinogens in industrial chemicals from reaching the environment.

• • •

The Solid Waste Disposal Act of 1965 acknowledged that waste had become a nationwide problem. Domestic waste alone amounted to 250 million tons a year, and local communities were tired of "sweep-it-under-the-rug" solutions. Congress responded with this act, which called for research and for assistance to the states. It dealt again with the issue in the Resource Recovery Act of 1970, the thrust of which was not merely to get rid of the stuff but to use it. The act was designed to lighten the $4.5 billion annual burden carried by the nation in disposing of solid waste. The act emphasized reduction of the amount of waste, improved disposal methods, and recovery of its usable materials and energy. In drafting the Resource Conservation and Recovery Act of 1976, a congressional committee observed that "solid waste" is more accurately described as "discarded materials." Accordingly, the act established an Office of Discarded Materials, under EPA, to replace the Office of Solid Waste Management. The act strengthened the government's hand in regulation. "The [drafting] Committee believes that the approach taken by this legislation eliminates the last remaining loophole in environmental law, that of unregulated land disposal of discarded materials and hazardous wastes."

Two tragedies in 1980 prodded Congress into acting more vigorously on the hazardous waste issue. On April 22, an abandoned warehouse of the Chemical Control Company in New Jersey blew up, burned for ten hours out of control, and released clouds of deadly smoke which would have drifted into New York City had the wind been right. And on May 16, the EPA announced that eleven out of thirty-six residents of Love Canal had apparently suffered chromosome damage. The idea that industrial poisons could penetrate even to the genetic core of life was, of course, played up by the media.

So, on December 11, Congress enacted the Comprehensive Environmental Response, Compensation, and Liability Act of 1980, widely known as Superfund. It provided for a $1.6 billion fund for cleaning up toxic dump sites and oil spills; the money to be accumulated from taxes on petroleum and certain chemicals and from federal appropriations. The "Battle of '79–'80" from which Superfund emerged was fought during Jimmy Carter's administration. It was especially fierce because the citizenry (acting through Congress) and industry could not agree either upon the urgency of the problem or who should pay the great costs of solving it. Superfund was the latest government move, starting with the Solid Waste Disposal Act of 1965, to deal with hazardous waste. But no one really knew the total number of abandoned chemical plants, illegal ("midnight") dumps, spills from vehicles, and incinerator plants across the country. The EPA put the total at more than 18,000, but surely that figure was low. It could not have included the myriad small-town dumps where, year after year, chemicals with names reciting the alphabet from asbestos to xylene were discarded in ignorance of their hazard to health.[25]

• • •

**Outdoor Values.** It was far easier for President Eisenhower and his successors in the 1960s to sell Americans on the value of saving outdoor recreation and natural beauty than of saving "environmental quality"—that new notion having overtones of bureaucratic management and expense to the taxpayers. Recreation and beauty are motherhood words. In 1959, Eisenhower had appointed an Outdoor Recreation Resources Review Commission (ORRRC), with Laurance Rockefeller as chairman. Social geographer Gilbert F. White praised the commission as "the first public agency to attempt an orderly canvass of consumer demand for qualitative use of environment."[26] Its careful, three-year study, reported on in 1962, led to new federal systems (wilderness, trails, and wild rivers), to the Land and Water Conservation Fund for buying parkland, to a Bureau of Outdoor Recreation, and to other recreational breakthroughs.[27]

In 1960, the *Reader's Digest* urged us to "Save a Spot of Beauty for America," including Walden Pond and other lovely places on the point of being scarred by the developers.[28] The Sierra Club made a pitch for beauty with a folio presentation of Ansel Adams's stunning landscapes: *This is the American Earth.*[29] In 1966, President Johnson appointed a Council on Recreation and Natural Beauty which, two years later, produced an elaborate picture book, *From Sea to Shining Sea: A Report on the American Environment.*[30] It argued for federal intervention to restore the health, beauty, and permanence of the environment. And in 1968, Johnson sent a special message to Congress on conservation, "To Renew a Nation." (Recorded also for radio and television broadcast.) He called upon "all Americans—every mother and father, every businessman and worker, every Governor and every mayor—to join us in this urgent task of conserving America the beautiful."[31]

The Highway Beautification Act of 1965 called for controls on advertising along interstate and primary highways, and for the screening of junkyards. One might suppose that a beautification bill would have moved easily through Congress. Not so. While the garden clubs and environmental groups lobbied for it, business interests were against it. Florida Congressman William C. Cramer sounded off when the bill was being debated: "I am for beauty. As a matter of fact, I married, I think, one of the most beautiful girls in the world. Nobody can say I am not for beauty, and no one can say that I am not for beautification of our highways. I am, and my record is clear in support of beautification of our highways."[32] Then he ripped into the bill on the grounds that it would hurt advertising. The act was doubtless the strongest measure that could have been enacted in its time.

Franklin D. Roosevelt had offered us a New Deal, John F. Kennedy had offered to lead us across the New Frontier, and in 1964 Lyndon B. Johnson would help us create the Great Society. In a talk to the students at the University of Michigan he spoke of America the beautiful. "Today that beauty is in danger," he said. "Our parks are overcrowded, our seashores overburdened. Green fields and dense forests are disappearing. . . . [Once] our natural splendor is destroyed, it can never be recaptured. And once man can no longer walk with beauty or wonder at nature his spirit will wither and his sustenance be wasted."[33]

Johnson harped on natural beauty before and after his election in 1964, and again in his messages to Congress in January and February 1965. In May 1965, he convened the historic White House Conference on Natural Beauty, attended by at least eight hundred.[34] Henry L. Diamond (later a Washington lawyer) recalled twenty years after the event that

> once inside [the White House], Cabinet members and Congressmen and concerned citizens sat around on the floor. The conferees told the President of the United States firsthand what ought to be done about natural beauty in America. They urged strong controls on strip mining. They told utility companies to get their power lines underground. They urged an urban beautification program. They proposed a program of landscape grants for the countryside. They urged

> increased efforts at educating their fellow citizens so they
> could better understand the environment. . . . Most im-
> portant of all, the word went out from the White House
> that the President and First Lady cared.[35]

We must thank Ladybird Johnson, a perceptive, courageous, and energetic woman, for stimulating White House interest in those outdoor values which in her day were called simply "beauty." (Some of us recall another First Lady—Eleanor Roosevelt—who likewise prodded a reluctant husband into tackling social problems which were low on his personal worklist.)

National interest in outdoor values left its mark in legislation. The Multiple-Use Sustained-Yield Act of 1960 acknowledged that our national forests have important amenity values. It declared that consideration must be given "to the relative values of the various [forest] resources, and not necessarily to the combination of uses that will give the greatest dollar return or the greatest unit output." The Bureau of Outdoor Recreation, created in 1962, assumed most of the planning functions then being performed by the National Park Service. The Public Land Law Review Commission, authorized in 1964, spent more than seven million dollars studying public land policies and laws. Its report, *One-third of the Nation's Land*,[36] was denigrated by a reviewer as "a bland and somewhat unctuous document . . . weighted heavily on the side of mining, timber, and other commercial users."[37] But it did quash a proposal to sell off the public domain, an idea which time and again has been brought to the floor of Congress by selfish Westerners (most recently during the Reagan administration).

The Wilderness Act in 1964 passed by voice vote: 73 to 12 in the Senate and 373 to 1 in the House. It gave legislative (in contrast to administrative) protection to 9.1 million acres. Of all the conservation laws enacted in our nation's history, the Wilderness Act most clearly reflects the inner glow of environmentalism. A 1960 public letter from Wallace Stegner, novelist and historian, was credited with generating strong support for the act. It was a long and moving appeal ending with these words: "We simply need that wild country available to us, even if we never do more than drive to its edge and look in. For it can be a means of reassuring ourselves of our sanity as creatures, a part of the geography of hope."[38] Wilderness regions were set aside in later years, always over the opposition of vested interests. Notably, with the signing of the National Parks and Recreation Act of 1978, the area of wilderness within the national parks was nearly tripled.

In 1968, the Redwood National Park Act set aside 58,000 acres of spectacular forest in northern California. Here live some of the world's oldest and tallest trees, uniquely American. In preserving the redwood groves, Congress rated their symbolic value above their lumber value and bore witness to a maturing national ethic. In the same year, Congress passed the National Trails System Act and the Wild and Scenic Rivers Act. The latter was a bold step in social legislation. While we Americans had long conceded the government's right—indeed obligation—to acquire private *lands* for public parks and preserves, we were not so sure about its right to acquire *rivers*. These are the nation's arteries, valued as routes of transportation; places of recreation and inspiration; sources of hydropower; sources of agricultural, domestic, and industrial water; and habitats for fish and wildlife. Congress took three years to decide that sections of eight free-flowing rivers should be saved: in total about seven hundred miles in California, Idaho, New Mexico, Oregon, Missouri, Minnesota, and Wisconsin.

The conservative Forest Service moved in a direction that would have irritated its bearded-and-booted "timber beasts" of an earlier day: it began to hire landscape architects. By the end of 1971 it was listening to the advice of about 170 outdoor design professionals on ways to avoid, minimize, or shorten the duration of unsightly side-effects of forest engineering. Meanwhile during the seventies, Congress enacted five important laws designed to reconcile the management of the national forests and rangelands with a growing public demand that broad societal values be given greater weight. The Forest and Rangeland Renewable Resources Planning Act of 1974 emphasized long-range planning. "For too long," declared Senator Hubert Humphrey, "we have marched backwards in our forest policies. In my judgment this Act comes to grips with tomorrow's resource problems now before we have irreversible crisis in our forests."[39] The act called for periodic assessment of renewable resources (in 1975, 1980, and every ten years thereafter) and for periodic programming of multiple-use goals (in 1975, 1980, and every five years thereafter). Authority for research was updated and broadened in the Forest and Rangeland Renewable Resources Research Act of 1978.

The Federal Land Policy and Management Act of 1976—the long overdue "BLM Organic Act"—appeared after six years of Congressional wrestling with the best way to manage 337 million acres of public land: acres "so diverse in land forms and resources as to be almost beyond the comprehension of the average citizen who is co-owner of this vast domain." Passed during the Gerald Ford administration, the act was a compromise. The Senate favored more protection, the House more exploitation, of public lands. It remains to be seen whether the act will continue to protect vast regions of America from overgrazing, from abusive mineral development, and from the human locusts who swarm from the city to the country where they tap the groundwater, scar fragile grassland with ORVs (off-the-road vehicles), and leave junk of infinite diversity.

The National Forest Management Act of 1976 brought Congress more deeply into the management of the national forests and opened its deliberations wider still to public scrutiny. A triggering impulse for the act was national debate that followed a 1975 legal decision. A federal judge had declared that the Forest Service did not have the right to clearcut in the Monongahela National Forest of West Virginia (and, by implication, other forests). Only dead or mature trees, selected individually, could be felled. The decision marked the end of a confrontation between the tiny Izaak Walton League and the giant U.S. Department of Agriculture. At the heart of the 1976 act was a requirement that each of the nation's 120 national forests prepare a fifty-year management plan, each of which would serve as a blueprint for future timber cutting, mining, oil-and-gas drilling, road building, wilderness preserving, and other activities. The Forest Service was not, I think, happy with its new assignment. It would have preferred more freedom to move with shifting political currents. But that very freedom was partly to blame in the first place for creating the forest-and-rangeland crisis of the seventies.

• • •

Alaska had won statehood in 1959, becoming the nation's largest state. It then fidgeted for two decades while the ownership of millions of acres of supremely wild and beautiful land was being disputed among Native Americans, the new state, and the federal government. The dispute seemed near an end in 1978 when the Alaska National Interest Lands Conservation Act bill (HR 39, known informally as the Alaska Lands Act) was passed by the House 277 to 31. But in the Senate, "one man decided he would have an oratorical contest to prevent the other 99 senators from voting . . . and so we lost it," explained Morris K. Udall.[40] However, the bill was not a total loss. Later in 1978 Jimmy Carter, under authority of the Antiquities Act (1906) and the BLM Organic Act (1976) boldly withdrew certain lands from state selection and designated other lands as national monuments. The effect was to save 113.5 million acres, some permanently and some *pro tem*. Never before had a President used his power of office and his pen for such an extensive land withdrawal. Two years later, Congress, in spite of intense lobbying by mineral and timber industries, did pass the great Alaska Lands Act. When Carter signed it on December 2, 1980, he called it the environmental vote of the century. It added to the nation's dedicated lands:[41]

| | |
|---|---|
| National parks, monuments, and preserves | 43.585 million acres |
| National wildlife refuges | 53.720 |
| National forests | 5.362 |
| National wild and scenic rivers (outside national parks) | 1.200 |
| Total | 103.867 million acres |

Public agitation to save vanishing wildlife gave the environmental movement one of its strongest pushes. Congress, through the prototype Endangered Species Preservation Act of 1966, moved "to provide for the conservation, protection, and propagation of native species of fish and wildlife." In the same act, it established the National Wildlife Refuge System, thereby consolidating the administration of more than two hundred federal refuges, the oldest dating to 1903. The act protected endangered vertebrates (mammals, birds, reptiles, amphibians, and fishes). It could be called an educational act, for it implied that even the least of species, like the Devil's Hole pupfish, is precious if only as a mark of our commitment to environmental values. The pupfish, which lives in one deep, water-filled limestone sink in Ash Meadows, Nevada, had been threatened by land developers. The 1966 act challenged them to trade economic gain for the lives of fewer than a thousand fish, none as long as two inches. Land developers and water engineers were slow to grasp—and slower to accept—the ethical implications of the act, for it seemed written in a foreign language. Its only precedent in federal law was, I believe, the Bald Eagle Protection Act of 1940 (later amended to include the golden eagle), a purely symbolic recognition of a living treasure.

The Endangered Species Conservation Act of 1969 extended protection to mollusks and crustaceans. It spoke for "threatened" as well as "endangered" species. It also gave Walter J. Hickel, Secretary of the Interior, an excuse for placing eight species of great whales on the endangered list. He did so in 1970, banning the import of whale products into the United States and putting a stop, at the end of 1971, to American whaling. His action was calculated. For petty political reasons, President Nixon had just moved the administration of whales and whaling from Hickel's jurisdiction to that of the Secretary of Commerce. Hickel now saw a way to get even by declaring whales, in effect, "noncommercial." Perhaps he sensed also that Nixon was about to fire him.[42]

Congress, in drafting the Endangered Species Act of 1973, reaffirmed the importance of wildlife habitat. The lawmakers spoke for the preservation both of populations and of the surroundings in which they are peculiarly adapted for survival. Two revisions followed: the Endangered Species Act Amendments of 1978 and of 1979. But, because the 1973 act had focused on the protection of "critical habitats," and because many of these happen also to be prizes in the ongoing struggle for ownership between private and public interests, the habitat provision of the act was not, for close to a decade, administered the way Congress had intended.[43] Even today, strong differences of opinion exist as to the meaning of "critical." The habitat provision made national headlines in 1977 when construction of the $116 million Tellico Dam on the Little Tennessee River threatened the future of the snail darter. After a two-year legal battle, President Carter signed "with regret" legislation which permitted completion of the dam. The bulldozers were at work twelve hours later. The Endangered Species Act of 1973 was due to expire in the fall of 1978. Congress did, in fact, extend and amend it, but (with the snail darter ruckus fresh in mind) nearly crippled it by requiring additional red tape and greater consideration of economic, as against biological, factors. This shifted the nature of the listing process in the direction of "social balancing."[44] The act may have come too late to save the prairie dog, black-footed ferret, ivory-billed woodpecker, dusky seaside sparrow, and California condor. Time will tell.

The Fish and Wildlife Conservation Act of 1980 documented a very important shift in public thought, namely, that wild animals are more than pests or game or targets; they are a universal good. The act was the first national recognition of the "ecological, educational, esthetic, cultural, recreational, economic, and scientific value" of all native species of wild vertebrates. It was the first federal law specifically to protect animals which are neither hunted

*Black-footed Ferret Stamp*

nor endangered. The Fish and Wildlife Service was authorized to allocate $20 million over four years to state fish and wildlife agencies for so-called "nongame conservation." (No money had been allocated through 1986, which does not detract from the value of the act as a progressive statement of policy.)

Congress turned its attention to oceanic, as well as terrestrial, wildlife. It enacted two important measures to protect America's coastal wildlife habitats: the Coastal Zone Management Act of 1972 and the Marine Protection, Research, and Sanctuaries Act of 1973. Oddly, to some environmentalists at least, administration of the two was left to the Department of Commerce. Because competition for seacoastal values is fierce, the Department has always found difficulty in reconciling the many claims upon the shores under its jurisdiction.

The Fishery Conservation and Management Act of 1976 "fostered the new concept of governing international fishery agreements which are required before any foreign vessel can fish in the U.S. 200–mile fishery conservation zone."[45] Within this zone, the act claimed U.S. authority for fish and "all other forms of marine plant and animal life other than marine mammals, birds, and highly migratory species [certain tunas]." The "Pelly Amendment" (1971) and the "Packwood-Magnuson Amendment" (1979) to the Fishermen's Protective Act of 1967 gave the United States authority to penalize, through economic sanctions, any foreign nation whose fishery operations diminished the effectiveness of a marine mammal treaty which the United States had ratified. If, for example, Japan were to ignore a decision of the International Whaling Commission (IWC), the United States could ban imports of Japanese fish products and could curtail Japanese fishing privileges in U.S. coastal waters. The two amendments gave new protection to endangered marine mammals. (However, for political reasons, the leverage of the acts proved difficult to apply. Thus, in 1986, the Supreme Court would rule 5 to 4 that enforcement of Packwood-Magnuson is strictly up to the Secretary of Commerce. Only he or she can decide whether a foreign nation is acting "to diminish the effectiveness" of an IWC decision.)

Popular demands for the protection of endangered species became emotionally entwined with demands for anti-cruelty legislation. Before the environmental age, Congress had evidently felt that kindness to animals was an issue to be dealt with at personal and community levels. But the lawmakers "came along," as the Quakers say, and showed their collective change of heart by enacting humane-treatment laws, all of which were later strengthened.[46] The Wild Horses and Burros Act (1959) banned the use of motorized vehicles to capture these animals and banned the poisoning of waterholes. The Laboratory Animal Welfare Act (1966), amended in 1970 and 1976, imposed a sweeping set of regulations to protect dogs, cats, laboratory animals, and many species of wild animals from abuse. It prohibited animal fighting—though not dog racing—as a sport. Nor did it ban the use of live animals for target practice. As I write, the town of Hegins, Pennsylvania, has just celebrated its annual Fred Coleman Memorial Shoot, a sociable affair in which several thousand pigeons are released, one by one, to be shot from the air by "sportsmen."[47]

The Wild, Free-Roaming Horses and Burros Act (1971) was rooted in two convictions: first, that these animals are "living symbols of the historic and pioneer spirit of the West" and second, that they were being cruelly treated. They were being harassed for sheer sport and killed for pet food and fertilizer. The Airborne Hunting Act in 1971 provided a penalty for shooting wild animals and birds from the air. It contained loopholes, though, as witness the shooting of wolves by Alaska game wardens in the 1980s. The Marine Mammal Protection Act of 1972 banned the taking, importing, or holding of seals, dolphins, and other sea mammals "inhumanely," and defined humane taking as that "which involves the least possible pain and suffering practicable to the mammal involved." Moreover, it banned the importation of any marine mammal which was pregnant or nursing, or was less than eight months old. These humane clauses, inserted in legislation designed primarily to protect dwindling populations, were criticized by some biologists as being sentimental. Others maintained that sentiment, as well as biology, should be weighed in lawmaking.

• • •

Federal lawmakers during the sixties and seventies were obliged—as had been their precursors—to deal with a cluster of problems surrounding the conservation of material resources and energy. But these problems were growing ever more acute because the human population was increasing while the supply of cheap materials and energy was decreasing. President Kennedy had been in office barely a month when, on February 23, 1961, he sent to Congress a special message on natural resources. It was a reckoning of America's slow progress toward a national policy for resource management. It was an appeal for agreement among state and federal agencies that such a policy was vital. It was a shopping list of improvements needed in the areas of water, electric power, forests, public lands, ocean resources, and outdoor recreation. "We cannot," said Kennedy, "delude ourselves—we must understand our resources problems, and we must face up to them now. The task is large but it will be done."[48]

He followed by asking the National Academy of Sciences to make recommendations for a new natural resources policy: an assignment which the Academy completed in 1962. Its report was praised at the time as "an extraordinary document [focusing] new attention on the neglected importance and essentiality of the life sciences, and the fundamental need to understand and nurture the complex environment that is an ecological unity."[49] It did more than give an inventory of America's holdings in land, water, minerals, energy sources, and wildlife; it asked a very important economic question: how seriously would the nation commit itself to living within its natural means? More specifically, who would bear the stepped-up costs of conservation and how—through government action—could they be persuaded or induced to do so?

In May 1962, Kennedy convened a White House Conference on Conservation, orchestrated by Secretary of the Interior Udall.[50] (Teddy Roosevelt's similar White House Conference of 1908 had been orchestrated by Chief Forester Gifford Pinchot.) It was followed in 1963 by a weighty book addressed to government planners and entitled *Resources in America's Future: Patterns of Requirements and Availabilities, 1960–2000*. Published by Resources for the Future, it became one of that organization's most widely read resource references. Its projections were based on population growth, labor force, gross national product, progress of technology, current consumption levels, estimated size of resources, and other factors. Its authors faced the future with optimism; they saw the prospect of "sustained economic growth." Where they fell short was first, in equating growth with welfare and second, in failing to consider the effect of social ferment—including the environmental revolution already under way—on future patterns of resource use. The authors of *Resources* were strong on technology and weak on sociology.[51]

In the fall of 1970, Congress established a National Commission on Materials Policy, under the Resource Recovery Act of 1970. The Commission classified about 150 materials by five groups: minerals, forest products, paper materials, plastics, and ceramics. It offered certain recommendations (paraphrased here):[52]

1. Environmental costs should be taken into account in any cost-benefit analysis of materials extraction and use.

2. Except where social benefits are paramount, the extraction should be limited to areas where the ecosystem can be restored.

3. The government should support research on "the dynamics of materials-energy-environment interplay" and should expedite decision-making in this area.

4. Market forces, rather than government subsidies, should determine the mix of imports and domestic production. But government should provide "a congenial economic and institutional climate." (Meaning what?)

5. To foster the search for scarce materials, the government should "facilitate access to public and private lands."

6. The highest priority should be given to efforts "to free this

Nation from dependence upon fossil fuels for its primary energy needs."

7. Government and industry working together should set standards for consumer products that last longer, can more easily be repaired, and can be recycled; thus indirectly conserving raw materials.

8. Because land-use decisions will shape the evolution of both the economy and the society, a single "Department of Natural Resources" should be established. "More than 63 executive branch organizations have responsibilities in the energy area alone," observed the Commission. "The interactions of materials, energy, and the environment are now too numerous, too subtle, and too complex to be managed effectively in such a decentralized manner."

9. "We have concluded," stated the Commission, "that it is impossible to understand, much less solve, problems in one part of the interlocking materials-energy-environment system without recognizing that all parts of the system are interrelated."

The Commission's report was based on ecological wisdom. It was generated by nine men working in the full light of the environmental dawn. And the nine were a good mix: four cabinet members (active or retired), three businessmen, a professor of political science, and the president of Rockefeller University.

After debating for nearly four decades, Congress finally made it harder for stripminers to scar the nation's landscapes; it enacted the Surface Mining Control and Reclamation Act of 1977. The act specified that, within three years, the individual states must either pass laws as tough as those contained in the act or yield jurisdiction over their strip-mines to the new Office of Surface Mining Reclamation and Enforcement. The act did not fully satisfy the environmentalists, for it covered only coal; not minerals and oil shale. What is worse, it was not enforced after 1979. Tennessee Senator Albert Gore called its administration "a national disgrace."[53]

The price of oil quadrupled in 1973–74, stirring Congress to new levels of fear for the nation's energy future. The price again increased in 1978–79. The Three Mile Island nuclear plant "blew" in 1979, bringing antinuclear protesters out on campuses and streets. Is it little wonder that, in the late seventies, many Americans gave serious thought for the first time to the meaning of *energy* in their lives?

The Trans-Alaska Pipeline Authorization Act was signed in the fall of 1973. It ended an Environmental Protection Agency ban on construction of the line and put a closure on further judicial review on environmental grounds. Three energy acts followed in the next year. The complicated Federal Energy Administration Act of 1974 established the Federal Energy Administration. The Energy Supply and Environmental Coordination Act of 1974 gave automobile manufacturers two years' grace "for the development of emission control technology" so that they might "focus attention on improving automobile fuel economy." It also provided for "a limited program to convert powerplants and other major fuel-burning installations from the use of petroleum products and natural gas to the use of coal."[54] The Energy Reorganization Act of 1974 was praised by President Ford as "the most important and far-reaching energy conservation program in history."[55]

A method of using the power of the atomic nucleus for peaceful ends had been developed in the early 1940s under a cloak of military secrecy. For several years thereafter, responsibility for using it in the service of humankind remained in the hands of the military. In 1946, however, Congress established a five-man civilian Atomic Energy Commission (AEC) broadly charged with overseeing government control of the production, ownership, and use of fissionable material. (Significantly, until the National Environmental Policy Act was signed in 1970, the AEC insisted that it had no authority to consider environmental quality as a factor in the licensing of nuclear power plants.[56]) By 1974, the AEC was revealed as having been poorly designed. As both the promoter of, and the regulator of, the atomic energy industry it was wide open to conflict-of-interest charges. So, in late 1974, its duties were split between a Nuclear Regulatory Commission and an Energy Research and Development Administration.

From 1975 to 1980, Congress considered hundreds of bills, the intent of which was to lessen America's dependence on foreign oil, to develop alternative sources of energy, and to promote energy conservation. Among those that became law were the Energy Policy and Conservation Act of 1975; the Department of Energy Organization Act of 1977, which created the Department of Energy; the Public Utility Regulatory Policies Act of 1978; the National Energy Conservation Policy Act of 1978; the Energy Security Act of 1980; and the Ocean Thermal Energy Conversion Act of 1980.

One of the forelisted, the Public Utilities Regulatory Policies Act (or PURPA), was welcomed by advocates of the "small-is-beautiful" philosophy. It *required* electric utilities to buy power from small private producers at the going per-kilowatt rate. Any kind of source would do, be it wind, biomass, hydro, or other. As a result of this and other new energy laws, the government received, between 1977 and 1983, applications for licenses to build or rebuild 6,328 dams.

But, as has been discovered time and again, when we disturb one of nature's freshwater arteries, we must expect harmful side effects. While environmentalists welcomed PURPA as an endorsement of alternative energy, they soon found that a rash of hastily designed dams was bringing damage to fishing streams and riparian forms of wildlife.[57]

"Thou canst not stir a flower," reflected poet Francis Thompson, "without troubling of a star."

# 18

# *Environmental Trends*

*No problem is insoluble in the creation of a balanced and conserving planet save humanity itself. Can it reach in time the vision of joint survival? Can its inescapable physical interdependence—the chief new insight of our century—induce that vision? We do not know. We have the duty to hope.*[1]

Barbara Ward (1982)

These words were written by an international economist and consultant to the United Nations, a woman who saw life with clarity. The certain dependence of human beings upon their natural bases of support is, indeed, the chief new insight of our century.

The sixties and seventies brought environmentalism: a revelation and a revolution. What changes would the future bring? What changes in public values as environmentalism penetrated to untouched layers of society? What changes in organizational leadership and tactics? Assuming the goal of the environmentalists to be an integrated, harmonious, steady-state Earth, what steps would they take toward that goal?[2] If I may speak for the environmentalists, I venture to answer the last question first. Eight steps seem absolutely necessary:

1. Placing more emphasis on reducing human overpopulation.
2. Measuring the carrying capacity of local ecosystems and managing them accordingly.
3. Restoring (insofar as possible) and protecting the agricultural base: the ancient and forever nursery of humankind.
4. Carefully rationing the use of irreplaceable minerals and fuels.
5. Stop disposing of wastes by dumping them somewhere else.
6. Measuring the health effects of the myriad anthropogenic poisons which, unrecognized, enter our bodies every day.

7. Placing more emphasis on protecting the purity of shared world environments such as tropical forests, the ocean, the atmosphere, and the stratosphere.

8. Preserving biological diversity, the earth's greatest treasure.

In taking these steps we will try more seriously to learn from the organic systems around us, for they found the answers long before *Homo sapiens* evolved. We will simplify our daily lives, changing, though not really lowering, our standard of living. And we will show greater concern for posterity, a word that now threatens to disappear from the vocabulary. "As far as I know," said historian Henry Steele Commager the other day, "no modern president has used it in any presidential address, though in the era of the Enlightenment, Washington and Adams and Jefferson couldn't give a speech or write a letter without invoking posterity."[3]

**Trends in Public Values.** Aldo Leopold, naturalist and philosopher, wrote a seminal essay in 1948, "The Ecological Conscience." Herein he observed that "no important change in human conduct is ever accomplished without an internal change in our intellectual emphases, our loyalties, our affections, and our convictions."[4] And Robert Cahn, one of the three initial members of the Council on Environmental Quality, spoke in 1980 on the conservation challenges of the coming decade. Foremost, he said, will be to develop *environmental citizenship* in parallel with political citizenship. The few decision makers in high places who are now practicing environmental citizenship "have a personal sense of values that is essentially different from the prevailing value system. This sense makes them willing to go against the power structure of their community or company or legislative body or government agency. Environmental citizenship will not be widespread, therefore, until a major shift in values takes place."[5]

Thirty-five years ago the Ecological Society of America appointed a committee to "review and formulate, so far as possible, the function and status of ecology in science and society." (A social conscience was stirring.) When the committee reported back, it asked a question that must trouble everyone who has thought seriously about the future of environmentalism: "Quite bluntly, profit is a driving force molding the ecosystems of man, but to what extent does a strict profit orientation have ecological survival [value]?"[6] The question might have been put in another way: Can market-driven economics conceivably be kind to the planet?

There will always be friction between environmentalism and capitalism. An economy that rests on private ownership of land (conferring more privilege than responsibility), on "healthy growth" (the magic words), and on profits now (never mind the cost to the grandchildren), is one that strains the laws of both nature and ethical society. When dollars are the goal, uses of nature's bounty too easily become abuses.

One would hardly expect to find a leading chemist at the Oak Ridge Plutonium Project predicting the demise of capitalism in America, yet Harrison Brown did just that, in *The Challenge of Man's Future* (1954). He baldly predicted that "sooner or later the entire world will become an agrarian one. . . . The first major penalty man will have to pay for his rapid consumption of the earth's nonrenewable resources will be that of having to live in a world where his thoughts and actions are ever more strongly limited, where social organization has become all-pervasive, complex, and inflexible, and where the state completely dominates the actions of the individual."[7]

In a sobering book, *Who Rules America Now?*, G. William Domhoff, professor of psychology and sociology at the University of California, argued that any reforms in environmental protection must start with recognition that "dominant power in the United States is exercised by a power elite . . . a property-based ruling class." That elite contains only 0.5 percent of all Americans yet owns from 20 to 25 percent of all wealth. Through its wealth it controls the most important corporations, commercial banks, investment banks, and law firms. Also through its wealth it influences government. Its members arrange to be seated on policy-planning commissions and take an active part in selecting candidates for office who will show sympathy for their own elite positions.[8]

A common image of the corporate world is of a world run by conservatives. If a conservative is one who cherishes a people's inheritance and wants to pass it on unchanged to new generations, then the inhabitants of the corporate world should have welcomed the dawning of the environmental age. They did not, for what conservatives really conserve is the established political order. A perceptive writer in the *New Yorker* declared in 1972 that

> today's conservatives should give their primary allegiance to an establishment much more ancient, much more majestic, and more fundamental than a government. They should give it directly to nature itself. [Edmund Burke] paid his respects to nature by envisioning a society as patterned after it, but he doubtless never dreamed that nature—the pattern

itself—could be threatened. Today, however, we hold a
dagger to the very heart of life.[9]

Conservation and conservatism, flowing from a common spring,
eventually became separate streams.

As environmentalism gains wider influence, Americans will, I
believe, demand many of the changes offered by socialism—such
as the redistribution of wealth and political power, fair sharing of
the commons, and a dimming of the lure of technology—without
giving up capitalism altogether. Capitalism will become more
yielding and democratic. I shall continue to believe this until, and
unless, there should appear on earth a true socialism proving that
people can live freely together by the Marxian ideal: "from each
according to his ability, to each according to his needs." The models
of "Marxian socialism" now in existence provide poorly for the
progression of government toward that ideal system described by
Garrett Hardin as *mutual coercion, mutually agreed upon by the majority of the people affected.*

The environmental age brought new awareness of an old truth:
that the earth is an inconceivably complex set of limits. These are
physical limits which we must either respect or face cultural degradation. The earth has a finite store of minerals, arable land,
breathable air, and potable water, as well as space to dispose of
wastes and poisons. Engineering cleverness can delay, but not prevent, us from reaching one limit after another. The question thus
looms: how fast should we move toward those limits? This is the
"drifting sailor" question. Limited to one jug of water, the sailor
must—as he rations it—weigh his hopes against his fears in order
to maximize his chance of being rescued before he dies of thirst. I
don't mean that we will (or should) soon give up industrial society.
With growing awareness of the environmental risks we run, we
will buy time to discover how we can live more simply, economically, and cleanly. We will gamble that we can phase out the old
ways of living before they destroy us.

**Trends in Organizational Leadership.** Many of the young idealists
who fueled the early environmental movement will quite certainly
be replaced by management professionals familiar with promotion,
fund raising, and lobbying. Within the environmental organizations, board members having expertise in ecology or natural history will be replaced by others having political clout. At the same
time, the organizations will add chemists, engineers, and economists who, during environmental disputes, will match their oppo-

nents in government or in industry blow for blow. Seth Zuckerman has wisely observed that, "One of the tools that the
environmental movement has adopted from the mainstream is economic analysis. First trotted out by conservationists in 1970 against
the supersonic transport plane, this type of study is now indispensable to their arguments."[10]

Environmental leaders will woo those in America—including the
poor, the hardhat workers, and the city dwellers—who have shown
little understanding of, or sympathy with, the environmental
movement. In a 1980 talk, Gus Speth (as chairman of the CEQ)
advised the leaders to build four bridges to "natural allies," namely:[11]

1. The urban poor, who bear the heaviest burden of ill health,
and lost beauty and recreation, because of environmental degradation.

2. The working people, who serve unwittingly as society's guinea
pigs, testing chemical and radiation hazards in industry.

3. The nation's farmers, whose lands are being destroyed by soil
impoverishment or are being taken for nonagricultural uses.

4. Those in business who are the more concerned and enlightened; those whose cooperation is necessary if progress is to
be made.

The environmental organizations will strengthen their links
abroad.[12] All humanity is affected by the destruction of tropical
forests, by the loss of wild species wherever they occur, and by
atmospheric degradation through acid rain, "greenhouse" gases,
and ozone depletion. British ecologist Frank Fraser Darling once
proposed that all nations should pay for the conservation of world
treasures. All should pay to save the finest forests of the Matto
Grosso, the finest salmon rivers, and the finest herds of African
wildlife. (I would add the fur seals of Alaska and the gorillas of
Rwanda.) Indeed, one Amherst professor told a scientific group
that "on ecological grounds, the case for world government is beyond argument."[13]

• • •

At this writing, an American waste-disposal firm has offered the
government of the Turks and Caicos Islands, in the West Indies,
$25 million a year for the privilege of dumping sewage sludge on
West Caicos. The sludge, laced with toxic metals, would be shipped
from a Philadelphia dump. Environmentalists are objecting, for the
turquoise waters around West Caicos support commercial fishing
and tourism. This impasse sharply illuminates the difference between local and international perspectives on land use.

*Logo of World Wildlife Fund*

**Trends in Strategy.** Congress will fine-tune its procedures for dealing with environmental issues. In 1975, a few House members began to hold weekly breakfast sessions to talk about environmental legislation. These grew into a standing Environmental and Energy Study Conference which, by the end of 1985, included 345 lawmakers from both chambers and supported a staff and a weekly newsletter. It grew from recognition that Congress is poorly designed to deal with environmental protection. The traditional committee system can easily handle specific jobs but hardly the overall job of managing the environment. Moreover, Congress has always been cozy with special interests, a relationship which breeds short-term legislation and even corruption. Lastly, congressional action lags behind public demand. Witness the prolonged, agonizing end of the Vietnam War and the failure, as yet, to enact handgun control, to end tobacco subsidies, and to enforce Superfund. As Senator Henry M. Jackson once said, "the public sense of priorities and those of government are poles apart with respect to the importance of environmental matters."[14]

Environmental activists will win greater political power. Ecological principles will gain greater understanding and acceptance on Capitol Hill and will enter the national agenda. Americans will increasingly use the ballot, the lobby, and letters to Congress to insure that the government *does* take the environment seriously. Americans, through democratic funding of federal elections, will curb the runaway power of political action committees (PACs). From 1977 to 1987, the number of PACs tripled.[15] As Common Cause concludes, "we are facing government of, by, and for the PACs of America unless this fundamental flaw in our political system is corrected."[16]

Will environmental law become tougher? I think so. The Law Reform Commission of Canada, after consulting with jurists and environmentalists, recently recommended that a new and distinct *Criminal Code* offense be added to the code: that of crime against the environment. Criminals would be those who, by intent, recklessness, or negligence, "seriously [compromise] a fundamental societal value and right, that of a safe environment or the right to a reasonable level of environmental quality." The explicit aim of the new code offense would be to protect human life and health, not to protect property (already protected under civil law) nor to protect "the environment for its own sake in the absence of any identifiable human values, rights or interests." Thus, the new law would stop short of granting rights to nonhuman entities.[17] We have seen considerable enthusiasm for enshrining environmental ethics in Magna Cartas of one kind or another. That enthusiasm was demonstrated anew in the work of the Law Reform Commission.

Fears for personal health continue to darken and distort the meaning of the word "environment." Many associate the word with poisons in their surroundings: asbestos, toxic water, poisonous fumes, unseen killers in hamburger, mysterious radiations from space . . . the list is endless. William Ruckelshaus said the other day that toxic waste is America's most serious environmental problem, followed by acid rain and polluted groundwater. Thus, for a few years to come, spending for pollution cleanup and control will increase faster than the GNP. According to the Bureau of Economic Analysis, about $69 billion, or 1.8 percent of GNP, was spent for that purpose in 1984 by all governments and corporations.[18] With ongoing efforts to flush old poisons from America's system and to defend her against new ones, the costs will (in my opinion) rise to 3 percent of GNP or higher.

Throughout my narrative I have left unmentioned the ultimate environmental issue: nuclear war. A nuclear exchange would bring global ruin. The alternative chosen by world leaders has been to engage in an arms race which, by wasting natural resources, brainpower, and capital, seems likely to bring ruin "not with a bang but a whimper." Although I have chosen not to discuss this issue, it is one which a few environmentalists are beginning to address. Some see the prevention of nuclear war as a necessary extension of environmentalism, while others fear that ongoing environmental activism will suffer if it tries to add arms control to its already long list of concerns.

Decision makers in government and industry will increasingly plan on the basis of acceptable risk. They will ask, What is the risk—based on historical data—that this or that proposed action will harm the environment? Next they will ask, What is its foreseen benefit in relation to that risk? And finally, What is the public *perception* of the risk-benefit ratio? Consider, if you will, the following real issues: What is the risk that an oil spill on the California coast will exterminate its relict population of southern sea otters? Is that risk low enough to warrant the exploitation of inshore waters for oil? What is the risk that nuclear waste, now buried at Hanford, will leak from its tomb before the year 10,000? How many trees can be taken from the Olympic National Forest before erosion, stream sedimentation, and diminishing watershed capacity become unacceptable social and economic costs? The answers to these and thousands of similar questions will be sought through research into both engineering feasibility and public opinion. I emphasize the importance of public opinion. "We are," says the Irish writer, Sean O'Faolain, "for a great part of our lives at the mercy of uncharted currents of the heart."[19]

We will become true stewards of the land to the extent that we develop land-use policies, implemented by multipurpose planning and zoning, which place the needs of society above the needs of the individual. Virtually anywhere in America a man can legally excavate and sell "his own" land by the truckload, from topsoil down to bedrock. He reckons its value in three dimensions only, ignoring its dimension in *time*. Ingrained American convictions about private property rights and individual enterprise will weaken as governments act vigorously to control land-abusive practices. Many small governments will lose their identity and blend with regional bodies such as King County's Metro and San Diego's Integrated Regional Environmental Management system.

Mediation groups like ACCORD Associates (Boulder, Colorado) and the Mediation Institute (Seattle, Washington) will proliferate. These are private, nonprofit groups which offer services in conflict management. They promote dialogue, negotiation, and binding arbitration as alternatives to litigation. ACCORD, founded in 1968, has helped to resolve conflicts over Superfund site treatment, radiation monitoring around Three Mile Island, big-game damage to property in Colorado, expansion of a park in Hawaii, and scores of other resource-use conflicts. The Mediation Institute (1975) has successfully dealt with conflicts over the development of the Columbia River estuary, a flood control project in Massachusetts, water diversion of the Platte River threatening a whooping crane marsh, protection of Indian rights to virgin timber in Alaska, and fair sharing—between Indians and others—of Pacific salmon and steelhead. This fishery conflict brought to the legal arena no fewer than twenty-five tribes and seventeen state and federal agencies.[20]

A speaker at a National Conference on Environmental Dispute Resolution explained that, while the ability to sue provides the leverage that environmentalists need to bring their adversaries to the bargaining table, mediation provides the solutions that courts alone cannot decree. The main advantages of mediation over litigation are, he said, that:[21]

1. The courts simply can't handle the increasing case loads. In 1973, about 47,000 environmental cases were filed in Federal District Court; in 1983, about 206,000. Keeping pace is easier through cooperation than confrontation.

2. Litigation is essentially injunctive; courts can say "no" but not "yes." Mediation offers alternatives which can permit both sides to win.

I would add that mediation is a learning process which can lead to mutual understanding, tolerance, and even respect. The environmentalist may change his perception of "the businessman" as one selfish and myopic, living in an unreal world, while the businessman may change his perception of "the environmentalist" as one arrogant, holier-than-thou, and likewise living in an unreal world.

Who commonly are the adversaries in resource-use conflicts? The Conservation Foundation sponsored a study of disputes in the 1970s and 1980s in which the adversaries aligned themselves as follows:[22]

| The Adversaries | Their Involvement in Disputes (%) |
|---|---|
| Government units: local, state, and federal | 81 |
| Local citizens groups [usually *ad hoc*] | 44 |
| Organized environmental groups | 33 |
| Private companies | 33 |

A greater proportion of the nation's GNP will be spent on environmental research. Like children entering a strange country, we face dangers of which we are but dimly aware. We need to identify them before we can avoid them. Nowadays, research (as, for example, by the EPA) is nearly all directed toward solving "brush fire" problems such as those presented by a toxic waste dump in New Jersey, an acid rainfall in industrial Illinois, or a selenium-poisoned valley in California. Far more basic, long-scale research is called for. The many new and unconventional questions that rise continuously in our progression toward environmental equilibrium are so disturbing as to call for deep and persistent exploration.

Professor Joseph M. Petulla, at the University of San Francisco, a long-time observer of environmental management, believes that this new species of management is destined to win higher status in tomorrow's industry. He has written that

> it does not make sense for the environmental manager to report to a production engineer or any part of industrial management whose goals primarily are focused on costs of production. The position needs its own independent department or needs to be placed under a company vice president in charge of research and engineering. . . . Thus, the director of environmental management would take a position beside the director of engineering and, in large companies, beside the director of research. . . . [There] the role of the environmental manager could be spelled out more clearly as a negotiator and maintainer of the firm's environmental quality.[23]

•   •   •

Relying on the natural systems of the earth to carry us as far, or farther, into the future as they have in the past, we will strive to perfect the *land ethic*. The term is Aldo Leopold's, and we who use it pay homage to his memory. What Bach gave to music, Leopold gave to environmentalism: its basic vocabulary. Leopold wrote forty years ago that the land ethic is a product of social evolution developing through the interplay of emotion and intellect. It will never be complete, he affirmed, for "nothing so important as an ethic is ever 'written.' Only the most superficial student of history supposes that Moses 'wrote' the Decalogue; it evolved in the minds of a thinking community, and Moses wrote a tentative summary of it for a 'seminar.'"[24] The spiritual descendants of Leopold are many. (If I were pressed to choose which living American does best at preserving and extending Leopoldian thought, it might be writer

*The Knot of Eternity*

Wendell Berry, though the choice would not be easy.)[25] Primitive peoples respected the earth. We who know it more fully than they are just beginning to offer it respect. We are slowly adopting an ethic which signals that respect.

Environmentalism, while retaining its links with the natural sciences and resource management, is coming to resemble a social science. It is increasingly involved in politics (the manipulation of human behavior) and education (arguably the most vital of all cultural activities). Environmentalism grew out of memories of cleaner, brighter, and richer surroundings. Its practitioners called for a return to remembered values (though not necessarily for giving up such props as satellite messages, credit cards, and silicon chips). They were shocked by the damage wrought by humans upon their natural bases of support. Aiming to minimize future damage and to heal the wounds of damage past, they set about to change ingrained public attitudes and customs. They recognized that environmentalism is radical (in the dictionary sense of favoring fundamental change). They sensed intuitively that caring deeply about the birthplace of the human race is a mark of individual and societal maturity and that—whatever else—it is good practice in *caring:* the most difficult assignment borne by Homo, the animal still climbing toward a state of civilization.

# 19

# *Epilogue: The 1980s*

The scope of the present narrative was originally limited to the decades 1960 to 1980 when environmentalism became a pervasive and necessary part of American thought. But political changes from 1980 to 1989—the Reagan years—so affected the course of the environmental movement as to prompt an extension.[1]

**The Reagan Legacy.** Ronald Reagan was elected in 1980 by a landslide, carrying forty-four of the fifty states. Amiable, relaxed, and incurious, he remained popular throughout his two terms in office. At the end, a Gallup poll inquired, "How do you think Ronald Reagan will go down in history?" Fifty-two percent replied outstanding or above average; 20 percent, below average or poor. (The rest, average or no opinion.)[2] Formerly a movie actor, Reagan spoke persuasively, if not always accurately or thoughtfully. While defending the beliefs that had guided him in his past political career—such as lower taxes, get the government off the back of business, and return responsibility to the private sector—he depended almost completely on White House advisers for new ideas. In 1981 he cut the U.S. contribution to the United Nations Environment Programme from $10 million to $2 million (the Congress later restored it to $7.85 million). A long-time foe of job-creation programs, he ended President Carter's Young Adult Conservation Corps, and in 1984 he vetoed a measure that would have created an American Conservation Corps.

In spite of his conviction that least government is best government, average federal expenditures during his administration climbed to 80 percent higher than those in the previous one. When he left office, he left the government about $1.4 trillion deeper in debt. As Stewart Udall, former Secretary of the Interior, stated in 1988: "History will confirm that Ronald Reagan's legacy created a massive fiscal debt restricting the options of his successors and of the American people for positive action on behalf of their air, water, and land."[3]

What dismayed environmentalists as much as the president's lack of leadership was his choice of appointees to key positions: James G. Watt to head Interior and Anne M. Gorsuch to head the EPA.

Watt, a former lobbyist for the U.S. Chamber of Commerce, startled senators at his 1981 confirmation hearings by leaving the impression that long-term planning for public land conservation is pointless, for the Second Coming will render moot the decisions of mortal beings. He confessed, though, that he did not know how many future generations will pass before the Lord returns. In 1981 he proposed to open for oil drilling the shallows along the scenic northern and central California coasts, and in 1983 those along the entire Outer Continental Shelf (OCS), an area roughly half the size of the continental United States. A Westerner, he endorsed the Sagebrush Rebellion against federal control of public lands. After two and a half years in office, he was forced to resign. Contributing to his fall was the Powder River Basin scandal, exposed by a congressional committee in 1983. In a shady, if not downright illegal, deal the Department of the Interior had leased coal mining rights in Montana and Wyoming to private companies at a loss to the Treasury of $60 to $132 million.

Anne M. Gorsuch, a lawyer, former Colorado legislator, and friend of Watt, was confirmed as EPA administrator in mid-May 1981. She quickly revealed herself as unwilling to delegate authority nor yet to provide clear policy guidance. Bowing before big business, she attacked the EPA's most influential branch: its division of law enforcement. Her high-handed moves were eventually halted by automatic brakes built into the federal machinery: the Civil Service structure, the powerful Office of Management and Budget, and the Legislature. Congress cited her for contempt for failing to turn over EPA files on 160 toxic waste dumps in three states where EPA was allegedly not enforcing the Superfund. She resigned in the spring of 1983.

In 1989, an association (Environmental Safety) with long experience in managing America's conservation institutions assessed the impact of the Reagan administration on environmental protective programs (see table, page 180).

"EPA currently is operating with the same level of resources it had in 1975," concluded Environmental Safety, "yet its workload doubled in the early 1980s and then grew sharply again as Congress enacted yet new responsibilities in the mid 1980s."[4]

### Percent Change in EPA Budget, 1981–89
*(without overhead, inflation adjusted)*

| | | | |
|---|---|---|---|
| air | −25 | pesticides | −20 |
| water | −43 | toxic substances | −34 |
| drinking water | −11 | other | −27 |
| hazardous waste | +25 | management support | +11 |

Political scientists Norman J. Vig and Michael E. Kraft summarized Reagan's style in these words: "Policy making that violates constitutional norms, democratic accountability, and empirical evidence is doomed to frustration and failure. . . . The ability to exercise presidential power is not an adequate criterion for evaluating presidential leadership."[5]

A Gallup poll near election time in 1988 asked for opinions on the single most important issue which would face the incoming president. The leading answers were (in this order): federal budget [i.e., deficit], environmental protection, and further arms negotiations. Although the environmental movement had been obliged to travel cautiously through the minefields laid by Reagan and his advisers, it had evidently lost neither its vision nor its energy.

**The Reaction.** For example: environmentalism developed a firmer and broader organizational base. Individuals who had never belonged to a conservation group, or even an "outdoor" group, began to swell the ranks of the Sierra Club, Defenders of Wildlife, Wilderness Society, Nature Conservancy, and similar organizations. (Many of the joiners were clearly reacting to the anti-environmentalism expressed by Reagan.) By the close of the 1980s, between 450 and 500 national organizations were promoting environmentalism by one means or other.[6] Moreover, some organizations had begun to join forces in *ad hoc* or permanent alliances to increase their clout. The following table lists eighteen organizations which cooperated to sponsor the publication, in 1989, of a pace-setting book, *Blueprint for the Environment*.[7] They are not representative; they simply impart the flavor of organized environmentalism in the United States in 1989.

Growth in the number of organizations was paralleled by growth in news coverage of environmental threats and disasters ranging

## Selected National Environmental Organizations, 1989[a]

| | Year | Members | Year | Budget, $$ |
|---|---|---|---|---|
| National Wildlife Federation[b] | 1989 | 5,800,000 | 1989 | 74,000,000 |
| National Audubon Society | 1988 | 550,000 | 1988 | 38,193,998 |
| Sierra Club | 1989 | 505,000 | 1989 | 28,000,000 |
| Wilderness Society | 1988 | 220,000 | 1988 | 10,932,448 |
| Natural Resources Defense Council | 1989 | 104,000 | 1988 | 11,070,228 |
| Union of Concerned Scientists | 1989 | 94,142 | 1989 | 2,717,000 |
| Defenders of Wildlife | 1989 | 80,000 | 1989 | 4,125,000 |
| National Parks & Conservation Foundation | 1988 | 70,000 | 1987 | 3,516,700 |
| Trout Unlimited | 1989 | 63,000 | 1988 | 1,406,409 |
| Izaak Walton League | 1988 | 50,000 | 1985 | 1,156,582 |
| Environmental Policy Institute[c] | 1988 | 45,000 | 1989 | 2,500,000 |
| Oceanic Society[c] | 1988 | 30,000 | 1988 | 421,788 |
| Zero Population Growth | 1989 | 25,000 | 1989 | 1,210,000 |
| Environmental Action | 1989 | 20,000 | 1988 | 940,335 |
| Friends of the Earth[c] | 1988 | 15,000 | 1988 | 850,000 |
| Renew America | 1989 | 7,000 | 1989 | 960,910 |

[a] Eighteen that cooperated to produce Blueprint for the Environment. Two not listed are consortia: The Global Tomorrow Coalition and the Natural Resources Council of America. Source of data: correspondence and the Conservation Directory, 1989.
[b] "Members and supporters"
[c] The Environmental Policy Institute, the Oceanic Society, and Friends of the Earth merged in early 1989; their combined budget to be "about $2.5 million."

from the discovery of PCBs in a neighborhood dump to the Bhopal accident (1984) which sent more than 200,000 people to the hospital and the Chernobyl accident (1986) which spewed a radioactive cloud across Europe.

**New Insights.** The two most important new (or rediscovered) insights in environmental thought during the 1980s were these: First, almost every environmental issue has significance beyond its immediate locale to the whole biosphere.[8] In a world now diminished in size through rapid communication and transport, all people are neighbors. Environmentalism is becoming less elitist or chauvinistic than it used to be; more willing to help the Third World countries develop sustainable resource-use systems. Rather suddenly, political parties known as "greens" are on stage at European elections, pushing for environmental reforms.[9] The seven leading industrial nations represented at the Fifteenth Economic Summit (or Summit of the Arch) in Paris in June 1989, issued an economic declaration, fully two-thirds of which dealt with environmental problems.[10]

Second, most of the environmental problems of our time are rooted in overpopulation. There are simply more people than the earth can support. Says Gro Harlem Brundtland, prime minister of Norway, "In spite of all the technological and scientific triumphs of the present century, there have never been so many poor, illiterate, or unemployed people in the world, and their numbers are growing. Close to one billion people are living in poverty and squalor. . . ."[11] Four scientists have calculated that, as of 1986, "nearly 40% of potential terrestrial net primary productivity [was] used directly, co-opted, or foregone because of human activities."[12] If the present rate of population growth continues, many persons now living will still be alive in a world of ten billion.

Future efforts to cut waste and consumption will fail in the absence of determined efforts to halt population growth. This truth was denied by James L. Buckley, U.S. representative at the International Conference on Population, in Mexico City, in August 1984. "We reject," he said, "the notion that we are caught up in a global population crisis."[13] Shortly thereafter, the U.S. Agency for International Development withheld a scheduled grant of $17 million to the International Planned Parenthood Foundation. The grant would have furnished about one-quarter of IPPF's annual budget.

**The Threat of Climate Change.** I turn now to certain environmental issues that captured—and are still holding—public attention during the 1980s. The threat that human activities may be changing irreversibly the world atmosphere and all that it touches seems ever more real. The consequences are predictable: drought intensification in most tropical and temperate areas and melting of the polar ice caps, followed by a rising sea level and flooding of coastal habitations around the world. Already in the present century, sea level has risen an estimated four to eight inches. And the ultimate consequences to agriculture, forestry, and fisheries are mind-boggling. However, all predictions of a greenhouse effect revolve around the interpretation of models, and these depend on data which are very incomplete. For example, which of the observed, year to year climate changes are "natural," that is, independent of human action? What are the effects of volcanic dust in the upper atmosphere, and of clouds, and of uneven solar activity? What separate roles do the oceans, tundras, and forests, with their photosynthesizing populations, play in absorbing and releasing carbon dioxide?

A World Conference on the Changing Atmosphere—first of its kind—convened in Toronto in June, 1988. Sponsored by Canada and the United Nations, it recommended an initial global reduction of carbon dioxide emissions by about 20 percent of 1988 levels by the year 2005.[14] Although inadequate to stabilize the atmosphere, it was a step in the right direction.

James E. Hansen, director of NASA's Goddard Institute of Space Studies, testified to Congress in May 1989 that greenhouse warming is already here and may get worse. The Office of Management and Budget (OMB), however, attached a caveat to his written testimony: "these changes should be viewed as estimates from evolving computer models and not as reliable predictions."[15] This bureaucratic editing by the OMB seems to have stemmed from an ongoing disagreement between the Environmental Protection Agency, which favors international action on global warming, and the Department of Energy, which is worried about the economic disruption that would follow a truly effective ban on industrial air pollution. In any event, a treaty conference on global warming will probably be called in 1990.

Aside from a measured rise in atmospheric carbon dioxide (from 1872) and a measured, though slight, rise in global temperature (from 1880), *we have no clear signal that the planet is warming up.* Nonetheless, if and when we receive that signal we will be helpless to reverse the trend that we started when we began to burn fossil fuels, lay waste to the tropical rainforests, poison the plankton of lakes and seas, and in other ways tamper with the earth's sensitive thermostat.

In the dark austral winter of 1987, concentrations of ozone above Antarctica dropped to about half in a region of sky as large as the United States. Atmospheric scientists urged that ozone-destroying chemicals be phased out as soon as possible. By February 6, 1989, representatives of thirty-four countries had signed the Montreal Protocol [to the Vienna Convention of 1985] on Substances that Deplete the Ozone Layer. It called on the industrialized nations to reduce their use of eight chemicals—five CFCs and three halon gases—by half over a ten-year period.[16] It was the first international agreement to curb an air pollutant. And it was one of Reagan's environmental achievements, dimmed only slightly by his Secretary of the Interior's view that "personal protection" was preferable to laws. Here was an opening for the cartoonists, who hastened to portray us wearing hats, sunglasses, and suntan lotions to shield us from ultraviolet radiation.

More progress. In Helsinki in early May 1989, eighty-one nations agreed in principle to ban by the year 2000 the eight ozone-damaging chemicals.[17] Unfortunately, troubling questions remain. Can the poor nations afford substitutes for CFCs? While the substitutes may not harm the ozone, may they not contribute to climate warming? (There is some evidence of this effect.)

The national problem of acid rain seemed in 1989 to be moving beyond stalemate. For eight years, environmentalists had been engaged in a dispute with the coal, auto, and electric-utility industries over remedial legislation. In one year alone, according to the Associated Press, the industry lobby known as Citizens for Sensible Control of Acid Rain spent $3,028,235.[18] The prospect for a cleanup bill is now encouraging. Canada has received a promise from the United States to start negotiating a bilateral acid-rain agreement as soon as U.S. legislation is introduced. In the meanwhile, the scientific community has learned a good deal about the damage done by acid rain and its chief culprit, sulfur dioxide. Some of the damage, unfortunately, is lasting; it cannot be cured by legislation.

The worst atmospheric pollutants in America were slated to be reduced by the Clean Air Act of 1970. Indeed, the 210 million tons of these being spewed into the air in 1970 had, by 1989, been cut by a third, despite population growth. Yet "the reality is that urban America is not within reach of the standards in the Clean Air Act, declared a *Science* writer in May 1989.[19] (The act technically expired in August 1988, during the Reagan regime.) Congress and President Bush are preparing to write a new act which will more effectively rule out delays, concessions, and exemptions to gross polluters. It will be among the most important acts of the 101st Congress and among the most difficult to draft. It must balance the large health costs of living in dirty air against the large economic costs of living more cleanly.

The 1980s brought several new scenarios picturing the effect on world climate of a nuclear war of mutual assured destruction. In the summer of 1982, three hundred scientists from more than thirty countries joined forces to model this effect. They envisioned a "nuclear winter" of darkened skies, subfreezing temperatures, and widespread toxic and radioactive pollution.[20] In the meanwhile, American scientists were studying similar scenarios, with horrifying conclusions. One group reported that, "When combined with the prompt destruction from nuclear blast, fires, and fallout and the later enhancement of solar ultraviolet radiation due to ozone depletion, long-term exposure to cold, dark, and radioactivity could pose a serious threat to human survivors and to other species."[21] Another group reported that "the population size of *Homo sapiens* conceivably could be reduced to prehistoric levels or below, and extinction of the human species itself cannot be excluded."[22] These are not scenes from a science-fiction movie but the tempered thoughts of scientists including Anne and Paul Ehrlich, Stephen Jay Gould, Ernst Mayr, Carl Sagan, George M. Woodwell, and eighteen others. (During the last thirty years, the world community has moved slowly toward a law of the sea. It should be thinking also about a law of the atmosphere.)

**Biodiversity.** In the 600 million years that animal life has existed it has survived three catastrophic periods of extinction: near the close of the Permian, the Triassic, and the Cretaceous. During each period, thousands of years passed before species fell to half their previous richness. But the present, ongoing loss of biodiversity—half the species in less than two centuries—will be the greatest of all catastrophes. The Tapestry of Life is disintegrating through our plundering of plant and animal habitats.

This hard truth is gradually capturing the attention of men and women in political power. The National Academy of Sciences and the Smithsonian Institution sponsored a biodiversity symposium in Washington in 1986. It received wide press coverage at the time, and its proceedings, condensed in a book by sixty professionals, became the leader in its field.[23] Congress, through its Office of Technology Assessment, was offered in 1987 a plan called "technologies to maintain biological diversity."[24] In addition to beefing up a score of conservation laws already on the books, the plan

*Logo of the Animal Welfare Institute*

would establish a National Endowment for Biological Diversity and would provide for greater leadership in the international arena. After all, the greatest loss of biodiversity is taking place in the tropical and subtropical lands and waters of the globe, not in the United States. Congress in 1988 passed a Joint Resolution to Encourage Increased Cooperation to Protect Biological Diversity, and later considered several biodiversity bills (as yet unenacted). While biodiversity legislation is supported by most life scientists and by the environmental community, it still seems rather arcane to some members of Congress.

Someone has said that compromise is essential in a democratic society, but in nature-conservation the great compromise has already been made.

186

**Wastes.** The 1980s saw the beginning of the end for landfill sites. America was running out of open space where wastes could be dumped and left to release methane and putrid odors into the air and to seep toxic chemicals into the groundwater. The NIMBY (Not in My Back Yard) response from the taxpayers was challenging land-use managers to find alternatives to practices that had served the citizenry for five hundred years. Incineration of wastes at high temperature was repeatedly suggested, though it left unanswered where to dispose of the toxic residues (mostly metallic). "Bribing" the poor Third World countries to take U.S. wastes could never be a permanent solution, as was demonstrated in 1986–88 when a cargo ship loaded with 15,000 tons of Philadelphia's incinerator ash headed for Panama but was turned away. It wandered the seas for two years in search of a friendly port, illegally dumping 3,000 tons on a beach at Haiti and the rest (it is believed) into the Indian Ocean.[25]

The UN General Assembly adopted in 1983 a resolution introduced by 23 countries to ban the importation of hazardous wastes without the permission of the importing country.[26] (Reagan's representative cast the only dissent in a 146 to 1 vote, arguing that the measure would create excessive legislation and would restrict free trade.) And in 1989, the UNEP Convention on the Control of Transboundary Movements of Hazardous Wastes and Their Disposal was signed at Basel by representatives of thirty countries.

The wastes we have "swept under the rug" for many years are still there. A writer in a local newspaper asks, "Will advertisements offering commercial land for sale someday carry an environmental pedigree?" Clearly, buyers don't want to learn that the land they have just bought contains hazardous chemicals. Someday they may demand a clean bill of land-health along with a clear title of ownership. "Testing for toxics," continues the writer, "is a late-arriving manifestation of the closing of the frontier. We can no longer just pull up stakes and move on, confident of a clean beginning farther out."[27]

**Energy.** So very slow to change is our economic system that in 1989 we still do not have a sensible energy policy. We depend heavily on fossil fuels while showing no serious intent to explore the possibilities of renewable, especially solar-based, sources. In the spring of 1981, renewable sources provided only 6 percent of our energy, as against fossil sources, including uranium, at 94 percent. That ratio moved up from 6 to 8 percent during the 1980s.[28]

Federal outlays for energy dropped from $14.6 billion in fiscal year 1981 to $2.3 billion in fiscal year 1990. The OMB made clear that "the best way to meet [the energy] need is to rely on the private market and limit the role of the Federal government."[29] Federal funding for solar research sank to about one-fourth between the Carter and the Reagan administrations. Yet America needs an integrated, farsighted energy strategy which will not be shaken by each new Three Mile Island explosion or Valdez oil spill. That strategy *must* include more conservation of energy-use and more reliance on permanent sources.

A 1987 proposal by the Department of the Interior to open the Arctic National Wildlife Refuge to oil exploration brought quick objection from the environmental community. At stake is the 1.5–million-acre coastal plain of the refuge. Interior argues that, for security reasons, America must free herself from dependence on foreign oil, and that the impacts of drilling will be temporary. Environmentalists counter that snow geese, muskoxen, caribou, and bowhead whales will be dispossessed from their ancient migratory routes. Moreover, Interior admits that the likelihood of finding a substantial pool of oil (3.2 billion barrels) under the coastal plain is only 19 percent—a pool which, if drained, would meet only 4 percent of the nation's oil demand until the year 2005. (The grounding of the *Exxon Valdez* in 1989 may have put Interior's proposal on the back burner.)

The poor track record of Big Oil in policing its own technology, along with the certainty that oil pools won't last forever and that the burning of oil aggravates the greenhouse effect, all give hope to the champions of nuclear power. They say it is cheap, clean, and limitless. But the American public has yet to be reassured (a) that a radwaste dump site good for thousands of years really exists and (b) that a foolproof nuclear power plant can be built. Over 100 licensed plants in the United States are (in 1989) producing 20 percent of our electricity, yet all orders for new reactors placed after 1974 have been canceled. The Bush administration is trying to keep the state of New York from taking over and dismantling a plant at Shoreham, demonstrators are protesting the start-up of the Seabrook plant in New Hampshire, Californians have voted to shut down the Rancho Seco plant near Sacramento, and the FBI is investigating the contractor who runs the Rocky Flats, Colorado, nuclear weapons plant.

An acceptable repository for the radwastes steadily being produced has yet to be found, although Nevada—thinly populated and politically weak—is targeted for high-level wastes and New

Mexico for those that are higher: the transuranic ones with a life of twenty-four millennia or so. Moreover, there is growing evidence that the number of accidents in nuclear plants has long been under-reported.[30] Weapons plants are the worst offenders. According to a Department of Energy estimate, the cost of cleaning up these facilities will run over $100 billion.

**Public Lands.** From the beginning of land use in America, the lands owned in common by the people have served as testing grounds for democratic ideas: arenas where men and women have tried to choose the "right" uses from the "wrong" ones. They are places where developers (interested in immediate values) and conservationists (interested also in future ones) still compete for land control. What now seems to be emerging is a social economics in which common sense prevails. Thoughtful Americans are agreeing that there must be less mining of Nature's bounties as though they were limitless. The old excuse, "by the time they're gone, we'll have developed substitutes," is no longer convincing. Nowhere are land-use debates more heated than in the nation's regions that have not yet been exploited, or only minimally so.

The issue of the Arctic National Wildlife Refuge has been mentioned; that of the ancient forests of Alaska, Oregon, and Washington are equally controversial. (Loggers call these forests mature or overripe; they are older than rotational age 50 to 120 years.) Because of their great size, their slowness to replace themselves, and their high market value, the trees of the ancient forests—like the great whales of the World Ocean—have become symbolic of national treasures on the point of being destroyed for temporary gain.

In 1978, the Forest Service picked the northern spotted owl as indicator species for the old-growth ecosystem.[31] Now the environmental organizations which were out to save examples of the ancient forests had a lever they could use. They asked the Fish and Wildlife Service to declare the owl "endangered," for they knew that the habitat, as well as the population, of an endangered species must legally receive protection. On June 23, 1989, the Fish and Wildlife Service did propose to list the owl as "threatened," partly because only about 1,500 pairs remained in the entire range of the species from southern British Columbia to San Francisco Bay.[32] Although final listing can take up to two years, the Forest Service has already moved to protect the ancient stands in thirteen forests. Its plan calls for a ban on logging and other development on 347,700 acres in Oregon and Washington having a carrying capacity for about 270 pairs of owls. If the plan carries, owl protection will annually "cost" 163 million board feet of lumber having a net value of $28 million, while 455 to 910 jobs will be lost. And the plan will "cost" a thousand pairs of owls.[33]

The Forest Service continues to sell the people's timber below cost, a practice which puzzles the taxpayers. Robert Repetto, analyst for the World Resources Institute, writes that "large areas in the Rocky Mountain, Intermountain, Alaskan, and Eastern regions [of the national forest system] that are economically unsuitable for timber production continue to be used for this purpose, at a substantial economic cost unlikely to be offset by net non-timber benefits. Significant efficiency gains could be achieved if timber operations were subordinated to other objectives. . . ." In a recent six-year period, the timber sale receipts from 82 forests or forest groups amounted to $475 million; the costs of sales, $983 million; the loss, 52 percent.[34]

Another land-use debate swirls around the "let-burn" policy which the National Park Service adopted in 1972 (at least for Yellowstone). The public has not been able to grasp why most lightning-caused fires, as long as they remain small, should be left to burn themselves out. On June 1, 1989, the Park Service, under intense political pressure, almost entirely abandoned its policy. In the summer of 1988, more than 200 fires had seared about 1.3 million acres of Yellowstone National Park and surrounding national forests. From the evidence of tree-ring studies, no fire of such magnitude had ever struck the Yellowstone within the lifetime of the oldest living tree. Although public outrage was understandable, no human action could have stopped the fires from spreading on the dry winds of summer, 1988. And the let-burn policy will quite surely be reinstated, though with modifications based on the Yellowstone experience. Wildfire *does* confer many benefits: it recycles bound-up mineral nutrients, it thins crowded timber stands, and it leaves patchwork landscapes rich in plant and animal habitats.

The Land and Water Conservation Fund of 1965 (LWCF) provided for acquiring and enhancing parks and other green spaces at federal, state, and local levels. During its early years, the fund helped to preserve millions of acres for outdoor recreation but, after 1978, its potential was not fully tapped. By the end of fiscal year 1987, the fund's account contained about $5.7 billion in "unspent" money.[35] President Reagan did, however, appoint a commission to study the nation's needs for outdoor recreation and, in 1987, the commission recommended that one billion dollars a year be spent on land acquisition under terms of a new and improved LWCF.[36]

Some members of the Reagan administration, however, grumbled that the report called for federal land-use planning in disguise.

The Bureau of Land Management "Organic Act" of 1976 mandated that "areas of critical environmental concern" must be identified and protected. These areas (ACECs) require special management "to protect and prevent irreparable damage to important historical, cultural, or scenic values, fish and wildlife or other natural systems or processes." The BLM manages some of the nation's wildest and most scenic lands in Alaska and twelve other states—all told about 332 million acres. By the end of 1988, *less than 2 percent* of this acreage—mostly in Alaska—had been designated as critical.[37] Moreover, many of the designated ACECs were already under special management, while many new ones were too small to protect the values which had led to their designation.

James Watt discouraged the ACEC program. It has remained barely alive with the help of environmental organizations and sympathetic members of Congress. Persons still opposed to it include the champions of recreational use (too often, abusive, motorized use), of mineral, oil, and gas development, and of livestock grazing.

**Agriculture.** Environmentalists were encouraged by the enactment of the "Farm Bill" in 1985. It has proved quite successful in restructuring farm programs to eliminate government subsidies and harmful farming practices such as "sodbusting" and "swampbusting." By 1989 it had retired 30.6 million acres of fragile cropland.[38] However, weak administration of its provisions by the Department of Agriculture continues to allow valuable land to deteriorate.

John Reganold, a soil expert at Washington State University, tells the history of two farms in the Palouse region of Washington, one of the world's most productive regions for dry farming. Although both farms have been worked for eighty years, one has always relied on the natural fertility of the soil, boosted with green (leguminous) manure plowed under, and on crop rotation. The other became a conventional farm in 1948–1950 and began to rely on chemical fertilizers and pesticides, as well as on crop rotation. The yield of winter wheat on the two farms held similar, but the topsoil on the conventional farm wasted steadily through wind and water erosion. It will be gone in another fifty to one hundred years.[39]

A similar study of organic, or sustainable, farming focused on a region of the Midwest producing corn, soybeans, wheat, oats, and hay. The leaders of the study reported that "slightly lower gross production . . . on the organic farms was largely offset by comparable reductions in operating expenses." The organic farms required less fossil energy (and thus would be hurt less by a deteriorating energy supply). The organic crops ranked slightly below conventional crops in available and crude protein. The leaders concluded that "there may be intermediate systems that, from the combined viewpoints of productivity, profitability, and resource use, would prove more attractive than either of the two systems we studied." (Organic farming with some use of chemical fertilizers.)[40]

Interest in sustainable agriculture seems to be escalating, along with interest in the "organic" foods that it yields. Shoppers are seeing produce labeled, for example, "NutriClean Certified" or "Organically Grown." Although organic produce now supplies only one percent of the U.S. market, the percentage may increase to ten by the end of the century.[41]

One front of the sustainable agriculture movement is a push to develop integrated pest management (IPM), a kind that depends on biological controls, insofar as possible, in place of chemical insecticides. Thus, early planting of wheat reduces Hessian fly infestation; ground-up crab shells nourish a microorganism that preys on harmful nematodes; tilling the soil at the right time destroys the eggs of insect pests and slugs; distracting pests with man-made pheromones can be as effective as poisoning them—and kinder to the ecosystem. Since 1986, New York's Cornell University has been successfully promoting IPM to thousands of state farmers.[42] Clearly, though, IPM can win only slowly against the pesticide manufacturers, for it is not a new product but a new decision-making process that can gain public favor only through long education.

Biotechnology is certain to change the lives of farmers and rural communities. Computer-based livestock management systems and new drugs—especially growth hormones—will benefit large farms more than small ones. The Office of Technology Assessment predicts that, "if present trends continue to the end of this century, the total number of farms will continue to decline from 2.2 million in 1982 to 1.2 million in 2000." Small farms will go first. Two farm-policy analysts agree that "not even the most ambitious family-farm proposals will reverse the century-long trend toward fewer, larger, more highly capitalized commercial farms."[43] (But will not this trend grind to a halt when the petroleum is gone?)

Genetic engineering, once a research curiosity, drew public attention in 1980 when the Supreme Court ruled that a genetically altered microbe could be patented.[44] The first proposed field test of an altered plant was stopped by a federal judge on May 16,

1984, at the behest of environmental activist (some say gadfly) Jeremy Rifkin. The test called for spraying potato vines with a bacterium that had been altered to protect plants from frost. However, the judge ruled on procedural grounds, not on the safety of the experiment. Optimists predict that genetic engineering will introduce a second Green Revolution. Invented varieties of farm plants that fix nitrogen, or grow faster, or thrive in marginal soils and climates, or resist weedicides and natural enemies, have obvious advantages. Public uneasiness over the idea of gene-tampering is grounded partly in the fear that altered "germs" to which living things have no resistance may escape the laboratory and cause pandemics. But the Ecological Society of America has given a qualified blessing to the release of genetically engineered organisms, and the Environmental Protection Agency is expected to rule on the final form of regulations controlling such releases.[45]

Annual rainfall and snowfall may well be the ultimate factors that limit the growth of America's population. Historian Walter Prescott Webb described vast areas of the American West collectively as "desert unqualified and absolute."[46] He was right. The image of deserts greened by irrigation water—an image painted by the Bureau of Reclamation and the Army Corps of Engineers from the 1930s onward—is partly mirage. Billions have been spent on dams, canals, and deep wells to "reclaim" the arid lands, with consequences that could have been predicted: sinking levels of groundwater, salt on the farmers' fields, and silt deposits in the reservoirs. The situation is dangerous, with no relief in sight. As for the desert cities kept alive on water from increasingly deep and distant sources, writer Marc Reisner asks, "Was it folly to allow Los Angeles and Phoenix to grow up?" His book, *Cadillac Desert*, is a telling indictment of the faulty reasoning, both economic and technological, that underpins the great reclamation projects of the 1930s and 1940s.[47]

**The Ocean.** Murray Bookchin is director emeritus of the Institute for Social Ecology at Plainfield, Vermont. He writes that "we do not simply live in a world of problems but in a highly problematical world, an *inherently* anti-ecological society."[48] His point was illuminated by the grounding of the *Exxon Valdez* and the spilling of 11.2 million gallons of dark brown oil on the waters and beaches of Prince William Sound, Alaska. It was America's most disastrous oil spill. It was not an accident; it was certain to have happened in the course of time. It originated in America's profligate use of oil, in corporate penny-pinching, in unhealthy political game-playing with the people's resources, and in errors of the kind that humans will forever be making. Within a month, hundreds of sea otters had died. Seafowl by the tens of thousands, landing on shimmering surfaces, were doomed to death. The commercial fishery suffered losses caused by actual damage to salmon, herring, and other food fishes and by public fear of buying catch that might be oil-tainted. The cost to Exxon will easily exceed one billion dollars, which may not be a crippling blow to a company that earned $5.3 billion in 1988.

"Exxon should have to reimburse the public and affected private parties for damages caused by the oil spill at Valdez," declares a consultant in institutional investments. "If this rule had been in place 10 or 15 years ago, Exxon would likely have opted for prevention as the best economic decision."[49] *Science* magazine editorialized: "Although the entire story is not yet known, it seems apparent that the oil company in this case was cavalier in regard to its responsibility."[50] Slade Gorton (Republican) spoke on the floor of the Senate: "I am appalled that a company like Exxon, after having received immense monetary benefits from public oil resources, would be so reckless in its preparation for, or prevention of, a clearly foreseeable disaster."[51]

The Valdez spill will lead to tighter federal rules covering the sea transport of oil. In the meanwhile, the House of Representatives has voted to impose a permanent ban on drilling in the new Cordell Bank National Marine Sanctuary, comprising about 400 square miles off Marin and Sonoma Counties, California. The vote is historic, being the first one to propose a *permanent* federal ban on offshore drilling.[52] Whether the vote means an eventual law remains to be seen (President Bush is a former Texas oilman).

And the Department of the Interior is listing the dollar value of species killed by the spill.[53] A fur seal, for example, is "worth" $15 and a wild goose is "worth" $35.74. This is disturbing news. One hopes that it will be followed by an assessment of the shock felt by the millions who, either in Prince William Sound or via the media, saw the dark oil stretching to the horizon. Interior could at least add something for the value of wild goose music falling from the April skies.

Another kind of damage to the ocean developed gradually during the 1980s by way of the pelagic gillnet fishery. About a thousand Asian-based vessels are now casting each night on the Pacific Ocean a total of 30,000 miles of nylon net. Each net is 30 to 40 miles long and is nearly invisible in the water. It drifts like a wall or curtain, held at the top by floats and at the bottom by weights. It kills blindly, not only fish and squid but seals, dolphins, and small whales; turtles and birds. When a net is lost or abandoned in rough weather it becomes a "ghost net," continuing to kill whatever comes its way.[54] While no international rules govern the fishery, the 1973 International Convention for the Prevention of Pollution from Ships (MARPOL) and its amendments ban the deliberate dumping of plastic debris. Because not all fishing nations are bound by MARPOL, and because the convention is hard to enforce, it can prevent only some of the damage caused by pelagic gillnets.

As Americans take over the nation's seacoasts and estuaries for residential, commercial, and industrial uses, pollution grows correspondingly in the waters along shore. Many of us became aware of ocean pollution for the first time in the summer of 1988 when East Coast beaches were closed as hazards to public health. Contaminated fish and shellfish, too, were listed as threats.

Witness the finding by biologist Laurence Alexander, first in 1983, of about 7,500 dead loons on Dog Island, off the Gulf coast of Florida. In later years he found thousands more. Laboratory tests showed high mercury levels in their tissues. Mercury is known to affect behavior (the "Mad Hatter" response); the bird bodies are typically emaciated; the conclusion can be drawn that mercury inhibits the ability of the birds to feed.[55]

**An Expanding Ethic.** The National Geographic Society devoted the December 1988 issue of its magazine to a report on "the endangered earth," while *Time* dedicated its 1989 New Year's cover to "the planet of the year." The gains made by the environmental movement during the 1980s reflect growth in the vitality and reach of its *ethic*, or set of moral principles that guide and energize it. To emphasize that the proper study of mankind is not solely man, some environmentalists are calling the ethic biocentric or ecocentric, as against anthropocentric. There are signs that the ethic is becoming part of the national dialogue. It is "greening" many fields. Let me touch on three: education, finance, and religion.

The number of environmental studies curricula in colleges and universities is multiplying rapidly. During the years around Earth Day they numbered only half a dozen but, by 1989, a national conference on environmental issues could attract scholars and educators from sixty institutions of higher learning.[56] Books on the philosophical aspects of environmentalism are appearing yearly.[57] These try to make sense of a morality which is not really new but is close to that old sense of surroundings which enabled the earliest humans to survive.

The environmental ethic as revealed through "social investing" is beginning to influence corporate behavior. Thus the Council on Economic Priorities has sold nearly 300,000 copies of a book entitled *Shopping for a Better World,* a guide that rates 138 companies and 1,300 products by socially responsible criteria, of which environmental protection is one.[58] Opportunities for social investing are offered by small firms and by a few traditional, large investment houses, including Shearson Lehman Hutton, the Calvert Group, Dreyfuss, and Merrill Lynch. During the early 1980s, sociologist Ritchie Lowry tracked the stocks of thirty socially responsible companies and found that their average value actually outpaced the Dow Jones Average.[59]

The environmental ethic overlaps and complements the moral principles held by conventional religions. Consider the World Wildlife Fund, the largest worldwide private conservation organization. While celebrating its twenty-fifth anniversary, in 1986, at Assisi, it launched the WWF Network on Conservation and Religion.[60] Leaders of five faiths—Buddhist, Christian, Hindu, Muslim, and Jewish—offered "declarations of nature" drawn from their wellsprings of belief. All the leaders felt the need to inject "powerful moral perspectives into conservation's ill-defined ethical foundations." In his essay, "The Greening of Religion," historian Roderick F. Nash gives an absorbing account of the evolution of *ecotheology,* which is more than a new word, it is a "compelling world view."[61]

We are watching, I think, a sort of ecumenical movement in which religious persons are reaching out to touch scientific conservation, rather than one in which scientists are reaching out to touch religion. Perhaps the distinction is unimportant; both groups would agree that "the future will be no less complicated if we proceed with a sense of the sacred in nature and are guided by the cardinal virtues of prudence, justice, fortitude, and temperance."[62]

•　•　•

Environmentalism usefully describes our perception of, and treatment of, our surroundings. We now realize that we have passed a point-of-no-return, for never again will we live as "naturally" as before we began to degrade our surroundings faster than they could recover. Science and technology enable us to understand and to exploit our surroundings but can never free us from dependence upon them. The goal of the environmental movement, then, is to somehow strike a balance between idealism and realism; to preserve the diversity and wondrous beauty of our world while recognizing that billions must steadily draw upon its substance for survival.

# Notes

## Preface

1. Eric Ashby, *Reconciling Man with Environment* (Stanford, Calif.: Stanford University Press, 1978), p. 3.
2. A. Clay Schoenfeld, *The Environmental Communication Ecosystem: A Situation Report* (Columbus, Ohio: SMEAC Information Reference Center, Ohio State University, 1981), p. 28.
3. James Fenimore Cooper, *The Pioneers* . . . (New York: Charles Wiley, 1823) and *The Prairie* . . . (London: Henry Colburn, 1827); Henry David Thoreau, *Walden, or Life in the Woods* (Boston: Ticknor and Fields, 1854); George Perkins Marsh, *Man and Nature, or, Physical Geography as Modified by Human Nature* (Cambridge, Mass.: Harvard University Press, 1965 [first 1864]).
4. Mary Anglemyer, Eleanor R. Seagraves, and Catherine C. LeMaistre, *A Search for Environmental Ethics: An Initial Bibliography* (Washington, D.C.: Smithsonian Institution Press, 1980); Mary Anglemyer and Eleanor R. Seagraves, *The Natural Environment: An Annotated Bibliography on Attitudes and Values* (Washington, D.C.: Smithsonian Institution Press, 1984.

## 1. The Roots of Environmentalism

1. Samuel P. Hays, *Conservation and the Gospel of Efficiency: The Progressive Conservation Movement, 1890–1920* (Cambridge, Mass.: Harvard University Press, 1959), pp. 1–2.
2. Charles Elton, *The Ecology of Animals,* 2d ed. (London: Methuen, 1946), p. 1.
3. John Steinbeck and Edward F. Ricketts, *Sea of Cortez: A Leisurely Journal of Travel and Research* (New York: Viking, 1941), pp. 85, 270.
4. Eugene P. Odum, "The New Ecology," *BioScience* 14, no. 7 (1964), p. 14.
5. Pierre Dansereau, "Ecological Impact and Human Ecology," in *Future Environments of North America,* ed. F. Fraser Darling and John P. Milton (Garden City, N.Y.: Natural History Press, 1966), p. 426.

6. Marston Bates, *The Forest and the Sea* (New York: Vintage Books, 1960), p. 247.

7. Marston Bates (1962) quoted in William Bowen, "Our New Awareness of the Great Web," *Fortune* 81, no. 2 (1970), p. 198.

8. The Rachel Carson Council, letter of May 8, 1979; Edward Welles, "The Great Blue Herons of Nanjemoy Creek," *Washingtonian*, September 1978, pp. 149–55.

9. Robert L. Burgess, "Introduction," in *Handbook of Contemporary Developments in World Ecology*, ed. E. J. Kormondy and J. F. McCormick (Westport, Conn.: Greenwood Press, 1981), p. 87.

10. Harrison Wellford, "On How to Be a Constructive Nuisance," in *The Environmental Handbook*, ed. Garrett De Bell (New York: Ballantine, 1970), p. 268.

11. John C. Whitaker, *Striking a Balance: Environmental and Natural Resources Policy in the Nixon-Ford Years* (Washington, D.C.: American Enterprise Institute for Public Policy Research, 1976), pp. 22–23.

12. Charles R. Morris, *A Time of Passion: America 1960–1980* (New York: Harper and Row, 1984), p. 71.

13. Theodore H. White, *America in Search of Itself: The Making of the President, 1956–1980* (New York: Harper and Row, 1982), p. 19.

14. Robert Cahn, *Footprints on the Planet: A Search for an Environmental Ethic* (New York: Universe, 1978), pp. 64–65.

15. Joseph Harry, "Causes of Contemporary Environmentalism," *Humboldt Journal of Social Relations* 2, no. 1 (1974), pp. 3–4.

16. Clarrissa Kitchen, *The Ecology Hymnal: New Words for Old Songs* (Austin, Tex.: Sharing Co., 1974), p. 8.

17. John Muir, *Our National Parks* (Boston and New York: Houghton Mifflin, 1901), p. 76.

18. Liberty Hyde Bailey, *Universal Service* (New York: Macmillan, 1923), p. 164.

19. René Dubos, *A Theology of the Earth* (lecture at the Smithsonian Institution, October 2, 1969; Washington, D.C.: Government Printing Office.)

20. Gordon Harrison, "Preface," in Alton A. Lindsey, Damian V. Schmelz, and Stanley A. Nichols, *Natural Areas in Indiana and Their Preservation* (Lafayette, Ind.: Purdue University, Dept. Biological Sciences, 1969), p. vii.

21. Lynn White, Jr., "The Historic Roots of Our Ecologic Crisis," *Science* 155, no. 3767 (1967), p. 1207.

22. Robinson Jeffers, "The Answer," in *Such Counsels You Gave to Me* (New York: Random House, 1937), p. 107.

23. Paul E. Klopsteg, "Environmental Sciences [editorial]," *Science* 152, no. 3722 (1966), p. 595.

24. Anonymous, "Redford OK's Institute for Resources," *Seattle Times* (AP), February 6, 1982, p. B-9.

25. Julian L. Simon, in Ben Wattenberg and Karlyn Keene, "Is the Era

of Limits Running Out? A Conversation with Garrett Hardin and Julian Simon," *Public Opinion* 5, no. 1 (1982), p. 48.

26. Julian L. Simon and Herman Kahn, eds., *The Resourceful Earth: A Response to Global 2000* (New York: Basil Blackwell, 1984), p. 2.

27. E. F. Schumacher, *Small Is Beautiful: Economics As If People Mattered* (New York: Harper and Row, 1975), pp. 255–56.

28. Barry Commoner, *The Closing Circle: Nature, Man, and Technology* (New York: Knopf, 1971), pp. 33–48.

29. John Maddox, *The Doomsday Syndrome* (New York: McGraw-Hill, 1972), pp. 18, 280.

30. John Maddox, *The Doomsday Syndrome* , pp. 5, 188.

31. J. Peter Vajk, *Doomsday Has Been Cancelled* (Culver City, Calif.: Peace Press, 1978), pp. xiv, 122, 165.

32. Theodore Roszak, *Where the Wasteland Ends: Politics and Transcendence in Postindustrial Society* (Garden City, N.Y.: Doubleday, 1972), p. 401.

33. Richard Neuhaus, cited in Stephen R. Fox, *John Muir and His Legacy: The American Conservation Movement* (New York: Little, Brown, 1981), p. 372.

34. Fox, *John Muir and His Legacy,* p. 373.

35. Joseph Wood Krutch, *Grand Canyon* (New York: Doubleday, 1962), p. 199.

36. Stephen R. Kellert and Joyce K. Berry, *Knowledge, Affection and Basic Attitudes Toward Animals in American Society.* Phase III. (Washington, D.C.: Fish and Wildlife Service, 1980), pp. 102–7.

37. National Council of Churches in Christ of the U.S.A., *Policy Statement: The Ethical Implications of Energy Production and Use* (New York, May 11, 1979), 4 pp.

38. Timothy O'Riordan, *Environmentalism* (London: Pion, 1976), p. ix.

## 2. The Societal Background

1. Daniel Bell, *The Winding Passage: Essays and Sociological Journeys 1960–1980* (Cambridge, Mass.: ABT Books, 1980); Charles R. Morris, *A Time of Passion: America 1960–1980* (New York: Harper and Row, 1984); Theodore H. White, *America in Search of Itself: The Making of the President, 1956–1980* (New York: Harper and Row, 1982).

2. Archibald MacLeish, quoted in *This Island Earth* (Washington, D.C.: National Aeronautics and Space Administration, 1970), p. 3.

3. Archibald MacLeish, *Riders on the Earth: Essays and Recollections* (Boston: Houghton Mifflin, 1978), p. 26.

4. Herbert Gold, review of *The Haight-Ashbury,* by Charles Perry, in *New York Times Book Review,* August 12, 1984, p. 10.

5. Ralph J. Gleason, "The Flower Children" (1968 *Britannica Book of the Year,* copyright 1969, with the permission of Encyclopaedia Britannica, Inc., Chicago, Illinois), p. 791.

6. Annie Gottlieb, review of *The Life and Times of the Underground Press,* by Abe Peck, in *New York Times Book Review,* July 7, 1985, p. 12.

7. Carol Polsgrove, "From Walden Pond to Love Canal," *Progressive* 48, no. 7 (1984), p. 24.

8. Barbara Dean, *Wellspring: A Story from the Deep Country* (Covelo, Calif.: Island Press, 1979).

9. Sam Keen and John Raser, "A Conversation with Herbert Marcuse," *Psychology Today* 4, no. 9 (1971), p. 37.

10. Wendell Berry, "Think Little," *The Last Whole Earth Catalog* (1971), p. 24.

11. "Ecology Special," *Ramparts* 8, no. 11 (1970), pp. 2, 4.

12. Douglas Moore, quoted in "The New Raid on Nader," *Christian Century* 87, no. 40 (1970), p. 1176.

13. Anonymous, "Notes and Comments," *The New Yorker,* May 13, 1972, p. 30.

14. Jeffrey L. Fox, "Tentative Agent Orange Settlement Reached," *Science* 224, no. 4651 (1984), pp. 849–50; Judith Perera, review of *Herbicides in War,* by Arthur H. Westing, in *New Scientist,* no. 1427 (1984), pp. 37–38.

15. Jeffrey L. Fox, "Agent Orange: Guarded Reassurance," *Science* 225, no. 4665, August 31, 1984, p. 909.

16. John R. Seeley, "Youth in Revolt," *Britannica Book of the Year,* 1969, p. 315.

17. Glenn W. Frank, Thomas R. Hensley, and Jerry M. Lewis, *The May Fourth Site* (Kent, Ohio: Kent State University brochure distributed at the Memorial Site, 1980).

18. Archibald MacLeish, *Riders on the Earth* (Boston: Houghton Mifflin, 1978), p. vii.

19. Daniel Bell, *The Winding Passage* (Cambridge, Mass.: ABT Books, 1980), p. 60.

20. Anonymous, "The '60s: Decade of Tumult and Change," *Life* 67, no. 26 (1969), special double issue, p. 9.

21. Charles R. Morris, *A Time of Passion* (New York: Harper and Row, 1984), p. 123.

22. Abigail McCarthy, "International Women's Year [1975]," *Britannica Book of the Year,* 1976, p. 691.

23. Barbara Milbauer, *The Law Giveth: Legal Aspects of the Abortion Controversy* (New York: Atheneum, 1983).

24. Barry Sussman, "Public Opinion Is Catching Up with the Women's Movement," *Washington Post,* Natl. Weekly Ed., June 25, 1984, p. 37.

25. Shana Alexander, *State-by-State Guide to Women's Legal Rights* (Los Angeles: Wollstonecraft, 1975), p. 215.

26. *Britannica Book of the Year,* 1961, p. 634.

27. Mark Barry Sullivan, "Ralph Nader," *Britannica Book of the Year,* 1972, p. 143.

28. Joseph Wood Krutch, *The Voice of the Desert: A Naturalist's Interpretation* (New York: William Sloane, 1955), p. 185.

29. International League for Animal Rights, *Universal Declaration of the*

*Rights of Animals* (proclaimed October 15, 1978, in a conference room adjacent to UNESCO headquarters, Paris, but not a UNESCO document); "The Animal Kingdom at the U.N.," *Washington Star*, October 27, 1978, editorial (unpaged reprint seen).

30. Scientists Center for Animal Welfare, "College Courses on Ethics and Animals," *SCAW Newsletter* 5, no. 2, May 1983, pp. 3–6.

31. Victor B. Scheffer, "Benign Uses of Wildlife," *International Journal for the Study of Animal Problems* 1, no. 1 (1980), pp. 19–32.

32. Christopher D. Stone, "Should Trees Have Standing? Toward Legal Rights for Natural Objects," *Southern California Law Review* 45, no. 2 (1972), pp. 450–51; " 'Should Trees Have Standing' Revisited: How Far Will Law and Morals Reach? A Pluralist Perspective," ibid. 59, no. 1 (1985), pp. 1–154.

33. David Paterson and Richard D. Ryder, eds., *Animal Rights: A Symposium* (London: Centaur Press, 1979), p. 240.

34. Peter Singer, *Animal Liberation: A New Ethics for Our Treatment of Animals* (New York: New York Review/Random House, 1975), p. 272.

35. Peter Singer, review of *Animals, Men and Morals*, edited by Stanley and Roslind Godlovitch and John Harris, in *New York Review of Books*, April 5, 1973, p. 17.

36. Kurt P. Richter, "Experiences of a Reluctant Ratcatcher: The Common Norway Rat—Friend or Foe?" *Proceedings of the American Philosophical Society* 112, no. 6 (1968), pp. 403–15.

## 3. Croplands, Rangelands, and Forests

1. Council on Environmental Quality and the Department of State, *The Global 2000 Report to the President* (Washington, D.C.: 1980–81), vol. 2, p. 97, tbl. 6–12.

2. Sandra S. Batie, *Soil Erosion: Crisis in America's Croplands?* (Washington, D.C.: The Conservation Foundation, 1983), p. xiii; Lester R. Brown and others, *State of the World 1984* (New York: W. W. Norton [A Worldwatch Institute Report] 1984), p. 58; David Pimentel and others, "World Agriculture and Soil Erosion," *BioScience* 37, no. 4 (1987), p. 278, tbl. 1.

3. Brown, *State of the World 1984*, p. 185.

4. David Sheridan, *Desertification of the United States* (Washington, D.C.: Council on Environmental Quality, 1981), p. 121.

5. Edward Abbey, "Even the Bad Guys Wear White Hats: Cowboys, Ranchers, and the Ruin of the West," *Harpers* 272, no. 1628 (1986), pp. 51–55; Jon R. Luoma, "Discouraging Words," *Audubon* 88, no. 5 (1986), pp. 86–104.

6. John Baden, ed., *Earth Day Reconsidered* (Washington, D.C.: Heritage Foundation, 1980), p. 73.

7. Ronald C. Tobey, *Saving the Prairies: The Life Cycle of the Founding School of American Ecology, 1855–1955* (Berkeley: University of California Press, 1981), p. 5.

8. John Fowles, *The Tree* (New York: Ecco, 1983), pp. 78–79.

9. Anonymous, "Oldest Trees in Oregon Fall," *News Journal of the National Audubon Society* (June 1986), p. 14.

10. Edward C. Crafts, quoted in Daniel R. Barney, *The Last Stand* (New York: Grossman, 1974), p. 41.

11. S. Blair Hutchinson, "Bringing Resource Conservation into the Main Stream of American Thought," in *Enclosing the Environment*, ed. Channing Kury (Albuquerque: University of New Mexico School of Law, 1985), p. 29.

12. Marion Clawson, "The National Forests," *Science* 191, no. 4227 (1976), p. 762.

13. Congressional Research Service, *State-by-State Estimate of Situations Where Timber Will Be Sold by the Forest Service at a Loss or a Profit* (Washington, D.C., March 7, 1984).

14. F. Kaid Benfield, "The Forest Service: Can It Learn to Listen?" *Environment* 27, no. 7 (1985), p. 4.

15. Orris C. Herfindahl, "What Is Conservation?" in *Readings in Resource Management and Conservation*, Ian Burton and Robert W. Kates, eds. (Chicago: University of Chicago Press, 1965), p. 230.

# 4. Natural Lands

1. Charles S. Elton, *The Ecology of Invasions by Animals and Plants* (London: Chapman and Hall, 1958), p. 145.

2. "Organic Act" of August 25, 1916 (39 Stat. 535).

3. Bernard DeVoto, "Let's Close the National Parks," *Harper's* 207, no. 1241 (1953), p. 52.

4. Anne Fadiman, "Nature Under Siege," *Life*, n.s. 6, no. 7 (1983), p. 112.

5. National Park Service, *State of the Parks: A Report to the Congress* (Washington, D.C.: January 2, 1981).

6. Roderick Nash, *Wilderness and the American Mind*, 3d. ed. (New Haven, Conn.: Yale University Press, 1982), pp. 317–19.

7. National Park Service, *Our Vanishing Shoreline* (Washington, D.C., 1955?).

8. Wilderness Society, *Memorandum for the Legislative Reference Service* (Washington, D.C.: Library of Congress, 1949), p. 3.

9. Donald L. Baldwin, *The Quiet Revolution: Grass Roots of Today's Wilderness Preservation Movement* (Boulder, Colo.: Pruett, 1972); The Wilderness Society, *The Wilderness Act Handbook* (Washington, D.C., 1984).

10. Oliver Wendell Holmes, opinion in *New Jersey* v. *New York*, 283 U.S. 336, 342 (1931).

11. Byron, *Journal*, September 19, 1814.

# 5. The Oceans

1. Lester R. Brown, *Resource Trends and Population Policy: A Time for Reassessment* (Washington, D.C.: Worldwatch Institute, Paper 29; 1979), p. 9, tbl. 1; United Nations Food and Agricultural Organization, *1982 Yearbook of Fisheries Statistics* (Rome, 1984), p. 80.

2. Victor B. Scheffer and Karl W. Kenyon, "The Rise and Fall of a Seal Herd," *Animal Kingdom* 92, no. 2 (March/April 1989), pp. 14–19.

3. Bruce S. Manheim, Jr., "The Oceans Are Choking on Plastic Debris," *New York Times,* March 1, 1986, p. 26; Michael Weisskopf, "Pollution from Plastics Ravaging Marine Life," *Washington Post,* December 15, 1986, p. A-1.

4. Michael H. Horn, John M. Teal, and Richard H. Backus, "Petroleum Lumps on the Surface of the Sea," *Science* 168, no. 3928 (1970), pp. 245–46.

5. Gladwin Hill, *Madman in a Lifeboat: Issues of the Environmental Crisis* (New York: John Day [New York Times Survey Series] 1973), p. 22.

6. E. B. White, "Letter from the East," *New Yorker* 33, no. 23 (1957), p. 43.

7. Anonymous, "Academy Changes Army Dump Plan," *Science* 165, no. 1957 (1969), p. 45.

8. Elisabeth Mann Borghese, "The Law of the Sea," *Scientific American* 248, no. 3 (1983), pp. 42–49; Norman Myers, ed., *The Gaia Atlas of Planet Management* (London: Pan, 1985), p. 96. A chronology of LOS conferences from 1958 to 1982 appears in: United Nations, *The Law of the Sea . . .* (New York, 1983), pp. 191–92.

9. Commission to Study the Organization of Peace, *The United Nations and the Oceans: Current Issues in the Law of the Sea* (New York, 1973), p. 7.

10. Philip S. Kelley, "International Control of the Ocean Floor," in *Congress and the Environment,* ed. Richard A. Cooley and Geoffrey Wandesforde-Smith (Seattle: University of Washington Press, 1970), p. 203.

11. Tony Loftas, "Law of the Sea III," *Britannica Book of the Year,* 1977, pp. 453–54; Elisabeth Mann Borghese, "The Law of the Sea," *Scientific American* 248, no. 3 (1983), p. 42; Bob Loeffelbein, "Law of the Sea Treaty: What Does It Mean to Nonsigners (Like the United States)?" *Sea Frontiers* 29, no. 6 (1983), p. 359.

12. Borghese, "The Law of the Sea", p. 42.

# 6. Fresh Water

1. Frank Graham, Jr., *Since Silent Spring* (Boston: Houghton Mifflin, 1970), pp. 93–108.

2. Public Health Service, quoted by Gladwin Hill, "The Great and Dirty Lakes," *Saturday Review* 48, no. 43 (1965), p. 33.

3. Anonymous, "The Ravaged Environment," *Newsweek* 75, no. 4 (1970),

p. 45; U.S. Congress, House Commission on Marine Science, Engineering, and Resources, *Panel Reports . . .* Vol. 1 (91st Congress, 1st Sess., House Doc. 91–42, part 2 (1969), pp. III-42 to III-45.

4. W. T. Edmondson, "Lake Washington," in *Environmental Quality and Water Development,* ed. Charles R. Goldman, James McEvoy III, and Peter J. Richerson (San Francisco: W. H. Freeman, 1973), pp. 281–98.

5. Dwight D. Eisenhower, "Veto of Bill to Amend the Federal Water Pollution Act," *Public Papers of the Presidents, 1960–61* (February 23, 1960), p. 208.

6. Joseph Tydings, quoted in "The Ravaged Environment," *Newsweek* 75, no. 4 (1970), p. 37.

7. Richmond Lattimore, "Report from a Planet," p. 131. Reprinted by permission of the publisher, Harry N. Abrams, Inc., N.Y., from the book *Fifty Years of American Poetry* (copyright 1984), Academy of American Poets. All rights reserved.

8. Anonymous, "Groundwater Contamination Bad, Getting Worse, Says Study," *Seattle Times* (AP), October 26, 1984, p. A-6.

9. Lester R. Brown and others, *State of the World 1984* (New York: W. W. Norton, 1984), pp. 15, 177; Kenneth D. Frederick, "Current Water Issues," *Journal of Soil and Water Conservation* 39, no. 2 (1984), pp. 86–91; Allen V. Kneese, "High Plains, Low Water," *Resources* [Resources for the Future] no. 78; 1984, pp. 7–9.

10. Environmental Protection Agency, *Protecting Our Ground Water* (Washington, D.C., 1985), 1 fold sheet, unpaged; Marjorie Sun, "Ground Water Ills: Many Diagnoses, Few Remedies," *Science* 232, no. 4757, 1986, pp. 1490–93.

11. Howard P. Brokaw, ed., *Wildlife and America: Contributions to an Understanding of American Wildlife and Conservation* (Washington, D.C.: Council on Environmental Quality and others, 1978), p. 158; Fish and Wildlife Service, *America's Endangered Wetlands* (Washington, D.C.: 1984), 1 folded sheet.

12. Jimmy Carter, *The President's Message on the Environment* (Washington, D.C.: Compiled by the CEQ; includes background material, Executive Orders, and two press statements, 1977), p. M-7.

13. Anonymous, "U.S. Loss of Swamps Is Called Alarming," *Seattle Times* (UPI), March 27, 1984, p. A-7; Ralph W. Tiner, Jr., *Wetlands of the United States: Current Status and Recent Trends* (Washington, D.C.: Fish and Wildlife Service, National Wetlands Inventory, 1984), p. 29; Milton W. Weller, review of *Wetlands of the United States . . .* and review of *Wetlands: Their Use and Regulation* (Washington, D.C.: Office of Technology Assessment, 1984) in *Environment* 27, no. 1 (1985), pp. 25–27.

14. Tom Harris, "The Selenium Question," *Defenders* 61, no. 2 (1986), pp. 10–19; Fish and Wildlife Service, Division of Refuge Management, *Preliminary Survey of Contaminant Issues of Concern on National Wildlife Refuges* (Washington, D.C.: April 1986), pp. 1–163; Richard W. Wahl, "Cleaning up Kesterson," *Resources* 83 (1986), pp. 11–14.

15. Eliot Marshall, "San Joaquin Flooded with Water Researchers," *Science* 230, no. 4728 (1985), pp. 920–21.

# 7. Air Quality

1. Walsh McDermott, "Air Pollution and Public Health," *Scientific American* 205, no. 4 (1961), p. 49.

2. Ralph I. Larsen, "Air Pollution from Motor Vehicles," *Annals of the New York Academy of Sciences* 136, no. 12 (1966), p. 298.

3. Charles Barber, quoted in "We Knew Tacoma Smelter Was Doomed . . .," *Bellevue Journal-American*, March 30, 1985, p. A-7.

4. Anonymous, *Acid Rain: A Teacher's Guide* (Washington, D.C.: National Wildlife Federation, 1984).

5. Leslie Roberts, "Studies Probe Unexplained Decline in Eastern Forests," *BioScience* 34, no. 5 (1984), p. 291.

6. P. A. Mayewski and others, "Sulfate and Nitrate Concentrations from a South Greenland Ice Core," *Science* 232, no. 4753 (1986), p. 975.

7. Anne La Bastille, "Acid Rain: How Great a Menace?" *National Geographic* 160, no. 5 (1981), pp. 652–80.

8. Ross Howard and Michael Perley, "Acid Rain," *Amicus Journal* 2, no. 3 (1981), pp. 24–26; National Commission on Air Quality, cited in *Acid Rain: A Teacher's Guide* (Washington, D.C.: National Wildlife Federation, 1984), p. 3.

9. Council on Environmental Quality, *First Annual Report* (Washington, D.C., 1970), p. 93.

10. Environmental Protection Agency, one-page press release on two 1983 publications: *Can We Delay a Greenhouse Warming?* and *Projecting Future Sea Level Rise* (Washington, D.C., 1983).

11. Robert L. Peters and Joan D. S. Darling, "The Greenhouse Effect and Nature Reserves," *BioScience* 35, no. 11 (1985), pp. 707–17; George M. Woodwell, "Global Warming and What We Can Do About It," *Amicus Journal* 8, no. 2 (1986), pp. 8–12; Environmental Protection Agency, *Unfinished Business: A Comparative Assessment of Environmental Problems* (Washington, D.C., 1987) Appendix III, p. 21; P. D. Jones, T. M. L. Wigley and P. B. Wright, "Global Temperature Variations Between 1861 and 1984," *Nature* 322, no. 6078 (1986), fig. 5.

12. Mario J. Molina and F. S. Rowland, "Stratospheric Sink for Chlorofluoromethanes: Chlorine Atomic-catalysed Destruction of Ozone," *Nature* 249, no. 5460 (1974), pp. 810–12.

13. J. C. Farman, B. G. Gardiner, and J. D. Shanklin, "Large Losses of Total Ozone in Antarctica Reveal Seasonal $ClO_x/NO_x$ Interaction," *Nature* 315, no. 6016 (1985), pp. 207–10. See also Paul Brodeur, "In the Face of Doubt," *New Yorker*, June 9, 1986, pp. 70–87.

14. Richard A. Kerr, "Taking Shots at Ozone Hole Theories," *Science* 234, no. 4778 (1968), pp. 817–18.

15. Norman Cousins, "The Noise Level Is Rising," *Saturday Review* 45, no. 9 (1962), p. 20.

16. Council on Environmental Quality, *Tenth Annual Report* (Washington, D.C., 1979), pp. 546–47.

17. Charles A. Lindbergh (letter to Congressman Yates), *New York Times*, July 27, 1972, p. 31.

18. Gaylord Nelson, "Noise Threatens Grand Canyon," *Seattle Times*, November 27, 1985, p. A-7.

19. Frederick Case, "Wild Music" (profile of Gordon Hempton), *Seattle Times*, October 21, 1985, pp. D-1, D-5.

20. Herbert Marcuse, quoted in "Noise Control Efforts Stir Up Many Disputes," *Conservation Foundation Letter*, June 1980, p. 3.

# *8. Minerals*

1. Thomas S. Lovering, "Mineral Resources from the Land," in *Resources and Man* (Washington, D.C.: National Academy of Sciences/National Research Council, Committee on Resources and Man, 1969), pp. 120, 128–29.

2. George Riley, "The Mining Law of 1872," *Amicus Journal* 2, no. 4 (1981), pp. 17–21.

3. Donella H. Meadows, Dennis L. Meadows, Jørgen Randers, and William H. Behrens III, *The Limits to Growth: A Report for the Club of Rome's Project on the Predicament of Mankind* (New York: Universe Books, 1972), pp. 56–60.

4. Council on Environmental Quality, *First Annual Report* (Washington, D.C., 1970), p. 158.

5. National Academy of Sciences/National Research Council, *Mineral Resources and the Environment* (Washington, D.C.: NAS Committee on Mineral Resources and the Environment; with NRC Commission on Natural Resources, 1975), pp. 1, 308.

6. John E. Tilton, *The Future of Nonfuel Minerals* (Washington, D.C.: Brookings Institution, 1977), pp. 6–7.

7. James M. Broadus, "Seabed Materials," *Science* 235, no. 4791 (1987), pp. 853–60.

8. National Science Foundation, Office for the IDOE, "International Decade of Ocean Exploration," *Progress Report*, vol. 2 (July 1972 to April 1973), pp. ii-iii; ibid., *Second Report* (program description]) (October 1973), pp. 2–3.

9. Claiborne Pell, "The Oceans: Man's Last Great Resource," *Saturday Review* 52, no. 41 (1969), p. 19; Samuel W. Matthews, "New World of the Ocean," *National Geographic* 160, no. 6 (1981), p. 814.

10. Lewis Mumford, *The Myth of the Machine*, vol. 2, *The Pentagon of Power* (New York: Harcourt, Brace, Jovanovich, 1970), p. 147.

11. Tony Velocci, "Minerals: The Resource Gap," *Nation's Business* 68, no. 10 (1980), p. 33.

12. Kenneth F. Weaver, "The Search for Tomorrow's Power," *National Geographic* 142, no. 5 (November 1972), p. 655.

13. Anonymous, "The Ravaged Environment," *Newsweek* 75, no. 4 (January 1970), p. 39.

14. David G. McCullough, "The Lonely War of a Good Angry Man," *American Heritage* 21, no. 1 (December 1969), pp. 13–15.

# 9. Energy

1. Anonymous, "The Disaster That Wasn't," *Time* 86, no. 21 (November 19, 1965), pp. 35–43.

2. David J. Rose, "Energy Policy in the United States," in *Readings from Scientific American: Energy and Environment* (San Francisco: W. H. Freeman, 1980 [orig. article, 1974]), pp. 40–52.

3. M. King Hubbert, "Energy Resources," in *Resources and Man* (Washington, D.C.: National Academy of Sciences and National Research Council, 1969), p. 205.

4. Hubbert, "Energy Resources," rearranged from p. 237.

5. Hubbert, "Energy Resources," p. 237; Kenneth F. Weaver, "The Search for Tomorrow's Power," *National Geographic* 142, no. 5 (November 1972), pp. 650–81; David J. Rose, "Energy Policy in the United States" reprinted in *Readings from Scientific American: Energy and Environment*, 1980, p. 49.

6. Hubbert, "Energy Resources," pp. 158–59. See also Richard A. Kerr, "How Fast Is Oil Running Out?" *Science* 226, no. 4673 (October 26, 1984), p. 426.

7. Joseph P. Riva, Jr., "Domestic Crude Oil Production Projected to the Year 2000 on the Basis of Resource Capability," *Congressional Research Service Report* no. 84–129 SPR (July 31, 1984), pp. 1–75.

8. Arthur R. Tamplin, "Issues in the Radiation Controversy," *Science and Public Affairs* 27, no. 7 (September 1971), p. 27.

9. Amory B. Lovins, *Soft Energy Paths: Toward a Durable Peace* (Cambridge, Mass.: Ballinger, 1977), p. 26; Lovins quoted in *Energy: A Special Report in the Public Interest* (Washington, D.C.: National Geographic Society, 1981), p. 73.

10. Department of Energy, *Renewable Energy: An Overview* (Washington, D.C.: DOE Conservation and Renewable Energy Inquiry and Referral Service, 1985), pp. 1–5.

11. National Academy of Sciences and National Research Council, *Mineral Resources and the Environment* (Washington, D.C.: NAS Committee on Mineral Resources and the Environment; NRC Commission on Natural Resources, 1975), p. 99.

12. William R. Catton, Jr., "Depending on Ghosts," *Humboldt Journal of Social Relations* 2, no. 1 (1974), p. 47.

13. Russell E. Train, "The Environment Today," *Science* 201, no. 4353 (1978), p. 321.

14. Christopher Flavin and Sandra Postel, "Developing Renewable En-

ergy," in *State of the World 1984*, ed. Lester R. Brown and others (New York: W. W. Norton, 1984), p. 149.

15. Jay Mathews, "A California Complex Finds Its Place in the Sun," *Washington Post National Weekly Edition*, March 20–26, 1989, p. 49.

16. Ibid., pp. 136–56; Christopher Flavin, "Electricity's Future: The Shift to Efficiency and Small-scale Power," *Worldwatch Paper* 61 (1984), pp. 1–70.

17. Flavin, "Electricity's Future," p. 139.

18. Hubbert, "Energy Resources," p. 212; John McHale, *The Ecological Context* (New York: George Braziller, 1970), p. 125.

19. Robert Cohen, "Ocean Thermal Energy," in *Harvesting Ocean Energy*, ed. Gerald L. Wick, Walter R. Schmitt, and Robin Clarke (Paris: UNESCO Press, 1981) pp. 83–110; Terry R. Penney and Desikan Bharathan, "Power from the Sea [OTEC]," *Scientific American* 256, no. 1 (January 1987), pp. 86–92.

20. Gayla A. Kraetsch, "Supplementary Conservation Practices with Alternative Energy Sources," *New Directions for Higher Education*, no. 34 (1981), p. 53; National Geographic Society, *Energy: a Special Report in the Public Interest* (Washington, D.C.: 1981), p. 51.

21. Mary Lou Van Deventer, "With a Grain of Salt," *Ecolibrium* 10, no. 4 (1981), p. 9–11.

22. Robert W. Rex, "Geothermal Energy—the Neglected Energy Option," *Science and Public Affairs* 27, no. 8 (1971), p. 52.

23. Hubbert, "Energy Resources," p. 218.

24. Bruce C. Netschert, "The Energy Company: A Monopoly Trend in the Energy Markets," *Science and Public Affairs* 27, no. 8 (1971), p. 14.

25. David Roe, *Dynamos and Virgins* (New York: Random House, 1984).

26. Judith Cummings, review of *Dynamos and Virgins* by David Roe in *New York Times Book Review* (April 7, 1985), p. 15.

27. U.S. Committee for Energy Awareness, brochures on non-renewable sources of energy (Washington, D.C.: USCEA [a nongovernmental association], 1985?).

28. United Nations, *1983 Energy Statistics Yearbook* (Rome, 1985), table 1.

# 10. Control of the Atom

1. Barbara Ward, *Progress for a Small Planet* (New York: W. W. Norton, 1982), p. 8.

2. Albert Schweitzer, quoted in *Putting First Things First: A Democratic View*, by Adlai Stevenson (New York: Random House, 1960), p. 29.

3. Harrison Brown, *The Challenge of Man's Future* (New York: Viking, 1954), p. 178.

4. Anonymous, "Atom Bombing of Antarctic Urged by Rickenbacker to Get Minerals," *Polar Times* (June 1946), p. 11.

5. Stewart L. Udall, "Foreword," in *Overshoot: The Ecological Basis of Revolutionary Change*, by William R. Catton, Jr. (Urbana: University of Illinois Press, 1980), p. xiii.

6. WGBY-TV (Springfield, Mass., Channel 57), "Nevada Fallout: The Hot Years," news release of September 4, 1981, p. 1; John W. Gofman and Arthur R. Tamplin, "Nuclear Radiation," in *The Social Responsibility of the Scientist*, ed. Martin Brown (New York: Free Press, 1971), p. 134.

7. Bruce S. Jenkins, *Irene Allen et al.* v. *The United States of America*, Memorandum Opinion, May 10, 1984, p. 317; quoted by Philip L. Fradkin, *Fallout: An American Nuclear Tragedy* (Tucson: University of Arizona Press, 1989), p. 230.

8. Charles Komanoff, cited by Carole Douglis in "The Economics of Contamination," *Atlantic* 254, no. 4 (October 1984), p. 32.

9. Flavin, "Electricity's Future," p. 26; Judith Perera, "Desperate Nuclear Firms Look to Middle East," *New Scientist*, no. 1448 (March 21, 1985), p. 9.

10. Colin Norman, "Assessing the Effects of a Nuclear Accident," *Science* 228, no. 4695 (April 5, 1985), p. 31.

11. Joan Sweeney, "A-Protesters: Single Issue, Many Groups," *Los Angeles Times*, November 18, 1979, p. 32.

12. Anonymous, "WPPSS Finally Makes Good News—and Power," *Journal American* (Bellevue, WA) (AP), May 29, 1984, p. A-3.

13. Bartle Bull, "Nuclear Welfare: Keeping Track," *Amicus Journal* 3, no. 3 (1982), pp. 11–13; Bull, "Voodoo Energy: Keeping Track," *Amicus Journal* 3, no. 4 (1982), pp. 4–6.

14. Dan Kirshner, "Dim Hopes for Nuclear Power," *Environment* 27, no. 6 (1985), p. 4.

15. Jay M. Gould and others, "Nuclear Emissions Take Their Toll," *Council on Economic Priorities Newsletter no. N86–12* (1986), pp. 1–9. (Mortality rates in nuclear and non-nuclear states are compared.)

16. Dean Abrahamson, "Radwastes: Still Homeless After All These Years," *Amicus Journal* 5, no. 2 (1983), p. 10.

17. Terry Lash, "Radioactive Waste: Nuclear Energy's Dilemma," *Amicus Journal* 1, no. 2 (1979), p. 27.

18. Thomas A. Sebeok, *Communication Measures to Bridge Ten Millennia* (Columbus, Ohio: Battelle Memorial Institute, Office of Nuclear Waste Information, [Publication] BMI DE 84–014459 BMI/ONWI 532, 1984).

19. Carole Douglis, "The Economics of Contamination," *Atlantic* 254, no. 4 (October 1984), p. 34.

20. Hannes Alfven, "Fission and Fusion Reactors: The Alfven Memorandum," *Science and Public Affairs* 27, no. 7 (September 1971), p. 36.

21. Norman Myers, *The Gaia Atlas of Planet Management* (London: Pan, 1985), p. 124.

22. Scott Fenn, *The Nuclear Power Debate: Issues and Choices* (New York: Praeger, 1981), p. 199.

# 11. Society's Wastes and Poisons

1. Anatole Broyard, "The Life That Is in Things," *New York Times Review of Books*, August 4, 1985, p. 13.

2. Council on Environmental Quality, *Environmental Trends* (Washington, D.C.: 1981), p. 86.

3. Garrett De Bell, *The Environmental Handbook* (New York: Ballantine, 1970), p. 214.

4. Norman Myers, ed., *The Gaia Atlas of Planet Management* (London: Pan, 1985), pp. 123–37.

5. Edward Segel and others, *The Toxic Substances Dilemma* (Washington, D.C.: National Wildlife Federation and EPA; Government Printing Office, 1980); Michael Dowling, "Defining and Classifying Hazardous Wastes," *Environment* 27, no. 3 (1985), pp. 36–41.

6. United Nations, *Consolidated List of Products Whose Consumption and/or Sale Have Been Banned, Withdrawn, Severely Restricted or Not Approved by Governments,* 1st issue revised (Rome: DIESA/WP/1 Rev. 1; 1984).

7. Peter A. A. Berle, "The Toxic Tornado," *Audubon* 87, no. 6 (1985), p. 4.

8. Resource Conservation and Recovery Act of 1976.

9. Albert L. Gore, Jr., quoted in *Hazardous Waste in America,* by Samuel S. Epstein, Lester O. Brown and Carl Pope (San Francisco: Sierra Club Books, 1982), p. 3.

10. Philip M. Abelson, "Waste Management," *Science* 228, no. 4704 (1985), p. 1145; Allen A. Boraiko, "Hazardous Waste," *National Geographic* 167, no. 3 (March 1985), pp. 318–51.

11. General Accounting Office, *Cleaning Up Hazardous Wastes* (Washington, D.C.: Report to the Congress by the Comptroller General; GAO/RCED-85–69; 1985), p. 5.

12. Environmental Protection Agency, *Environmental Progress and Challenges: An EPA Perspective* (Washington, D.C.: EPA Office of Management Systems and Evaluation, PM 222; 1984), p. 82.

13. Samuel S. Epstein, Lester O. Brown, and Carl Pope, *Hazardous Waste in America* (San Francisco, Calif.: Sierra Club Books, 1982), p.31.

14. Council on Environmental Quality, *Eleventh Annual Report* (Washington, D.C.: 1980), pp. 219–21; Wanda Veraska, *A Citizen's Guide to Toxic Substances* (Washington, D.C.: National Wildlife Federation, 1981), pp. 3–4.

15. Peter Borrelli, "Not in My Backyard: The Legacy of Love Canal," *Amicus Journal* 4, no. 2 (1982), p. 45.

16. Michael Castleman, "Toxics and Male Infertility," *Sierra* 70, no. 2 (1985), p. 50.

17. Ralph C. Dougherty and others, "Sperm Density and Toxic Substances: A Potential Key to Environmental Health Hazards," in *Environmental Health Chemistry,* ed. J. D. McKinney (Ann Arbor, Mich.: Ann Arbor Science Publishers, 1980), p. 275.

18. David Schottenfeld and M. Ellen Warshauer, "Testis," in *Cancer Epidemiology and Prevention,* ed. D. Schottenfeld and Joseph F. Fraumeni, Jr. (Philadelphia: W. B. Saunders, 1982), p. 950.

19. John C. Bailar III and Elaine M. Smith, "Progress Against Cancer?" *New England Journal of Medicine* 314 (May 19, 1986), p. 1226.

20. Herbert L. Needleman, Susan K. Geiger, and Richard Frank, "Lead and IQ Scores: A Reanalysis," *Science* 227, no. 4688 (1985), pp. 701–4.

21. John H. Trefry and others, "A Decline in Lead Transport by the Mississippi River," *Science* 230, no. 4724 (1985), pp. 439–41.

22. Fish and Wildlife Service, *Fish, Wildlife and Pesticides* (Washington, D.C.: 1966), pp. 1–12; George W. Ware, *Pesticides: Theory and Application* (San Francisco: W. H. Freeman, 1983).

23. Anonymous, "Pesticides: Facts and Figures," *PANNA Outlook*, no. 2, July 1983, p. 3.

24. George P. Georghiou and Roni B. Mellon, "Pesticide Resistance in Time and Space," in *Pest Resistance to Pesticides*, ed. G. P. Georghiou and Tetsui Saito (New York: Plenum, 1983), p. 9, tbl. 2; L. B. Brattsten and others, "Insecticide Resistance: Challenge to Pest Management and Basic Research," *Science* 231, no. 4743 (1986), pp. 1255–60.

25. Robert L. Metcalf, "Changing Role of Insecticides in Crop Protection," *Annual Review of Entomology* 25 (1980), pp. 219–56; also letter of October 3, 1985.

26. Robert W. Risebrough, "Pollution, Wildlife and Science," *Canadian Field Naturalist* 82, no. 4 (1968), pp. 241–43; Daniel W. Anderson and others, "Significance of Chlorinated Hydrocarbon Residues to Breeding Pelicans and Cormorants," *Canadian Field-Naturalist* 83, no. 2 (1969), pp. 91–112.

27. E. A. Sauter and E. E. Steele, "The Effect of Low Level Pesticide Feeding on the Fertility and Hatchability of Chicken Eggs," *Poultry Science* 51, no. 1 (1972), pp. 71–76.

28. Rachel Carson, *Silent Spring* (Boston: Houghton Mifflin, 1962), pp. 68–69.

29. Harrison Wellford, *Sowing the Wind: A Report from Ralph Nader's Center for Study of Responsive Law on Food Safety and the Chemical Harvest* (New York: Grossman, 1972); Lewis Regenstein, *America the Poisoned* (Washington, D.C.: Acropolis, 1983).

30. Wellford, *Sowing the Wind*, p. 187.

31. Anonymous, "The Poisoning of America," *Time* 116, no. 12 (September 1, 1980), p. 69.

# 12. Endangered Species

1. Stephen Vincent Benét, *Selected Works* (New York: Farrar and Rinehart, 1955), vol. 1, p. 402.

2. Norman Myers, "Tackling Mass Extinction of Species," *Horace M. Albright Lectureship in Conservation*, no. 26 (1986), p. 2.

3. Norman D. Levin, "Preservation Versus Elimination," *BioScience* 36, no. 5 (1986), p. 309; Benjamin C. Stone, letter to editor, *BioScience* 36, no. 8 (1986), p. 524.

4. Vincenz Zisweiler, *Extinct and Vanishing Animals: A Biology of Extinction and Survival* (London: English Universities Press, 1967).

5. Boyce Rensberger, "Our Vanishing World: 17,500 Species Are Becoming Extinct Each Year," *Washington Post National Weekly Edition* 3, no. 52 (October 27, 1986), p. 38.

6. John Ogden, quoted in "Lost Condors Spark Debate: Lead Poisoning Takes Two," by Ken Ketwig in *Audubon Action* 3, no. 4 (1985), p. 1.

7. Kenneth E. F. Watt, *Understanding the Environment* (Newton, Mass.: Allyn and Bacon, 1982), p. 319.

8. National Wildlife Federation, *List of Threatened and Endangered Plants and Wildlife of the U.S.* (Washington, D.C.: 1984). See also R. J. Hoague, ed., *Animal Extinctions: What Everyone Should Know* (Washington, D.C.: Smithsonian Institution Press, 1985).

9. Defenders of Wildlife, *Saving Endangered Species: A Report and Plan for Action* (Washington, D.C.: 1984), p. 11.

# 13. The Human Population

1. Paul K. Andersen, comp., *Omega: Murder of the Ecosystem and Suicide of Man* (Dubuque, Iowa: W. C. Brown, 1971), p. 3.

2. Heinz von Foerster, Patricia M. Mora, and Lawrence W. Amiot, "Doomsday: Friday, 13 November, A.D. 2026," *Science* 132, no. 3436 (1960), pp. 1291–95.

3. Thomas Exter, "Demographics," *Atlantic* 259, no. 4 (April), pp. 8–9.

4. Planned Parenthood Federation, *Birth Control U.S.A.* (New York, 1952[?]).

5. Ibid., p. 7.

6. National Academy of Sciences and National Research Council, *The Growth of U.S. Population* (Washington, D.C., Publication 1279, 1965), p. 21.

7. Ward E. Y. Elliott, "Federal Law and Population Control," in *Federal Environmental Law*, Erica L. Dolgin and Thomas G. P. Guilbert, eds. (St. Paul, Minn.: West Publishing, 1974), pp. 1518–1600.

8. Anonymous, "Gallup: '73% of Americans Will Pay More Taxes to Fight Conservation Problems'," *National Wildlife* 7, no. 2 (1969), p. 19.

9. Paul R. Ehrlich, *The Population Bomb: Population Control or Race to Oblivion?* (New York: Ballantine, 1968). See his bibliography, pp. 218–20.

10. Ehrlich, *The Population Bomb,"* p. xi.

11. Paul R. Ehrlich, quoted in "Fighting to Save the Earth from Man," *Time* 95, no. 5 (February 2, 1970), p. 59.

12. S. Fred Singer, ed., *Is There an Optimum Level of Population? An AAAS Symposium, Boston, December 1969* (New York: McGraw-Hill, 1971).

13. Singer, *Is There an Optimum Level of Population?* p. 88.

14. Ibid., p. 96.

15. National Academy of Sciences and National Research Council, *Resources and Man* (San Francisco: W. H. Freeman, 1969), pp. 238–39.

16. Donella H. Meadows and others, *The Limits of Growth: A Report for the Club of Rome's Project on the Predicament of Mankind* (New York: Universe Books, 1972), p. 165. For lively criticism of the Club of Rome, see Samuel C. Florman, *Blaming Technology* (New York: St. Martin's, 1981), pp. 132–47.

17. Paul H. Ehrlich in Meadows and others, *The Limits of Growth* (back cover).

18. R. Buckminster Fuller, "An Operating Manual for Spaceship Earth," in *Environment and Change: The Next Fifty Years*, ed. William R. Ewald (Bloomington: Indiana University Press, 1968), p. 388.

19. Alan Anderson, Jr., "Scientist at Large [Barry Commoner]," *New York Times Magazine* (November 7, 1976), p. 62.

20. Paul R. Ehrlich and John P. Holdren, "People in the Machinery: A Negative Comment on a Popular New Book," *Saturday Review* (January 1, 1972), p. 71.

21. Garrett Hardin, *An Ecolate View of the Human Condition* (Washington, D.C.: Environmental Fund, 1984), p. 9.

22. Garrett Hardin, "The Tragedy of the Commons," *Science* 162, no. 3859 (1968), p. 1244.

23. Garrett Hardin, "Living on a Lifeboat," *BioScience* 24, no. 10 (1974), p. 561.

24. Bureau of the Census, "Statistical Abstract of the United States, 105th ed." (1985), p. 6.

25. Bureau of the Census, "Population Profile of the United States," *Current Population Reports*, Series P-23, no. 145 (1985), pp. 8–9; Charles F. Westoff, "Fertility in the United States," *Science* 234, no. 4776 (1986), p. 555.

26. World Affairs Association, "Focus on World Population," *Intercom* 6, no. 1 (1964), p. 22.

27. Ward E. Y. Elliott, "Federal Law and Population Control," in *Federal Environmental Law*, ed. Erica L. Dolgin and Thomas G. P. Guilbert (St. Paul, Minn.: West, 1974), p. 1567.

28. Department of the Interior, "The Population Challenge: What It Means to America," *Conservation Yearbook* no. 2 (1966), p. 65.

29. James Reed, *From Private Vice to Public Virtue: The Birth Control Movement and American Society Since 1830* (New York: Basic Books, 1978), p. 379.

30. Anonymous, "The Environmental Crisis," *Christian Century* 87, no. 40 (special issue) (1970), p. 1530.

31. Richard M. Nixon, "Special Message to the Congress on Problems of Population Growth," *Public Papers of the Presidents*, July 18, 1969, pp. 521–30.

32. Richard M. Nixon, "Global Challenges: The New Dimension in Foreign Affairs," *Congressional Quarterly Almanac* (1971), p. 54-A.

33. John D. Rockefeller III, "Population Growth and America's Future," *Britannica Book of the Year* 1972, pp. 568–69.

34. James Reed, *From Private Vice to Public Virtue: The Birth Control Movement and American Society Since 1830* (New York: Basic Books, 1978), p. xiii.

# 14. The Citizens Organize

1. J. Clarence Davies III, "The Greening of American Politics," *Wilson Quarterly* 1, no. 4 (1977), p. 92.

2. E. Max Nicholson, *The Environmental Revolution: A Guide for the New Masters of the World* (New York: McGraw-Hill, 1970), p. 186.

3. Alexander B. Adams, *Eleventh Hour: A Hard Look at Conservation* (New York: Scribner's, 1970), pp. 336–37.

4. Joseph W. Meeker, "Nurturing Chaos," *Minding the Earth* 6, no. 4 (1985), p. 3.

5. Kathleen A. Ferguson, *Toward a Geography of Environmentalism in the United States* (Master's thesis, California State University at Hayward, May 1985), p. 89.

6. John G. Mitchell and Constance L. Stallings, eds., *Ecotactics: The Sierra Club Handbook for Environmental Activists* (New York: Pocket Books, 1970), p. 5.

# 15. The Educational Front

1. Richard W. Etulain, review of *The Uneasy Chair*, by Bernard DeVoto, *Pacific Northwest Quarterly* 67, no. 2 (1976), p. 93.

2. Wallace Stegner, ed., *This Is Dinosaur: Echo Park Country and Its Magic Rivers* (New York: Knopf, 1955).

3. E. B. White, "These Precious Days," *New Yorker* (May 16, 1959), p. 180.

4. Joseph Wood Krutch, *More Lives Than One: An Autobiography* (New York: William Sloane, 1962), p. 331.

5. William O. Douglas, *A Wilderness Bill of Rights* (Boston: Little, Brown, 1965); *The Three Hundred Year War: A Chronicle of Ecological Disaster* (New York: Random House, 1972).

6. Douglas, *The Three Hundred Year War*, pp. 198–99.

7. Loren Eiseley, *The Immense Journey* (New York: Vantage/Random House, 1957).

8. Loren Eiseley, *The Invisible Pyramid* (New York: Scribner's, 1970), pp. 1, 69.

9. Paul B. Sears, quoted in *Since Silent Spring*, Frank Graham, Jr. (Boston: Houghton Mifflin, 1970), p. 63.

10. Frank Fraser Darling, *Wilderness and Plenty* (Boston: Houghton Mifflin, 1970), p. 39.

11. Paul Brooks, *The House of Life* (Boston: Houghton Mifflin, 1972), p. 293.

12. Anonymous, "Pesticides: The Price for Progress," *Time* 80, no. 13 (1962), pp. 45, 48.

13. I. L. Baldwin, "Chemicals and Pests [review of *Silent Spring*]," *Science* 137, no. 3535 (1962), p. 1043.

14. New Alchemy Institute (East Falmouth, Mass.), brochures, 1984[?]; also, James K. Page, Jr., and Wilson Clark, "The New Alchemy: How to Survive in Your Spare Time," *Smithsonian* 5, no. 11 (1975), pp. 82–89; Nicholas Wade, "The New Alchemy Institute: Search for an Alternative Agriculture," *Science* 187, no. 4178 (1975), pp. 727–29.

15. Wendell Berry, quoted in "The Prairie Perspective: Setting Agriculture Back on Its Biological Feet," Dick Russell, *Amicus Journal* 6, no. 3 (1985), p. 34.

16. Robert Rodale, ed., *The Basic Book of Organic Gardening* (New York: Ballantine, 1971); Wade Greene, "Guru of the Organic Food Cult," *New York Times Magazine,* June 6, 1971, sec. 6, pp. 1–70 (with breaks); Carlton Jackson, *J. I. Rodale: Apostle of Nonconformity* (New York: Pyramid, 1974).

17. J. Tevere MacFadyen, "Behind the Natural-Food Facade," *Country Journal* (August 1984), pp. 36–41.

18. Ian Burton, "The Quality of the Environment: A Review," *Geographical Review* 58, no. 3 (1968), p. 479.

19. Russell E. Train, "The Role of Foundations and Universities in Conservation," *Horace M. Albright Lectureship in Conservation,* no. 7 (1967), pp. 15–16.

20. Robert S. Morison, "Education for Environmental Concerns," *Daedalus* 96, no. 4 (1967), p. 1210.

21. Ernst Mayr, *The Growth of Biological Thought* (Cambridge, Mass.: Harvard University Press, 1983), p. 892.

22. William Murdoch and Joseph Connell, "The Ecologist's Role and the Nonsolution of Technology," in *Ecocide—and Thoughts Toward Survival,* ed. Clifton Fadiman and Jean White (New York: Interbook, 1971), p. 47.

23. A. Clay Schoenfeld, *The Environmental Communication Ecosystem: A Situation Report* (Columbus, Ohio: SMEAC Information Reference Center, Ohio State University, 1981); A. Clay Schoenfeld and John Disinger, eds., *Environmental Education in Action* (Columbus, Ohio: ERIC Clearinghouse for Science, Mathematics, and Environmental Education, 1977–78), Parts I–III.

24. Carl P. Swanson, "The Role of the Humanities in Environmental Education," *American Biology Teacher* 37, no. 2 (1975), pp. 84–99.

25. *Congressional Record,* April 27, 1970, p. 13098 (Sen. Res. 399).

26. Peter Steinhart, "Teaching and Preaching," *Audubon* 87, no. 3 (1985), pp. 12, 13.

27. Environmental Action, *Earth Day: The Beginning; a Guide for Survival* (New York: Arno Press and the New York Times, 1970), foreword.

28. Rene' Dubos, quoted in "Five Who Care," *Look* 34, no. 8 (1970), p. 34.

29. Environmental Action, *Earth Day,* p. xvii.

30. Greenpeace U.S.A., *Greenpeace Capsule History, 1969–1984* (Washington, D.C.: 1984), 17 typescript pp.; Dick Russell, "Greenpeace: The Hippie Navy Gets Organized," *Amicus Journal* 6, no. "2" [ = no. 1] (1984), pp. 20–27; Peter Dykstra, "Greenpeace," *Environment* 28, no. 6 (1986), pp. 5, 44–45.

31. Conservation Foundation, *Concepts of Conservation: A Guide to Discussion of Some Fundamental Problems* (New York, 1963).

32. Conservation Foundation, *Conservation and Values: The Conservation Foundation's Thirteenth Anniversary Symposium* (Washington, D.C., 1979), 72 pp.; Fairfield Osborn, *Our Plundered Planet* (Boston: Little, Brown, 1948).

33. F. Fraser Darling and John P. Milton, eds. *Future Environments of North America* (Garden City, N.Y.: Natural History Press, 1966).

34. William K. Wyant, *Westward in Eden: The Public Lands and the Conservation Movement* (Berkeley: University of California Press, 1982), p. 376.

35. Katherine Barkley and Steve Weissman, "The Ecoestablishment," *Ramparts* 8, no. 11 (1970), p. 48.

36. National Wildlife Federation, "Our National EQ: The First National Wildlife Federation Index of Environmental Quality," *National Wildlife* 7, no. 5 (1969), pp. 2–13.

37. More than 400 organizations are listed in the annual *Conservation Directory* published by the National Wildlife Federation (Washington, D.C.).

38. Louis A. Iozzi, ed., *A Summary of Research in Environmental Education, 1971–1982* (Columbus, Ohio: ERIC Clearinghouse for Science, Mathematics, and Environmental Education, SE 045 290; 1984).

39. R. Rajagopal, "Environmental Education in the Marketplace: A Decade of U.S. Experience," *Environmental Conservation* 10, no. 3 (1983), p. 225.

40. Paul Shepard, "Ecology and Man: A Viewpoint," in *The Subversive Science: Essays Toward an Ecology of Man* (Boston: Houghton Mifflin, 1969), pp. 9–10.

# *16. The Litigational Front*

1. Environmental law was nominally recognized in 1970 when the Association of American Law Schools, in its annual listing of subjects taught in member law schools, first carried a listing for "Environmental Law."

2. Joseph L. Sax, *Defending the Environment: A Strategy for Citizen Action* (New York: Knopf, 1971), pp. xviii-xix.

3. Kenneth E. F. Watt, *Understanding the Environment* (Newton, Mass.: Allyn and Bacon, 1982), pp. 377–81.

4. Philip Soper, "The Constitutional Power of the Federal Government," in *Federal Environmental Law*, ed. Erica L. Dolgin and Thomas G. P. Guilbert (St. Paul, Minn.: West, 1974), p. 21ff.

5. Vincent Scully, quoted in "When Is the Pig in the Parlor? The Interface of Legal and Aesthetic Considerations," Richard C. Smardon, *Environmental Review* 8, no. 2 (1984), p. 156.

6. Michael Kitzmiller, "Environment and the Law," in *Ecocide—and Thoughts Toward Survival*, ed. Clifton Fadiman and Jean White (New York: Interbook, 1971), p. 141.

7. Stephen P. Duggan, quoted in "Militant Adversary of Progress," by Whitney North Seymour, Jr., *Amicus Journal* 2, no. 3 (1981), p. 12.

8. For discussion of standing see—among others—Joseph L. Sax, *Defending the Environment* (New York: Knopf, 1971); Norman J. Landau and Paul D. Rheingold, *The Environmental Handbook* (New York: Friends of the Earth/Ballantine, 1971); Frederick R. Anderson, *NEPA in the Courts: A Legal Analysis of the National Environmental Policy Act* (Washington, D.C.: Resources for the Future, distributed by Johns Hopkins University Press, 1973); Timothy O'Riordan, *Environmentalism* 2d ed. (London: Pion, 1981); Anonymous, "Good News from the Supreme Court," *Amicus Journal* 8, no. 2 (1986), p. 3, with reference to the Court's opinion in *Hunt v. Washington Apple Advertising Commission*, 432 U.S. 333, 343 (1977).

9. Frank Graham, Jr., *Since Silent Spring* (Boston: Houghton Mifflin, 1970), pp. 251–59.

10. Graham, *Since Silent Spring*, p. 255.

11. Joseph L. Sax, *Defending the Environment* (New York: Knopf, 1971), pp. 207–8.

12. Richard C. Smardon, "When Is the Pig in the Parlor? The Interface of Legal and Aesthetic Considerations," *Environmental Review* 8, no. 2 (1984), pp. 147–61.

13. U.S. Court of Appeals for the Ninth Circuit, *Northwest Indian Cemetery Protective Association, et al v. R. Max Peterson, Chief, U.S. Forest Service et al*, CA No. 83–2225 of July 9, 1984; decision filed June 24, 1985.

14. William S. Paley (chairman), *Resources for Freedom: Report of the President's Materials Policy Commission* (Washington, D.C., June 1952), 5 vols.

15. Michael J. Bean, *The Evolution of National Wildlife Law*, 2d ed. (New York: Praeger, 1983).

16. James S. Rummonds, "A Challenge to the Law," in *Ecotactics: The Sierra Club Handbook for Environmental Activists*, ed. John G. Mitchell and Constance L. Stallings (New York: Pocket Books, 1970), p. 119.

17. Marion Edey, "Eco-politics and the League of Conservation Voters," in *The Environmental Handbook*, ed. Garrett De Bell (New York: Ballantine, 1970), pp. 313, 316.

# 17. The Political Front: Congress

1. Theodore H. White, *America in Search of Itself: The Making of the President, 1956–1980* (New York: Harper and Row, 1982), p. 124.

2. Lynton K. Caldwell, "Environment: A New Focus for Public Policy?" *Public Administration Review* 23, no. 3 (1963), p. 134.

3. Stewart L. Udall, *The Quiet Crisis* (New York: Holt, Rinehart and Winston, 1963), p. viii; updated as *The Quiet Crisis and the Next Generation* (Layton, Utah: Gibbs Smith, 1988).

4. Geoffrey Wandesforde-Smith, "National Policy for the Environment: Politics and the Concept of Stewardship," in *Congress and the Environment*, ed. Richard A. Cooley and Wandesforde-Smith (Seattle: University of Washington Press, 1970), p. 208.

5. William D. Ruckelshaus, "The First Year of EPA," *Ecology USA 1971* (1972), pp. 441–42.

6. Lettie McSpadden Wenner, "The Misuse and Abuse of NEPA," *Environmental Review* 7, no. 3 (1983), pp. 229–54.

7. Council on Environmental Quality, *Fourth Annual Report* (Washington, 1973), p. 243; Paul Culhane, "Federal Agency Organizational Change in Response to Environmentalism," *Humboldt Journal of Social Relations* 2 (1974), p. 33.

8. Culhane, "Federal Agency Organizational Change," p. 34.

9. William R. Catton, Jr., *Overshoot: The Ecological Basis of Revolutionary Change* (Urbana: University of Illinois Press, 1980), p. 265.

10. Alex Shoumatoff, "The Skipper and the Dam," *New Yorker* (December 1, 1986), pp. 71, 94.

11. Environmental Protection Agency, Office of Research and Monitoring, *The Quality of Life Concept: A Potential New Tool for Decision Makers* (Washington, D.C., 1973), p. iii.

12. Ibid., Kenneth W. Terhune, "Probing Policy-Relevant Questions on the Quality of Life," p. II-24.

13. Health, Education and Welfare Department, Committee on Environmental Health Problems, "Reports of the Committee . . . to the Surgeon General," Pub. 908 (1962).

14. John W. Gofman, "Confronting the A.E.C.," in *Omega: Murder of the Ecosystem and Suicide of Man,* ed. Paul K. Anderson (Dubuque, Iowa: W. C. Brown, 1971), p. 260.

15. Garrett Hardin, *Filters Against Folly* (New York: Viking, 1985), pp. 43–44.

16. Health, Education, and Welfare Department, *A Strategy for a Livable Environment* (Washington, D.C., 1967), p. ix.

17. Anonymous, "The Ravaged Environment," *Newsweek* 75, no. 4 (1970), p. 34.

18. John Douglas Wellman, *Environmental Pollution: Legislation and Programs in the Areas of Water and Air Pollution and Solid Waste Management* (Library of Congress, Legislative Reference Service, TP 450 U.S.B. and 70–145 EP; 1970), pp. 1–17.

19. Philip P. Micklin, "Water Quality: A Question of Standards," in *Congress and the Environment,* ed. Richard A. Cooley and Geoffrey Wandesforde-Smith (Seattle: University of Washington Press, 1970), p. 130.

20. President's Science Advisory Committee, Environmental Pollution Panel, *Restoring the Quality of Our Environment* (Washington, D.C.: The White House, 1965), pp. 13, 16.

21. Lyndon B. Johnson, "Remarks upon Signing the Pesticide Control Bill, May 12," *Public Papers of the Presidents* (1964), p. 681.

22. R. Jeffrey Smith, "Supreme Court Orders Pesticide Data Released," *Science* 225, no. 4658 (1984), p. 150.

23. John Walsh, "EPA and Toxic Substance Law: Dealing with Uncertainty," *Science* 202, no. 4368 (1978), p. 598.

24. Russell E. Train, quoted in *The Apocalyptics: Cancer and the Big Lie,* by Edith Efron (New York: Simon and Schuster, 1984), p. 22.

25. Samuel S. Epstein, Lester O. Brown, and Carl Pope, *Hazardous Waste in America* (San Francisco: Sierra Club Books, 1982), pp. 202–22.

26. Gilbert F. White, "Formation and Role of Public Attitudes," in *Environmental Quality in a Growing Economy,* ed. Henry Jarrett (Baltimore: Johns Hopkins Press for Resources for the Future, 1966), p. 109.

27. Outdoor Recreation Resources Review Commission, *Public Outdoor Recreation Areas—Acreage, Use, Potential* (Washington, D.C., ORRRC Report no. 1 [of 23], 1962); William E. Shands, "New Recreation Commission Builds on Past," *Conservation Foundation Letter* (September-October 1985), p. 2.

28. William Hard, "Save a Spot of Beauty for America," *Reader's Digest* (January 1960), pp. 148–53.

29. Ansel Adams and Nancy Newhall, *This Is the American Earth* (San Francisco: Sierra Club, 1960).

30. President's Council on Recreation and Natural Beauty, *From Sea to Shining Sea: A Report on the American Environment—Our Natural Heritage* (Washington, D.C., 1968).

31. Lyndon B. Johnson, "Statement by the President on the Conservation Message, March 8, 1968," *Public Papers of the Presidents* (1968), p. 370.

32. William C. Cramer, *Congressional Record,* v. 111, part 19 (1965), p. 26252.

33. Lyndon B. Johnson, "Remarks at the University of Michigan," *Public Papers of the Presidents* (1964), pp. 704–7.

34. White House Conference on Natural Beauty, *Beauty for America: Proceedings of [the Conference] May 24–25, 1965* (Washington, 1965), pp. 1–782; Earl Hale, Jr., "Presidential Proposal and Congressional Disposal . . ." in *Congress and the Environment,* ed. Richard A. Cooley and Geoffrey Wandesforde-Smith (Seattle: University of Washington Press, 1970), p. 37.

35. Henry L. Diamond, "The Land, the City, and the Human Spirit," *Environmental Forum* 3, no. 8 (1984), pp. 12–13.

36. Public Land Law Review Commission, *One-third of the Nation's Land: A Report to the President and to the Congress . . .* (Washington, D.C., 1970), 342 pp.

37. William K. Wyant, *Westward in Eden: The Public Lands and the Conservation Movement* (Berkeley: University of California Press, 1982), p. 127.

38. Wallace Stegner, "Wilderness Letter" in *The Sound of Mountain Water* (Garden City, N.Y.: Doubleday, 1969 [letter originally 1960]), p. 153.

39. Hubert Humphrey, in *Conservation Milestones* (Council on Environmental Quality, 1984), p. 40.

40. Morris K. Udall, "Conservation of Natural Areas," in *Conservation and Values* (Washington, D.C.: Conservation Foundation, 1979), p. 32.

41. Anonymous, "Ah, Wilderness," *Amicus Journal* 2, no. 3 (1981), p. 11.

42. Department of the Interior, *Secretary Hickel Bans Imports of Products*

*from Eight Endangered Species of Whales* (Washington, D.C., news release of November 24, 1970).

43. Michael J. Bean, *The Evolution of National Wildlife Law* (New York: Praeger, 1983), pp. 334–41.

44. Bean, *The Evolution of National Wildlife Law*, p. 335.

45. Warren G. Magnuson, in "Treaties and Other International Agreements on Fisheries, Oceanographic Resources, and Wildlife Involving the United States," Senate, 95th Congress, 1st sess., Committee on Commerce, Science, and Transportation (October 31, 1977), p. iii.

46. Humane Society of the United States, *Report on Animal Welfare Laws* (Washington, D.C., 1983), 28 typescript pp.

47. International Society for Animals Rights, *Report* (Clarks Summit, Penn., 1984), p. 1.

48. John F. Kennedy, "Special Message to the Congress on Natural Resources, February 23, 1961," *Public Papers of the Presidents* (1961), p. 121.

49. National Research Council, Committee on Natural Resources (seven reports in the NRC Publications series, nos. 1000 to 1000–G [lacking 1000–F], all in 1962); Samuel H. Ordway, Jr., Wallace D. Bowman, and John Milton, "Research on Natural Resources: A Review and Commentary," *Natural Resources Journal* 4, no. 1 (1964), pp. 44–45.

50. White House Conference on Conservation, *Official Proceedings, May 24 and 25, 1962* (Washington, D.C., 1963).

51. Landsberg, Hans H., Leonard L. Fischman, and Joseph L. Fisher, *Resources in America's Future: Patterns of Requirements and Availabilities 1960–2000* (Baltimore: Johns Hopkins Press and Resources for the Future, 1963).

52. National Commission on Materials Policy, *Material Needs and the Environment Today and Tomorrow, Final Report* (Washington, D.C., June 1973), pp. 1–5 to 1–8.

53. Albert Gore, Jr., quoted in "The Miner's Watchdog Doesn't Bite," *Sierra* 71, no. 5 (1986), p. 32.

54. Richard M. Nixon, "Statement about Signing the Energy Supply and Environmental Coordination Act of 1974," *Public Papers of the Presidents* (June 26, 1974), pp. 548–49.

55. Gerald Ford, in *Conservation Milestones* (Council on Environmental Quality, 1984), p. 3. (His proclamation No. 4341 of January 19, 1975.)

56. Henry M. Jackson, *A National Policy for the Environment*, address to the National Audubon Society at St. Louis, Missouri, April 1969, p. 7 of typescript.

57. Marc Reisner, "America's Newest Old Energy Source: Hydro Power," *Amicus Journal* 6, no. 4 (1985), p. 45.

## *18. Environmental Trends*

1. Barbara Ward, *Progress for a Small Planet* (New York: W. W. Norton, 1982), p. 277.

2. Among the source materials for this chapter are writings by John H.

Adams, Lester R. Brown, Robert Cahn, Stephen P. Duggan, Erik P. Eckholm, Herman H. Field, William Ophuls, Gus Speth, Francis R. Thibodeau, Barbara Ward, and Seth Zuckerman.

3. Anonymous, "Henry Steele Commager," *Geo* 6 (June 1984), p. 16.

4. Aldo Leopold, "The Ecological Conscience," *Bulletin of the Garden Club of America*, September 1947, pp. 45–53.

5. Robert Cahn, "The Conservative Challenge of the 80s," *Horace M. Albright Lectureship in Conservation*, no. 19 (1980), p. 24.

6. Richard S. Miller, "Summary Report of the Ecology Study Committee with Recommendations for the Future of Ecology and the Ecological Society of America," *Bulletin of the Ecological Society of America* 46, no. 2 (1965), pp. 63, 72.

7. Harrison Brown, *The Challenge of Man's Future: An Inquiry Concerning the Condition of Man During the Years That Lie Ahead* (New York: Viking, 1954), pp. 218–19, 226.

8. G. William Domhoff, *Who Rules America Now?* (New York: Simon and Schuster, 1983), pp. 42, 56, 149–50, 222.

9. Anonymous, "Notes and Comments," *New Yorker* 48, no. 12 (1972), p. 29.

10. Seth Zuckerman, "Environmentalism Turns 16," *Nation* 243, no. 12 (1986), p. 368.

11. Gus Speth, "A Nation of Conservers: Environmental Quality in the 1980's," address given . . . at the Environmental Decade Conference sponsored by the Conservation Foundation, Estes Park, Colorado, April 13, 1980, pp. 1–9.

12. M. Taghi Farvar and John P. Milton, *The Careless Technology: Ecology and International Development; the Record* (Garden City, N.Y.: Natural History Press, 1972).

13. Leo Marx, "American Institutions and Ecological Ideals," *Science* 170, no. 3961 (1970), p. 945.

14. Henry M. Jackson, "A National Policy for the Environment," address to the National Audubon Society, St. Louis, Missouri, April 1969, p. 9 of typescript.

15. Federal Election Commission, "FEC Releases New PAC Count," Washington, D.C., press release, January 1987.

16. Common Cause, quoted in "A Nation of Conservers: Environmental Quality in the 1980's," Gus Speth, address given at the Environmental Decade Conference sponsored by the Conservation Foundation, Estes Park, Colorado, April 13, 1980, pp. 8–9.

17. Canada, Law Reform Commission, "Crimes Against the Environment," *LRC Working Paper* 44 (Ottawa) 1985, p. 67; Canada, House of Commons, "Canadian Environmental Protection Act," Bill C-74, 2d sess., 33d Parliament, 1986–87.

18. Kit D. Farber and Gary L. Rutledge, "Pollution Abatement and Control Expenditures," Department of Commerce, Bureau of Economic Analysis, *Annual Report* (1968), p. 103; Mark Crawford, "Hazardous Waste: Where to Put It?" *Science* 235, no. 4785 (1987), pp. 156–57.

19. Shawn O'Faolain, *Collected Stories* (New York: Atlantic, 1983), p. 584.

20. Celia M. Hunter, "This Our Land," *Alaska* 50, no. 12 (1984), p. 37.

21. Jay D. Hair, "Winning through Mediation," *Ecolibrium* 12, no. 4 (1983), pp. 19–20.

22. Gail Bingham, *Resolving Environmental Disputes: A Decade of Experience, Executive Summary* (Washington, D.C.: Conservation Foundation, 1985), p. 5. This is a 13–page summary of a book, same title, published in 1986.

23. Joseph M. Petulla, "Environmental Management: Defining the Profession," *Environment* 25, no. 8 (1983), p. 5.

24. Aldo Leopold, *A Sand County Almanac and Sketches Here and There* (New York: Oxford University Press, 1949 [1964]), p. 225.

25. See, for example, his essays in *Home Economics* (Berkeley, Calif.: North Point Press, 1987).

# 19. Epilogue

1. See also, Samuel P. Hays, "The Reagan Antienvironmental Revolution," in his book, *Beauty, Health, and Permanence* (New York: Cambridge University Press, 1988), pp. 491–526; Norman J. Vig and Michael E. Kraft, eds., *Environmental Policy in the 1980s: Reagan's New Agenda* (Washington, D.C.: Congressional Quarterly Press, 1984); David Vogel and Robert W. Crandall, "The Politics of the Environment, 1970–1987," *Wilson Quarterly* (Autumn, 1987), pp. 51–80.

2. *Gallup Report*, no. 278 (November 1988), p. 27.

3. Stewart S. Udall, *The Quiet Crisis and the Next Generation* (Layton, Utah: Gibbs Smith, 1988), p. 262.

4. William Drayton, *America's Transition: Blueprints for the 1990s* (Washington, D.C.: Environmental Safety), p. 21.

5. Norman J. Vig and Michael E. Kraft, eds., *Environmental Policy in the 1980s: Reagan's New Agenda* (Washington, D.C.: Congressional Quarterly Press, 1984), p. x.

6. *Conservation Directory*, 34th ed., 1989 (Washington, D.C.: National Wildlife Federation); *Directory of National Environmental Organizations* 3d ed., 1988 (St. Paul, Minn.: U.S. Environmental Directories).

7. T. Allan Comp, ed., *Blueprint for the Environment: A Plan for Federal Action* (Salt Lake City: Howe Brothers, 1989).

8. United Nations, World Commission on Environment and Development, *Our Common Future* [the "Brundtland Report"] (New York: Oxford University Press, 1987); World Resources Institute and International Institute for Environment and Development in collaboration with United Nations Environment Programme, *World Resources 1988–89: An Assessment of the Resource Base that Supports the Global Economy* (New York: Basic Books, 1988).

9. Diana Johnstone, "Europe's Green Light," *Progressive* 53, no. 7 (July 1989), pp. 12–13.

10. Department of State, *Economic Declaration* (Washington, D.C.: Press

release of July 16, 1989, from Summit of the Arch, Paris, July 14–26; 22 pp. ("Environment," pp. 12–19.)

11. Gro Harlem Brundtland, "Global Change and Our Common Future," *Environment* 31, no. 5 (June 1989), p. 17.

12. Peter M. Vitousek, Paul R. Ehrlich, Anne H. Ehrlich, and Pamela A. Matson, "Human Appropriation of the Products of Photosynthesis," *Bioscience* 36, no. 6 (June 1986), p. 368.

13. Bartle Bull, "Voodoo Demography: What Population Problem?" *Amicus Journal* 6, no. 1 (Fall 1984), p. 36.

14. Jill Jäger, "Anticipating Climatic Change: Priorities for Action," *Environment* 30, no. 7 (September 1988), pp. 12–15, 30–33.

15. Richard A. Kerr, "Hansen *vs.* the World on the Greenhouse Effect," *Science* 244, no. 4908 (June 2, 1989), p. 1041.

16. Anonymous, "Ozone Pact Takes Effect," *Atmosphere* (Friends of the Earth) 1, no. 4 (Winter 1989), pp. 1, 11.

17. Debora MacKenzie, "Countries Agree More Help for the Ozone Layer," *New Scientist*, no. 1663 (May 6, 1989), p. 25.

18. Larry Margasak, "After Years of Stalemate on Hill, Congress May OK Acid-rain Bill," *Journal-American* (Bellevue, Wash.), March 19, 1989, p. B-3.

19. Eliot Marshall, "Clean Air? Don't Hold Your Breath," *Science* 244, no. 4904 (May 5, 1989), p. 517.

20. International Council of Scientific Unions, Scientific Committee on Problems of the Environment (SCOPE), *Environmental Consequences of Nuclear War* (New York: John Wiley and Sons), *SCOPE* 28, vol. 1 (1986) and vol. 2 (1985).

21. Richard Turco and others, "Nuclear Winter: Global Consequences of Multiple Nuclear Explosions," *Science* 222, no. 4630 (December 23, 1983), p. 1283. See also Turco and others, "Nuclear Winter Revisited," *Amicus Journal* 9, no. 1 (Winter 1987), pp. 4–7; National Research Council, *The Effects on the Atmosphere of a Major Nuclear Exchange* (Washington, D.C.: National Academy Press, 1985).

22. Paul H. Ehrlich and others, "Long-term Biological Consequences of Nuclear War," *Science* 222, no. 4630 (December 23, 1983), p. 1293.

23. Edward O. Wilson, ed., *Biodiversity* (Washington, D.C.: National Academy Press, 1988).

24. Office of Technology Assessment, *Technologies to Maintain Biological Diversity: Summary* (Washington, D.C.: OTA-F-331; 1987). With list on pp. 12–13 of 29 federal laws (1988–78) concerned with biological diversity.

25. Mary Deery Uva and Jane Bloom, "Exporting Pollution: The International Waste Trade," *Environment* 31, no. 5 (June 1989), pp. 4–5, 43–44.

26. UN Resolution 37/137 of December 17, 1982.

27. Anonymous, "Testing for Toxic Land Marks End of Frontier," *Journal-American* (Bellevue, Wash., May 9, 1989, p. A-8. See also Melinda Beck, "Buried Alive," *Newsweek*, November 27, 1989, pp. 66–76; William L. Rathje, "Rubbish," *Atlantic*, vol. 264, no. 6 (December 1989), pp. 99–109.

28. Scott Denman and Ken Bossong, "Big Oil Makes Its Move," *Amicus*

*Journal* 2, no. 4 (Spring 1981), pp. 35–41; Nancy Rader and others, *Power Surge: The Status and Near-Term Potential of Renewable Energy Resources* (Washington, D.C.: Public Citizen, 1989), pp. 1–2.

29. Office of Management and Budget, *The United States Budget in Brief, Fiscal Year 1990* (Washington, D.C.: GPO, 1989), p. 55.

30. Debora MacKenzie, "Radioactive Pollution 'Underestimated by Six Times'," *New Scientist*, no. 1664 (May 13, 1989), p. 25; Tamara Jones and Dan Morain, "Secrets at Rocky Flats Nuclear Plant Slowly Surfacing," *Los Angeles Times*, reprinted in *Seattle Times*, June 22, 1989, p. A-6.

31. Randall O'Toole, *Reforming the Forest Service* (Covelo, Calif.: Island Press, 1988), pp. 77–79.

32. *Federal Register* 54 (120), June 23, 1989, pp. 26666–77.

33. U.S. Forest Service, *Final Supplement to the Environmental Impact Statement for an Amendment to the Pacific Northwest Regional Guide* (Portland, Ore., July 1988).

34. Robert Repetto in *Public Policies and the Misuse of Forest Resources*, ed. Repetto and Malcolm Gillis (New York: Cambridge University Press, 1988), pp. 378–79.

35. Robert B. Reed, "Shaping a New Fund for America's Heritage," *Conservation Foundation Letter*, 1988, no. 4, pp. 3–6.

36. President's Commission on Americans Outdoors, *Report and Recommendations to the President. . . .* (Washington, D.C.: January 28, 1987).

37. Faith T. Campbell and Johanna H. Wald, *Areas of Critical Environmental Concern* (New York: Natural Resources Defense Council, April 1989).

38. Justin R. Ward, "The Conservation Reserve and the Rural Environment," *Environment* 28, no. 7 (September 1986), pp. 3–4; Tom Kuhnle (Natural Resources Defense Council) letter to author, 1989.

39. John P. Reganold, "Comparison of Soil Properties as Influenced by Organic and Conventional Farming Systems," *American Journal of Alternative Agriculture* 3, no. 4 (Fall 1988), pp. 144–55.

40. William Lockeretz, Georgia Shearer, and Daniel H. Kohl, "Organic Farming in the Corn Belt," *Science* 211 (February 6, 1981), p. 546.

41. Nancy Shute, "Going Organic," *Amicus Journal* 11, no. 2 (Spring 1989), p. 40.

42. New York State Integrated Pest Management Program, *1988 Annual Report* (Geneva, N.Y.: State Agricultural Experiment Station, 1989).

43. Office of Technology Assessment, *Technology, Public Policy, and the Changing Structure of American Agriculture: Summary* (Washington, D.C.: OTA-F-268; 1986), p. 16; Kenneth A. Cook and Susan E. Sechler, "Agricultural Policy: Paying for Our Past Mistakes," *Issues in Science and Technology* 2, no. 1 (Fall 1985), p. 108.

44. Supreme Court, June 16, 1980, *Diamond v. Chakrabarty*.

45. Ecological Society of America, "The Release of Genetically Engineered Organisms: A Perspective," *Ecology* 70, no. 2 (April 1989), pp. 297–315.

46. Walter Prescott Webb, "The American West, Perpetual Mirage," *Harper's Magazine* 214, no. 1284 (May 1957), p. 26.

47. Marc Reisner, *Cadillac Desert: The American West and Its Disappearing Water* (New York: Viking, 1986), p. 497.

48. Murray Bookchin, "Death of a Small Planet: It's Growth That's Killing Us," *Progressive* 53, no. 8 (August 1989), p. 21.

49. Michael Edesess, "Figuring the Worth of an Otter or Whale," *Christian Science Monitor*, May 31, 1989, p. 18.

50. Daniel E. Koshland, "Low Probability–High Consequence Accidents," *Science* 244, no. 4903 (April 28, 1989), p. 405.

51. Slade Gorton (Senator), "Floor Statement on Exxon and Corporate Responsibility," U.S. Congress, May 3, 1989.

52. Anonymous, "Offshore Drilling Ban Is First Such Action," *Seattle Times*, June 28, 1989, p. A-2.

53. John Lancaster, "How Do You Price the Intrinsic Value of Lost Wildlife?" *Seattle Times,* June 26, 1989, p. A-3 (from the *Washington Post*).

54. David W. Laist, "Overview of the Biological Effects of Lost and Discarded Plastic Debris in the Marine Environment," *Marine Pollution Bulletin* 18, no. 6–B (1987), pp. 319–26.

55. Judith W. McIntyre, "The Common Loon Cries for Help," *National Geographic* 175 (April 1989), pp. 510–24.

56. American Society for Environmental History and the Northwest Association for Environmental Studies, "Solving Environmental Problems: The Past as Prologue to the Present" (Olympia, Wash., April 27–30, 1989).

57. Donald Edward Davis, *Ecophilosophy: A Field Guide to the Literature* (San Pedro, Calif.: R. & E. Miles, 1989). An annotated catalogue—emphasizing "recognizable benchmarks in the field"—of 283 books; 33 periodicals, journals, and newsletters; and 18 learning centers and professional organizations; Charles R. Magel, *Keyguide to Information Sources on Animal Rights* (Jefferson, N.C.: McFarland, 1989).

58. Anonymous, "Corporate Guide Allows You to Match Your Money with Ideals," *Seattle Times*, July 31, 1989, p. E-8.

59. Ronald Brownstein and Nina Easton, "Ethical Investing: Putting Your Money Where Your Heart Is," *Amicus Journal* 5, no. 3 (Winter 1984), pp. 16–19.

60. Issue no. 1 of *The New Road* (World Wildlife Fund, Gland, Switzerland, Winter 1986/87).

61. Roderick Frazier Nash, "The Greening of Religion," in his book *The Rights of Nature: A History of Environmental Ethics* (Madison: University of Wisconsin Press, 1989), pp. 87–120.

62. Peter Borrelli, "Epiphany: Religion, Ethics, and the Environment," *Amicus Journal* 7, no. 3 (Winter 1986), p. 41.

# Illustration Credits

1. Technological Man, p. 13: Mark S. Fisher (*The Progressive*, October 1986).

2. Ralph Nader, p. 27: Victor Juhasz (*The Progressive*, July 1984).

3. Logo of American Farmland Trust, p. 35: (Washington, D.C., 1986).

4. World production of edible whale oil, 1947–1976, p. 46: Margery L. Oldfield (U.S. Department of Agriculture, 1984).

5. Preserving wetlands (1984 stamp), p. 55: (U.S. Postal Service, 1984).

6. Man's annual production of carbon dioxide, from 1872, p. 61: Norman Myers (Multimedia Publications (UK) Ltd., 1984).

7. Energy consumption in the United States by sector, 1960–81, p. 71: (from *State of the Environment 1982* copyright The Conservation Foundation, 1982; after fig. 5.3).

8. (Untitled cartoon), p. 83: Paul K. Anderson (W. C. Brown, 1971).

9. World population growth through history, p. 101: Anne Firth Murray (*Environment* 27(6) July/August 1985, p. 33. Reprinted with permission of the Helen Dwight Reid Educational Foundation. Published by Heldref Publications, 4000 Albemarle St., NW, Washington, D.C. 20016. Copyright 1985).

10. Stabilized world model, postulated, p. 103: (from *The Limits to Growth: A Report for the Club of Rome's Project on the Predicament of Mankind*, by Donella H. Meadows, Dennis L. Meadows, Jørgen Randers and William W. Behrens, III. A Potomac Associates book published by Universe Books, N.Y., 1972. Graphics by Potomac Associates).

11. Number of environmental organizations and periodicals (combined) founded in the United States from 1901 to 1980 and still in existence in 1983, p. 114: Author, from *Conservation Directory* (1984) and *Ulrich's International Periodicals Directory* (1983).

12. Rachel Carson (1981 stamp), p. 121: (U.S. Postal Service).

13. Logo of Earth Day, 1970, p. 126: Yukihisa Isobe (George Braziller, 1970).

14. Black-footed ferret (1981 stamp), p. 160: (U.S. Postal Service).

15. Logo of World Wildlife Fund, p. 172: (WWF, Washington, D.C., 1989).

16. The Knot of Eternity, p. 177: logo of the World Resources Institute (Washington D.C., 1987).

17. Logo of the Animal Welfare Institute, p. 186: (Washington, D.C.).

# Index